JESSICA LOST

JESSICA LOST

A Story of Birth, Adoption
& the Meaning of Motherhood

BUNNY CRUMPACKER
AND
J.S. PICARIELLO

UNION SQUARE PRESS
New York

UNION SQUARE PRESS
New York

An Imprint of Sterling Publishing
387 Park Avenue South
New York, NY 10016

Library of Congress Cataloging-in-Publication Data
Crumpacker, Bunny.
  Jessica Lost : a story of birth, adoption & the meaning of motherhood / Bunny Crumpacker and J.S.
Picariello.
      p. cm.
  Includes bibliographical references and index.
  ISBN 978-1-4027-7570-3 (alk. paper)
  1. Adoptees--United States--Biography. 2. Birthmothers--United States. I. Picariello, J.S. II. Title.
  HV874.82.P53C78 2011
  362.734092--dc22
  [B]
                        2010039324

10 9 8 7 6 5 4 3 2 1

© 2011 by Faith (Bunny) Crumpacker and J.S. Picariello
Distributed in Canada by Sterling Publishing
c/o Canadian Manda Group, 165 Dufferin Street,
Toronto, Ontario, Canada M6K 3H6

Sterling ISBN 978-1-4027-7570-3

For information about custom editions, special sales, premium and
corporate purchases, please contact Sterling Special Sales
Department at 800-805-5489 or specialsales@sterlingpublishing.com.

All photos courtesy of Jil Picariello and Bunny Crumpacker

To my men: Lenny, Damien, Alex
—JSP

For Jil
—BC

*M*emoir comes from the Latin word *memoria*, which means "memory," or "reminiscence." This book is a remembering of the past, and is, as much as any memory can claim to be, a true story. Others may have different memories; that's not surprising: It is the very nature of memory to be as individual as fingerprints. Although this is a true story, some names and identifying characteristics have been changed to protect the privacy of individuals portrayed. And, of course, since we weren't carrying recording devices with us at all times, conversations are reconstructed to the best of our ability.

Bunny Crumpacker
J.S. Picariello

Contents

1. BUNNY: LOST   1
2. JIL: THE LETTER   3
3. BUNNY: THE NEW YEAR   4
4. JIL: THE CHOSEN BABY   11
5. BUNNY: EARLY DAYS   15
6. JIL: ANOTHER CHOSEN BABY   21
7. BUNNY: WAITING   28
8. JIL: NINE AND NEUROTIC   34
9. BUNNY: *WILKOMMEN*   45
10. JIL: MADISON   53
11. BUNNY: PARIS   58
12. JIL: WEDDING   64
13. BUNNY: WITH CHILD   70
14. JIL: LOSS   75
15. BUNNY: BIRTH   88
16. JIL: BIRTH   91
17. BUNNY: THE END AND THE BEGINNING   101
18. JIL: THE SECOND TIME   104
19. BUNNY: THE SECOND TIME   111
20. JIL: MEETING RUTH   116
21. BUNNY: HOPE   123
22. JIL: FINDING FAITH   127
23. BUNNY: FOUND   140
24. JIL: FOUND   146
25. BUNNY: GETTING TO KNOW JIL   160
26. JIL: FATHERS   165
27. BUNNY: EVERY WOMAN IS A DAUGHTER   180
28. JIL: MYSELF   185
EPILOGUE   207
ACKNOWLEDGMENTS   212
ABOUT THE AUTHORS   213

A NOTE ON NAMES

Alike in so many surprising and often stunning ways, my birth mother and I also shared a history of fluctuating names. In addition to the changes wrought by adoption and marriages on our surnames, our given names metamorphosed as well. I was born Jessica, became Jill Ann, changed it to Jilann, and am known as Jil. Inspired by a book she was reading while pregnant, Faith's mother put "Faith Ann" on her birth certificate, but nicknamed her newborn Bunny. The pet name (in both senses) took: Faith was Bunny to herself, her family, her friends. But I first heard of her as Faith, and it stuck.

I never thought of her as Bunny, and could not write of her as Bunny. She was Faith to me, and I loved the name, and found it fitting for her as a person, and for her role in my life. That's why, when she writes of herself in this book, she is Bunny. But when I write of her, she is, and always will be, Faith.

J.S. Picariello

1. BUNNY

{ LOST

The knowledge of the past has been as an overture
to what we have learned in the most recent ten and twenty years.
It gives the theme (all life from a single cell ...)
but leaves the subtle details still to be discovered.

GERALDINE LUX FLANAGAN
THE FIRST NINE MONTHS OF LIFE

B efore she found me, the last time I had seen my daughter was when she was four days old. When she found me, she was fifteen thousand, three hundred and ninety-one days old—just over 42.

In my mind, she was always four days old. She was always 'The Baby," the one I'd lost—the one I'd given away.

The adoption agency told me I could give her a name. Her adopting parents would keep the initial, they said. I named her Jessica, but I still thought of her as "The Baby."

I wasn't supposed to see her; the belief at that time was that it was harder for a birth mother to give up her child if she had seen it. But it isn't any harder than being pregnant for nine months with a baby you can't keep, or giving birth to a child who will not be your own. And what could be harder, after nine months, than not seeing the baby at all? There would be no way to know the shape of her mouth, the color of her hair. The baby would never be real, never have substance; and all those months of swelling and growing would have produced nothing but a few hours of pain. Flat again, myself again, but now with something missing; and how was I to know what I'd lost?

Fortunately, in the busy, crowded nursery, the nurses let me hold my baby. She was wrapped in a pink hospital blanket. A nurse placed her so that she rested on my arm in the classic pose. I wanted to hold her forever, watch her, forever. The love I felt was chemical, cellular, galactic—a flow as natural as that in the cord that had so recently connected us.

For four days, she was mine, not yet "The Baby," the name for loss. For those four days, I could touch her shoulder, examine her fingers, watch her eyes and her mouth, feel the softness of her hair, look at her, and tell her, over and over: I love you. I will always love you.

I try now to remember her face. She had a birthmark across the bridge of her nose. That's important. But the four days in the hospital, with her, remain something of a blur—like the nine months before them.

I think of myself then as numb, as if I had been pregnant with numbness, and was left with it after giving birth. The few things I remember about being pregnant are the times it was all right—I want to put that in capital letters—ALL RIGHT— to be pregnant: the days at the hospital clinic with the other women whose bodies were swollen like mine; the times I was alone, standing in front of the mirror, naked, looking at myself sideways.

But there are also many smooth and empty spots in my memory: What did I wear? How did I get to the hospital when I went into labor? What time of day was it? Was anyone with me during those long hours? I can't recall even getting from the hospital to the adoption agency for the formal transfer of "The Baby." It's all a wall of glass—smooth, cold, and blank.

I do remember that, afterward, I went to the movies, because there was nothing else I could bear to do. I don't know what I saw. Afterward, I remember standing on the corner of Third Avenue and 23rd Street in Manhattan, waiting first for the light to change; and then just waiting. I was unable to put one foot in front of the other to cross the street, or to move at all. If I took a step, I would be beginning the rest of my life—and I couldn't. I couldn't leave the first part of my life behind me, and I couldn't face what was to come. Paralyzed, having given away my baby, I could no longer claim myself.

I was too young to recognize how alone I was; but that's what I knew.

Not many people knew about the pregnancy then, or later. It was the great secret of my life. I can tell you how it began. I can tell you how it affected the rest of my life. I can tell you what kind of mother I turned out to be. But there is only a little I can tell you about the pregnancy, or the birth of that lost child. I kept my secret so successfully, for so long, that I no longer have it to share. For a long time, I no longer had it for myself to know.

2. JIL

THE LETTER

January, 1997

Dear Mr. Aylford,

This is a very difficult letter to write. You see, I am an adult adoptee currently searching for my birth parents. I believe my birth father's name was John Aylford.

I was born on November 15, 1954 at New York Hospital. I have been told my parents were a young couple who married in the early 1950s after a very brief courtship, and then were separated by my father's time in the service. After his return, they realized that their marriage was not going to work. Finding that they were going to have a baby, they made the decision to put that child up for adoption.

I am that child, now forty-two years old. I began searching for my birth parents about a year ago. I believe my birth mother's name may be Sara. I know little about her except that her father, a pharmacist, died several years before I was born of a brain tumor, and she had one sister.

My birth father was trying to make a living as a photographer when I was born. His father was an advertising executive who died, I believe, in the 1970s. His parents had divorced when he was younger, and he had one sister who died in an accident.

Mr. Aylford, I don't know anything about you except that you have the same name as the man I seek. If you are my birth father, please understand that I don't want to cause problems for anyone, or intrude on a life that may not welcome me. I am just trying to put the missing pieces of my life together—to find out who I am, and who I come from.

Although I found your telephone number, I hesitate to use it—I don't have the nerve, I guess. As I said earlier, this is a difficult letter to write. I hope that you will write back to me, or call me if you would rather (maybe you have more nerve than I). I would love any information you can offer about my birth family, especially my birth mother. If you are my birth father, I promise I will follow your lead. If you don't want a surprise forty-two-year-old baby in your life, I understand and I won't bother you. I would just like to *know*.

Thank you,

Jil Picariello

3. BUNNY

THE NEW YEAR

We were very tired, we were very merry—
We had gone back and forth all night on the ferry.
And you ate an apple, and I ate a pear,
From a dozen of each we had bought somewhere;
And the sky went wan, and the wind came cold,
And the sun rose dripping, a bucketful of gold.

EDNA ST. VINCENT MILLAY
RECUERDO

I n my first year of college, a small, nervous professor repeatedly told us, "If you don't know where you're going, any road will take you there." I didn't know what he meant; I liked being able to take any road. My official grade for the term was an incomplete.

I was very passive then. That was the year my father died. He had been ill for years with a brain tumor, though it was a long time before we knew what was wrong with him. At first, he had problems with his eyes, though the doctor could find nothing wrong. Then my father began to behave oddly, in a variety of ways no one understood, but that my mother and I resented. After he collapsed on the street suddenly, while waiting for a bus, we found out about the brain tumor.

The coffin we lowered into the ground contained a person who could not have been my father. He resembled my father, but only in unpleasant ways. The living man who behaved so strangely all those months could not have been my adored— and adoring—father, who suddenly wanted to touch me too often, who stared at me for no reason, or was frequently angry about nothing I had actually done. His long, slow decline and death left more than his absence: It left an inexplicable gap of love and sorrow for the father he had been, and a chilly mystery about the man he had become. After he died, I dreamt he was still alive, but as he had been when I was younger.

Going back to college, to Antioch, the year after my father died was a refuge. There were friends there, and laughter. There were classes, even ones I slept through; and there were boys. There was music, a pile of 78s, and the first long-playing records. Back in New York City, between times at school, there was jazz uptown, with guitar, harmonica, and washtub bass, Brownie McGee and Sonny Terry. There was sentiment and there was nostalgia: Though the present was intense, we knew we'd want to remember everything.

Somehow there were almost always three of us. Everything was drama, but we were all so innocent. We were neither ignorant nor stupid; we were simply unprepared.

I'd known Jake at college from afar. He was a year or two ahead of me, a transfer student. He acted in various plays; he directed one; he painted; he wrote. He went out with Carol, and was a friend of Ann's. The third was another Ann, called by her last name, who kept company with a trombone player. Carol was beautiful—tall, as tall, or taller, than Jake. She moved slowly and serenely. Her eyes were huge and still. Ann, her friend as well as Jake's, was full of good cheer, a soul of sympathy and wisdom. I wasn't sure which of them I wanted to be. They were both ideal. And they were part of how I saw Jake: They gave him an aura beyond his own.

He smiled and said hello if we passed on the diagonal paths that crisscrossed the grass between buildings. But, then, Antioch was famous for its friendliness, among other things.

Jake also went out with one of my roommates, Karla. Together with my other roommate, Mary, Karla and I made three as well as one. Karla even looked a little like me, with a round face, soft, dark eyes, full lips—a face well-set over its bones, full of sympathy and strength. The look in her eyes said she was funny and smart.

I really *met* Jake at a New Year's Eve party in New York City. Though he was supposedly there with Karla, she spent most of the evening with someone else. We did that; but it wasn't that we didn't take the boys seriously—we didn't take ourselves seriously.

Technically, I met Jake on the stairs outside the apartment where the party was taking place. I wasn't having a good time, but I wasn't ready to leave. If I left, I would have to go home. I wasn't ready for the Long Island Railroad and the long ride to my mother's house—the widow's house.

This was my first weekend away from my co-op job. Antioch was a cooperative college, which meant that students worked in areas related to their field of study for half the time we were there, to gain practical experience to complement theoretical ideas and choices. I was interning in the music therapy department of the Marlboro State Mental Hospital in New Jersey, and I hated it.

At nineteen, I wasn't ready for underground tunnels lit by bare lightbulbs, or nights spent in my room in the employees' hall, hearing screams echoing across the lawns. In the dining room, we used the same napkin for several days, rolling it up into its ring after every meal, and unrolling it—damp, greasy, dirty—when we sat down again. Patients waited on tables, and watched us eat. I didn't think these were the patients who screamed at night, but it was hard to be sure. Though I kept a light on in my room all night, I found only a little less discomfort in the brightly lit dining room.

As part of my job, I had to take a portable record player to the electroshock therapy room, and play carefully chosen music for the patients as they were brought, struggling and shouting—resisting—into the room. After they had convulsed, there was different music to accompany them as they emerged from the shock, weak and sick, in a stupor, smoke drifting away from their bodies.

I also played the piano for Sunday morning chapel, as the patients shouted hymns, boisterously or reverently, but always with intense feeling. The music was new to me; Jewish girls don't know hymns.

"Oh, He walks with me and He talks with me," I sang as I played, "and He tells me I am His own. . . ." I didn't believe it, but I loved the music, and I loved hearing everybody sing as we rollicked along. During the sermons, on sunny days, I sat on the chapel's front steps and smoked.

On weekdays, I collected patients for music therapy sessions, going from building to building through the underground tunnels, waiting for doors to be locked and unlocked, with the more dependable patients at the head and the end of the line. In the middle were the patients who mumbled all the time, or were silent, or stared too much. They made sure never to look directly at anybody.

I played the piano again for them in the big music therapy room, with the emergency button on the wall near the door. We sang songs, and we danced. There was supposed to be a pattern to the music: quiet and slow at first, then faster and louder—the patients loved polkas —then quieter and slower, until the end of the class. Then back through the tunnels in our disorderly line.

Before I came to Marlboro, I thought the patients would be just like everybody else, but with problems that were perhaps just a little worse than most. I had imagined sitting next to some sweet, unhappy soul on a piano bench and teaching him a scale, or a simple melody, thus touching both his mind and his heart. Ah! Cured!

It wasn't like that. They were not almost like everybody else. They stared at nothing; they didn't move, or they moved too much, yelling, jerking, hulking, curled into themselves.

It all terrified me. Where do you find sense and reason in a world where the people who are supposed to be sane are giving electric shocks to the ones who are called insane? The insane ones have the sense to resist, but the others drag them into the room, while they scream and try to get away. Still fighting, still resisting, they're tied onto platform beds and attached to equipment that, in effect, plugs them into electric sockets. Through the shouts and the shocks and the smoky recovery, distant melodies were played on a tinny portable record player.

I had been wrong about insanity; I might be wrong about sanity, too. This party was my first weekend away from all that, back in the world I had once thought was reasonable. It would have been very difficult for me to have a good time at any party, when I was so unsure, and so alone.

I was just old enough to have learned to set myself apart when I needed to— to be separate by choice. Before, I would have stayed at the side of the room, at the edge of the party's life. I learned to be physically separate by watching Karla, who sat under tables, oblivious to everything at parties when she wasn't having fun—full of mystery and an odd, introspective air. That's what I wanted to convey.

I sat on the stairs, leaning my head against the wall, and listened to the music, barely audible under the voices, though the apartment door was open. When Jake came out, I moved closer to the wall so that he could get by. Instead, he sat down next to me.

I have to imagine words I don't remember, but the imagining—like memory—is real.

Jake's smile was lopsided, and because it was not perfect, not what it should have been, it seemed intimate.

"Which were you—on your way in, or out?"

"Undecided," I said.

"I was thinking about leaving," he said. "New Year's Eve parties don't make it. You keep thinking you're supposed to be having a better time, and you never do."

"Last year was lovely," I said. "We all went to Karla's mother's house and at midnight, we called Mary."

"Doesn't Mary live in Texas?"

"Dallas. It wasn't midnight there yet."

"You could follow midnight around the world that way," Jake said. The planed, flat surfaces of his face connected when he smiled.

After dropping out of Antioch, Jake had been drafted. This was 1953, and there was a war on in Korea. He wasn't wearing his uniform; if I had to guess, I'd say he was wearing brown corduroy pants and a blue shirt. His hair, brown, hung straight and fine across his forehead, which rose flat and high over his dark eyes.

"Do you hate the Army?" I asked.

"It's worse than anything anybody ever says: Nothing redeems it."

"What do you do? March around, clean rifles, all that stuff?"

"I did. Now I'm in Special Services, not quite so bad. I'm in a photography school."

"That sounds as though it might be a little redeeming."

"I won't allow it. I can be redeemed, but not the Army. So my redemption—my revenge—is photography school. I'm learning to see through a camera, to be a camera. They made me say, 'Yes, sir,' and they made me wear khaki underwear, but now I'm learning what I want to learn."

"Khaki underwear? Even on your days off?"

"When I start wearing khaki shorts on my days off, I'll know they've got me."

"Do you get to do anything you really want to, when you're not looking through a camera?"

"Sure. You've always got to find something you really want to do, and then you just do it. I come into the city. I go to parties. I talk to you."

I could only smile.

"And you?" Jake said. "Do you do what you really want to do? If you could do anything you wanted to do tonight, New Year's Eve, on the edge of 1953, what would it be?"

Want was such a strong word. "I'd like to go someplace I've never been," I replied.

We paused for a minute.

"Have you ever been to Staten Island?" he asked.

The native New Yorker blushed. "No."

"We could go over on the ferry, and when we get there, we'll get off and walk straight ahead, wherever that takes us."

Jake was an explorer, not a surveyor; he would never stay to measure. He was a person who found new places, new things, and new people, and then told others about what he'd found. That was how he saw the world: always brand new. Everything he did was an adventure, and every place he went was newly discovered.

Life was a romance. He was the captain of the Staten Island Ferry, sailing through the dark and icy waters of the Hudson River for the first time; natives waited for him on the far shore, and though they might be wild, he would know them, and love them. They would enchant him.

The second lesson in Jake's charm, after his smile, was that it was like a politician's, totally focused on you while he was in your presence. Later he might forget your name; but while he was with you, he was hard to resist.

After our walk from the ferry, we wandered into a neighborhood bar, decorated with bits of pine and Christmas tinsel, to warm ourselves. A Schaeffer beer sign on the wall opposite the bar offered "Season's Greetings" in big red letters. A few men sat at the long, dark counter, ringing out the old year in wet circles on the bar's shiny wooden surface. These people were, for the moment, and for whatever reason, where they wanted to be. Their fellowship was no less deep for being fleeting. Circumstances made them friends, not anything else. One of them smiled at us, surprising me; I had never been in this kind of bar before, and expected it to be a sullen place.

"Cold?" the stranger asked.

"Freezing," Jake said, and we both smiled. "We've never been here before, and we thought we'd start the year off by seeing Staten Island."

The men laughed. "That's the way to start the year, all right," the bartender said.

"Listen," said the first man, "lotta good people on Staten Island."

"Name three," another man said.

"Him, him, and him," somebody else volunteered, pointing at the bartender.

"I like it here," I said.

I felt as though I'd been allowed into a new part of the world, one that I'd always thought was private and closed, especially to women. No one in my family drank—except before family dinners, when the men would gather in the kitchen for schnapps, each holding a shot glass, calling out the toast—*L'chaim!*—and then throwing their heads back to swallow the amber liquid in one gulp before going back to the dining room to rejoin the women and children for dinner. I was sixteen before I found out that people drank in living rooms before dinner, men and women sipping slowly together. I'd been in bars at Antioch, but those were college bars. It wasn't that nice girls didn't want to go into corner bars then; it was that they—or I—didn't think they'd be allowed past the door. Now I'd found a passport, stamped "Good for Tonight Only." My enjoyment must have showed.

They all smiled, and said in unison: "Happy New Year!"

"You live in the city?" one of them asked Jake.

He shook his head. "I'm in the Army. I'm on leave from Fort Monmouth." Fort Monmouth, New Jersey, was less than ten miles from Marlboro State Mental Hospital.

"Lucky you—you RA (Regular Army)?"

"No," Jake said. "I was drafted."

"I'll buy you a drink for the holiday; for a GI and his girlfriend." He smiled at me. "You know how Staten Island got its name?"

Everybody else groaned.

"You know Henry Hudson, the one they named the river after? He was the first white man who ever saw this place. He was sailing up the river and he saw this chunk of land, and he said to the other guys on the boat, 'S'dat an island?' Like he couldn't believe it was worth it. And that's why it's called Staten Island."

I laughed. We drank together, and wished each other "Happy New Year!" yet again when we left.

Jake took me to Penn Station and waited for the train with me. By the time I got to my mother's house, the sun had come up. On the first day of the New Year, the world was still and golden as I moved through it.

4. JIL

THE CHOSEN BABY

I've always known I was adopted. I don't remember my parents ever telling me. It was simply a fact that went without saying. After all, did your mother tell you she gave birth to you?

My parents gave me a book, the first one I can remember, a slim book with a dark-green cover, a little faded and worn. It had lost its dust jacket somewhere along the way, and thin threads floated delicately off the spine like spider's webbing. Published in 1939, *The Chosen Baby* was a must-read for decades of adopted children. The warm watercolor pictures tell the story of the perfect couple, Mr. and Mrs. Brown, who are very much in love: "Only one thing was wrong. They had no babies of their own, although they always longed for a baby to share their home."

A lady named Mrs. White helps Mr. and Mrs. Brown find "a rosy, fat baby boy." Peter is clearly not a newborn when Mr. and Mrs. Brown meet him; he looks at them and smiles, laughs, then kicks his legs and wiggles his toes. But there is no suggestion that Peter has come from anywhere but heaven, and Mr. and Mrs. Brown know right away that he is their chosen baby. Soon a sister arrives from the same magical place, and they grow up healthy and rosy: "Peter and Mary like to hear the story of how they were adopted. And Mr. and Mrs. Brown and Peter and Mary are a very happy family."

The book was read to me; eventually, I read it myself, and the message sank in: I was chosen. I was lucky. We were a very happy family.

It seemed so logical: You want a baby, you decide to acquire a baby, and then you go and get a baby—like a car, or a toaster. Early on, I thought every child was adopted. In the way children have of accepting a magician's trick as perfectly ordinary, I accepted the magic of adoption. It was orderly and comprehensible— much more comprehensible than the real story of how babies are made, one I learned a few years later.

Growing up, my best friend Linda lived across the street. She was everything I wasn't: daring, fierce, fearless. Only six months older, but vastly more sophisticated, Linda was the first person I ever heard say *fuck* out loud. Lying under the sprinkler in my backyard, Linda revealed the secret of the erection to me, which explained a great deal about the mechanics of sex. In the winter of first grade as we walked home from school Linda said, grinning, "My mother can't have children, and neither can I." Then she laughed.

I didn't understand. How did Linda know she couldn't have children? And if her mother couldn't, did that mean Linda was adopted, too? Was this her way of telling me?

As I tried to unravel the mystery, I realized that she was staring at me. "Don't you get it, dodo?" she asked, poking me in the side. "If my mother can't have children, how the heck can I be here? It's crazy!"

Finally, I got it: If your mother couldn't have children, then you wouldn't exist. Yet somehow I did.

By third grade I had it fully figured out: the facts of life, and the facts of my life. My mother didn't believe in skimping on the birds and bees. Given that her own mother was a Russian Jewish immigrant with an Old-World inability to talk about anything related to sex, my mother erred in the opposite direction. My brother and I were never allowed to say those cute words other families used, like *wee-wee* and *poopy*, *number one* and *number two*. We knew only the clinical words: *penis*, *vagina*, *rectum*, *bowel movement*. And *sexual intercourse*: Never *sleeping together*, or *making love*, or even just *sex*.

I knew all the right names for all the implicated body parts, but had no idea what really happened. Questions about where babies came from, or where I came from, were discouraged. I knew I was adopted, but once I was old enough to wonder about the story of "the chosen baby," it was clear that the door was closed. Any questions I asked were dismissed with an impatient, "I don't know."

"We're very open," proclaimed my mother. "We don't hide anything." But when something more specific came up, there was only discomfort, evasion, and a palpable desire to end the discussion.

So we pretended that what I had been told early on was enough. I learned to be quiet, and to live with the pale shadow of a story I'd been given.

It was a sweet, simple story, the story of my adoption, a story I was told at such a young age that I was never really sure I'd actually heard it. Maybe I had dreamed it, or made it up: A young couple, still in college, marry too quickly, and then plan to divorce, but she discovers she is pregnant. The marriage is over; she can't raise a baby alone, so she does what is best for the baby (she is selfless; it is never about what is best for *her*). She saves the baby, throws it ashore from the sinking ship, into the safe and loving arms of my personal Mr. and Mrs. Brown.

In the legal papers, it's called *abandonment.* In adoption terminology, it's called *putting up* for adoption, a term that comes from the infamous orphan trains of the late nineteenth and early twentieth century, when as many as a quarter of a million children from the cities of the East Coast were sent by train to the Midwest and West. At each town where the train stopped, children were placed on display in the station—"put up" on platforms—so local families could look them over and make a choice, usually a child who looked best suited for hard work.

I wasn't chosen for my ability to work hard; in fact, I wasn't "chosen" at all, despite the book's title. For many years, I believed I was. The story of the Brown family made such an impression on me that the image I had of my "birth" was of a long white room, like a hospital nursery, but larger. It looked the way heaven looks in the movies, glowing with warm, white light, soft and fuzzy at the edges, as if the walls weren't really there, the room unwinding into a glowing bright infinity. Down the length of the long, long room stood row upon row of bassinets, and in each one was a pink and white baby swaddled in a soft white blanket. In my vision, a nurse in a starched apron leads my mother and father down the rows. They stop and look into each bassinet, then look at each other and shake their heads, *no, not this one,* moving slowly down the rows, until they get to *the one*—the baby who is just right for them. And they scoop me up and take me home forever.

By the time I discovered the real story, the long room with its rows of bassinets was so firmly implanted in my personal geography that sometimes it is still the birth I see for myself.

We pretended we were open and honest. But we were able to lay claim to our honesty only because everything that might cause pain was walled off where it couldn't hurt us.

We pretended we looked alike. I was blond and my mother was brown-haired; her eyes were pale, cool blue; mine green. She was dark-skinned; I was pale. I had a large, pointy chin; she was always ashamed of what she called her recessive "Queen Elizabeth chin." But people saw a mother and a daughter, and they said, bending down, leaning in, *You look just like your mommy,* and *You're the spitting image.* We smiled and said, *Thank you,* nodding politely, never looking at each other.

She never commented, casually, "Isn't it funny," though it happened everywhere we went, for years. I was large-boned, a stocky child, healthy, with thick hands and short, broad fingers. She had tiny hands with thin fingers, *chicken hands,* my father called them, and small, pointy-toed feet, made for the high heels and the deep V of 1950s pumps. I was ashamed of my wide, flat feet, and took to standing with one foot planted on the other shin, storklike, embarrassed.

We didn't speak much, my mother and me; we rarely touched. I have no memory of her stroking my hair, of her cool hand on mine, the feel of her fingers circling my back, heavy on my shoulder. And years later when I found the woman whose eyes were green, whose feet were broad, whose chin was pointy, she put out her hand to me. I saw the thick small fingers, and I thought: *She has my hands. She has my hands.*

5. BUNNY

EARLY DAYS

In a sense, each new life actually has no definite beginning.
Its existence is inherent in the existence of the parent cells
and these, in turn, have arisen from the preceding parent cells.

GERALDINE LUX FLANAGAN
THE FIRST NINE MONTHS OF LIFE

One month later, we were married.

I wouldn't have to live any longer in my perfectly rectangular room in the employees' hall at Marlboro, where I kept the light on all night and listened to the screams, and Jake wouldn't have to sleep on a cot in the barracks at Fort Monmouth and be awakened by a trumpet playing reveille.

Jake said he loved me, and I said I thought I loved him, too. (It was hard for me to make a definitive statement.) He said we would love each other for eighty-seven years, exactly. I said that didn't seem long enough. By his count, I would have been 106 when we stopped loving each other, and undoubtedly still in my prime.

My mother tended to think we hadn't loved each other long enough quite yet.

"Who is he? What do you know about him?" she asked me. "What do you know about his life, his family? You don't have to rush. He'll still be here in six months, and so will you. What's the hurry? How do you know this one is the right one? Wait a while, see how you feel, and then if you still want to, you can marry him. Slow down. Get to know him *before* the wedding, not after."

Why was she so stubborn? Why couldn't she understand how I felt? Why was my sister on my mother's side?

I sounded so sure when I talked to my mother because anything else would have been capitulation. It was now or never, Jake or no one, true love or nothing. There was never a bridge between her point of view and mine. One of us had to be right; clearly the other one was then wrong. As an adult, a mother of my own children, I've tried to think of what my mother might have said that would have convinced me to wait, and not marry someone I had known for only a month.

But there is nothing she could have said that would have stopped me. If she had threatened not to come to the wedding, I would have been sorry she couldn't be there. If she'd forbidden me to marry him, I would have done it anyway. She tried to bribe me with a trip to Europe; I wasn't interested.

Though I would never have admitted it then, there was always a part of me that didn't take the marriage seriously: If it didn't work, we could always get a divorce—shrug. At least getting married solved a lot of problems: I didn't have to live at Marlboro. I didn't have to go back to school. I could be free, an adult. I would belong somewhere, and I would belong to someone. I only had one decision to make—to get married. After that, Jake would make decisions for both of us; there would be no problem he couldn't solve. I wouldn't have to feel as if I'd abandoned my mother, who was still new to widowhood, by going back to school in Ohio—though, of course, I was abandoning her in the worst possible way.

I tried to explain how I felt: "It's the pointlessness of waiting. If we can be married now, why should we wait? We know what we want."

She only had one answer, which always came back to the same thing: "If you love each other, you'll still love each other in six months. If you want to get married then, I promise I won't object. I don't object to Jake. I don't even know him. What I object to is the hurry. What for? Wait!"

Jake's father gave him a ring to give me, a single pearl, very large and rough, of a creamy pink, with two small glittery diamonds on either side. I wondered whether he had bought it for us, or if it had been reclaimed from one of his previous wives. There were three, I think—or was it four, or even five? His ring didn't match in spirit the wedding rings we had selected: Each of the two was like a squared silver chain—one line of the chain for Jake and one for me. The links formed where our lives met; it was the kind of symbol Kahlil Gibran wrote about.

We had only made love once or twice before the wedding, barely successfully enough to save me from being a virgin bride. I didn't wear white—only because the dress I liked was blue, an iridescent blue silk that shimmered and changed into shades of near-green as I moved. It reminded me of all the summers I'd spent at the beach, my eyes sunstruck from sand and sea, and the blue of the ocean.

My mother wore a black suit. Did she mean to mourn so publicly? Or was it a Freudian slip of the closet? As I recall, my sister wore a black suit, too. She insists she did not, and that she tried to persuade my mother not to, either. The image I have of my family—those who were present at the small civil ceremony held in

Jake's father's apartment on East 64th Street—is of a row of dark, solemn, unhappy figures, something like the totems on Easter Island.

Weddings are like pardons granted from reality. Of all our ceremonies, they are the most innocent—celebrations of hope, of trust, of the springtime of love. Inevitably, the weather changes later; but, for that moment, everyone believes like children again, in terms of happily-ever-after, "for better or for worse." Tears shed are not for what will surely follow. They are the tears of completion: We have arrived safely at this point. Let's pretend that the rest of the journey will be safe and happy, that this ceremony is a strong enough blessing. We remember the journey to this point; how incredible and wonderful it is that we are still safe. Now there will be joy; we celebrate.

Jake found a furnished apartment in Atlantic Highlands, a sweet, small town near the ocean, south of Sandy Hook, in New Jersey. It was a converted attic in a big old stone house. The wallpaper in the living room had roses all over it; the bed was tucked under one of the eaves in the bedroom; and the kitchen was a tiny square next to the bedroom.

Jake also found a 1938 four-door Ford touring sedan convertible, red, with leather seats, swooping fenders, and a wooden shelf between the front seat and the back to separate the passengers from the driver. Sometimes when we parked it on the street in Manhattan, we'd come back and find a note under the windshield wiper: "Call me if you want to sell this car."

In the mornings, I drove Jake to the base, and then went on to Marlboro; I picked him up in the afternoon after work. Everything was different, from taking buses to meet in the biggest town between Fort Monmouth and Marlboro, and meeting in bars, or going to the movies, wishing we had a room of our own. Now we had a room of our own—three rooms, in fact.

From Jake, I learned about photography as we went through endless books and magazines: I had to look at each photograph and say what I liked about it, and what I didn't. He taught me to frame a picture through the tunnel of a double-lens reflex camera, and how to hold a camera without feeling conspicuous, a kind of arrogant stealth. He taught me how to develop my photographs afterward. He taught me how to have my picture taken—as if I were completely unaware that there was a camera anywhere nearby.

He taught me how to make salads his way. I made them the way my mother did, with lettuce, tomato, green pepper, cucumber, onion. Too much, he said, with too many things. When his father came to dinner, I think I made a salad all of lettuce. I made a salad dressing of sour cream with lemon juice and dried thyme, from a cookbook a friend had sent as a wedding present. And, as I recall, I made my mother's stuffed cabbage. What did we talk about? Was one of his father's wives along? I don't remember anything but the salad.

We only had one fight: He used toothpaste neatly, from the bottom of the tube to the top, and I just picked up the tube and squeezed, leaving it crimped and bent. That made him angry.

When he said he was going out to get the paper, and was gone for hours, I wasn't angry: I was wildly jealous. Had he been to see Carol? She was in New York City. Tormented and desperately unhappy, I didn't say anything about these disappearances.

When he left letters he'd received on the top of our bureau: "Dear Jake, I loved seeing you again," he always had a good explanation: "I lent her my Robinson Jeffers books. That's all. Absolutely nothing happened."

We found an empty, silent house on the ocean, abandoned after a fire, with a boathouse next door, its own boardwalk, tennis courts, and weeds everywhere. We climbed through the ruined rooms, taking pictures. We found burned books, some with the ashes all blown away, but others with the words still visible. Everywhere we turned, there were charred silhouettes of what had been.

When the Army sent Jake to Germany, we had been married for less than half a year. We had already begun to wish we had never gotten married.

Jake had a leave coming, so before he left we drove out to visit his mother at her family's old beach house, near Benton Harbor on Lake Michigan. The lake was all about childhood summers in affluent middle America: barefoot walks, tall grasses on the sides of the roads, brown cow ice cream sodas in the middle of the afternoon, weeds and wildflowers, bees, sand dunes, dogs shaking themselves after swimming in the shallow water, voices everywhere—but no people to be seen.

Jake's mother was an older, more gracious-looking version of Jake, with the same aura—that of the enchanted explorer. She was tall and graceful. You could tell she had been somewhat bohemian when she was young. Jake said that when she was in college, she and her friends used to drive across the sand on moonlit nights with their headlights turned off. She was warm of heart, although a little remote; I liked her very much and felt comfortable with her, though she was far removed from my own intense, warm, open, and involved mother.

She talked a little about the girls Jake had gone out with before me; she'd met Carol and Ann. I thought she liked me, but I wasn't sure. I think she felt sorry for me, as she did for Jake. She knew we were unhappy.

The ride back from Lake Michigan progressed through what was then the farmland of borderline Midwest America: rolling patches of land, clutches of trees, Burma Shave signs, and eventually new turnpikes—dullards even then, though we talked about how beautifully the curves were banked. It ended in the surrealism of northern New Jersey, with car dealers, food, furniture, factories, dead marshes, smudgy skylines, smells. I remember that I was wearing a blouse Jake loved, and I wondered if that was why he said he thought we should try again.

Or maybe his mother had suggested it.

After dropping Jake off at the Army Embarkation Center in New Jersey, I got lost in the maze of bridge and tunnel approaches to New York City, and stopped at a diner for directions. There were enormous trucks parked in rows off to one side. As I started toward the diner, a brightly lit magnet in the back of the lot, a man emerged from the tunnel of dark trucks. Though he was imperfectly silhouetted, I could see that he was tall and thin, and had an intense look. The features of his face seemed crowded together.

"You looking for something?" he asked me.

"I seem to be lost," I said, smiling. "I'm trying to find the George Washington Bridge."

"Where you coming from?" he asked, as if that would help him decide which road I should now take.

"The Army Embarkation Center."

"Yeah?" He smiled. "Saying good-bye to a soldier?"

"My husband."

"You look too young to be married. You're gonna miss him, aren't you?"

"Yes."

"You scared?"

I couldn't imagine why I should be.

"No," I said. "I just want to find the bridge."

He pointed. "Right over there." He looked back at me again. "Want a cup of coffee or a drink?"

"No, thanks," I said. "I'm kind of tired."

"I have a place where you could rest . . ."

"No, thanks," I repeated. "Which way do I go to the bridge?"

"Come over here, I'll show you."

Before I could move, he grabbed me, and put one arm around my back, and the other on my shoulder. His mouth was on mine at the same instant, his tongue cold, wet, tasteless, and hard.

He let my rigid body go as suddenly as he had grabbed me. "I hope you did better for your soldier." His smile was a sneer.

He turned and walked toward the cave of trucks. I got back to the car, and remembered how to start it. Later I stopped at a gas station for directions.

All the way back to the city, I tried to wipe out the inside of my mouth, by spitting, and then rubbing with my fingers until I gagged. Jake was gone, and this was the sour taste I was left with.

6. JIL

ANOTHER CHOSEN BABY

I grew up in a classic suburban split level, a little white Monopoly house with three bedrooms and two-and-a-half baths. Our development spanned Francesco Drive and Rosaria Lane, named for the mother and father of the developer, Mr. Niccolini. My street, Francesco Drive, wound gracefully through turns and hills until it peaked and dove straight and sharply down into a big circle at the bottom, like a tilted exclamation mark with a large round dot. We didn't call it a cul-de-sac; that term was too fancy for us. We called it a dead end. For the six houses on the hill and loop at Francesco's conclusion, our world was defined by that peak and circle.

The hill was perfect for sledding in the winter and skateboarding in the summer; in the circle, we played kickball and tag and dodgeball all year round. The six families were all close. One Greek, one Italian, one Irish, two Jewish, one German—all the dads had served in the war, and then come home and left the Bronx and Washington Heights behind for backyards and trees and a good place for kids to play. There were fifteen kids living in those six houses, and the front doors were never locked.

In warm weather, the mothers gathered on back lawns or patios and brought out platters of meat for the grills and bowls of cold salads: potato salad, macaroni salad, cole slaw. In summer the children played in the circle and in the woods behind the houses all day and into the chill fire-flied darkness. The mothers drank pastel drinks with stylish names, whisky sours and Manhattans and Tom Collinses. The men drank in shades of amber: scotch on the rocks, seven and seven, rye and ginger.

This was my mother in her world: tightly wound, straight-backed, never slack, except after a drink or two. Head to toe she was a puzzle of pieces held firmly in place. Her hair was dyed blond, lacquered and rigid with hair spray, an arrangement she adjusted every Friday morning at the beauty parlor. It never stirred, not even in the wind. Her makeup was careful and always the same: pale blue shadow to complement her blue-gray eyes, mascara, rouge, and lipstick in a dark orangey-red. A substantial bosom compressed into cone-shaped brassieres, white in the daytime, black at night. She wore thin, pointy shoes to flatter her small feet, and a thick, powerful, ironlike girdle that squeezed and squashed her middle. Sometimes, for special occasions, she wore a model that combined the cones and the girdle and went all the way from the top of her breasts to the middle of her thigh—the formidable "all-in-one."

My father was her opposite—tall, lanky, and graceful. He mastered anything physical with ease. He was the best dancer I ever saw, the best driver. He played several instruments by ear, could draw anything from memory, could fix any machine, pull loose teeth painlessly, close a wound, and, so he said, set a broken bone.

My mother bullied her way through life, demanding, fighting, and pushing. Her world was filled with danger, forbidding and dark. My father glided through his sunny world with ease, welcomed by all. He rarely said no, was always ready to jump a car, climb a ladder, or lend a buck. She was his protector as much as she was ours, the harsh voice he would never use, the bad news he could not deliver—his wife, guardian, and mother.

When I was six, Billy Ciano asked me what I was.

"Jewish," I said, puzzled. He knew I was Jewish as well as I did. Everyone's ethnic background was up for discussion on the circle. We were all relatively recent immigrants, just one foot out of some ghetto or other, and the grown-ups were proud of themselves for getting along so well.

"No, what are *you*?" he said. "Not your parents—your *real* parents."

I looked at him, confused. And then I got it. I was stunned. I had never thought of this before. I felt embarrassed. How could I not know what I was? Everyone knew what they were; everyone was *something*.

"Jewish, too," I said. I didn't want Billy, so much more confident, to realize I didn't know this important fact.

"How do you know?" Billy asked.

"They told me," I lied.

That night at bedtime, I mustered my courage and asked my mother as she sat at the edge of my bed in the darkened room.

"Where do I come from?"

She answered quickly. "You were born in New York."

"I mean what country? Like Billy's parents came from Italy."

I couldn't see her face, but she sat up a little straighter.

"My parents came from Russia," she said. "And your daddy was born in Vienna—in Austria."

Even at six, I knew the discussion was supposed to end there. But in the dim light, I was brave.

"But where am I from?" I asked again. "Just me—what am I?"

She stood up, straightened the blanket. "My parents came from Russia," she repeated. "You're the same as me." She kissed my cheek and left the room.

In the darkness I tried to parse her statement. Was I the same as her because I was her daughter? Was I the same as her because the woman in my Chosen Baby story came from Russia, too? Was I the same as her because she said so? I had asked as much as I dared.

I learned to notice the things my mother did not say. The other mothers on the circle talked about what they called "women's problems": menstrual pain, husbands who demanded too much sex, or not enough, miscarriage, pregnancies, labor and delivery. After two or three whiskey sours, the other women didn't seem to notice that my mother had nothing to contribute. From around the corner of the patio I watched her, straight-backed in her chair, the only one not swaying into the circle of women, her lips compressed, her legs tightly crossed.

I knew a little of her story. As a teenager, her periods were heavy and horribly painful. My grandmother took her to a doctor, a *shtetl* doctor, an immigrants' doctor. He said she needed an operation, and they were not the kind of people to question a doctor's decision. He put her in the hospital and performed a hysterectomy. She knew, from what she overheard, that she could never have children. She didn't know why.

When she came home from the hospital, the dressing on her wound had to be changed every day. My grandmother couldn't bring herself to look; my grandfather had to do it. He was unwell, a man with a weak heart who was not allowed to exert himself in any way. But in addition to his bad heart, while my mother was in the hospital recovering from her surgery, he had developed hysterical blindness, losing first his sight, and then also his ability to speak. In his darkness and silence, he changed the dressing every day. Perhaps this was the only way he could allow himself to perform this intimate, horrific act: blind, mute, changing the bandages on a brutal wound.

As a child, I knew very little about all this. The story was pieced together over a lifetime, a fragment here, a detail there. My shadowy childhood was filled with secrets, whispers in corners, whispers on the telephone, whispers I wove together into stories that made sense of my existence.

When I was four, we adopted my brother. My mother bought me a big baby doll. This was to be *my* new baby, so I would not be jealous of *her* new baby. I named her Jessica, my favorite name, and I carried her everywhere. I carried Jessica on my lap in the back seat when we drove into the city to pick up my new brother.

Even to the untrained eyes of a four-year-old, I knew my mother's new baby was not beautiful. I couldn't figure out why she had picked him out from all the rows of bassinets in the long white room of my imagination. Kenny had a large head of thick, dark hair that stuck out damply from his skull in pointy clumps, like wet weeds. Over the next few weeks, the house filled with visitors welcoming the baby. My new brother was so unappealing that even the kindest grown-ups were hard-pressed to compliment him. "What a lovely chin," one woman clucked. "Such a lot of hair!" another offered. One that became a family favorite: a pause, a thoughtful moment, then, "He has a beautifully shaped head."

My brother didn't have a sweet story of a college romance and failing marriage. He didn't have any story at all. As I got older I wondered if he were the child of a prostitute, or a foundling, a baby in a basket—a Moses of Manhattan.

For two years after Kenny arrived, until the adoption was finalized, my father and I drove to the train station every other Monday to pick up Mrs. Tanner, the agency's caseworker, the same caseworker who had visited after my adoption. Mrs. Tanner walked through the house, making sure everything was clean and healthy; then she and my parents would chat briefly before we drove her back to the train. If my mother was nervous about this woman coming to judge her, to run her finger along the lintels and check the contents of her refrigerator, week after week for two long years, she hid it well.

Kenny was born with enlarged adenoids and tonsils, had difficulty swallowing and digesting food, and projectile-vomited on a regular basis. Until he was four and had surgery to remove his tonsils and adenoids, he would choke on even the mushiest of foods. Long before Dr. Heimlich invented his maneuver, my mother developed hers: She would grab Kenny by the ankles, lift him swiftly upside down, and pound on him until whatever was trapped got knocked free.

I was terrified of his choking and vomiting. I was sure Kenny would stop breathing, or explode, or die. When the gasping started, I would run from the room, hide under the dining room table or my bed, put my fingers in my ears and sing "Jingle Bells" until the danger passed. I didn't like my baby brother much; I didn't like how he had disrupted our family life. I didn't like his smell, or his sticky dark hair, or his noises, his snuffling and choking. I didn't see much use for him; at best he was boring, at worst, disturbing.

I spent a lot of time hidden in my room with a book. Like my green eyes and small hands, this passion seemed to have sprung from nowhere at all. Other than the supply catalog where he ordered equipment for his contracting business, I never saw my father read anything other than the newspaper. On Sundays I sat on his lap while he read the comics in the *Daily News*. I loved Brenda Starr, her red hair, the twinkle in her eyes. I loved that she was a reporter, and worked with words. All the men I knew worked with their hands, all the women I knew stayed home and raised a family. But sparkly Brenda Starr wrote things and was glamorous.

My father was too impatient to read to me, so week after week I tried to work out the markings for myself. Slowly, I unlocked the secrets to Little Orphan Annie and Li'l Abner. By the time I went to kindergarten at age four, I could read every word in the comics.

Our house held three books: the heavy Dr. Spock on my mother's bedside table, a Jewish family cookbook that was stained and oily despite the fact that I'd never seen my mother use it, and a rotating best seller that the women in the circle passed around from house to house like a fire bucket: Jacqueline Susann one week, Harold Robbins the next.

I was never without a book. Other than the kids on the circle, who were my friends by proximity, I was a lonely and unformed child. I played in the circle after school and on weekends, but I rarely went home with a friend; I was never invited to a birthday party. I had almost no sense of myself, no image of who I was, or how others saw me. In third grade I looked around the room and realized that I could label each child with just one or two words. Richard: He was the funniest boy. Susanne was giggly and helpless; the boys liked her. Peter was tough, aggressive. Donald was dumb; he still struggled to read. Clare was the smart one; even in third grade we all knew she would be a doctor someday, like her father. Elizabeth was the most popular girl; she ruled the social scene. Even Eric had an identity: He was strange; white flecks coated the sides of his mouth. He was the one we picked on.

But I was a cipher. I could not choose even one word that defined me. I could not imagine how the other children saw me; I wasn't sure they saw me at all. To them, and to myself, I was invisible and at the same time, hypervisible, sure that my oddness made me stand out. I felt both acutely self-conscious and completely unreal. Sometimes I would touch my chest, my arms, and my neck, to make sure I was really there.

I started writing stories—vivid, florid tales of princesses and dragons and wild, romantic rescues. As I read and I wrote, my mother yelled up the stairs, "Go outside and play. Get some fresh air." After a few minutes she'd march to the door of my room and stand there, hands on hips. "This isn't why we moved from the Bronx, for you to stay in your room all day with a book."

Once I showed her one of my stories in order to explain myself, and because I was proud of it. She laughed at the language, the flowery childish words. "This is so funny!" she crowed. "Better than Buddy Hackett!"

"It's not supposed to be funny," I said, clenching my jaw to hold back tears.

"But it is," she said. "It's very funny."

She called her friend across the street, Mrs. Spyros, and read her a couple of pages out loud. "Can you believe this?" she laughed into the phone. "It's hilarious."

After that, I kept my writing to myself.

I loved my books: *Nancy Drew, Little Women, Cherry Ames Student Nurse,* the *Five Little Peppers,* the *Oz* tales. I was happiest when I was in another world. I dragged heavy loads of books home from the library. "Stop carrying all those books. You're going to get a hernia," my mother warned. "You're going to hurt your eyes."

My mother had a warning about everything. I was not allowed to sleep at friends' homes, even Linda who lived just across the street and whose mother was my mother's closest friend. Until the day I left for college, I wasn't allowed to sleep in the home of someone I was not related to. I begged my mother, I asked her why; but she was as evasive as a Mafia don on the witness stand.

"You can have your friends sleep at our house."

"You see your friends all day; you don't need to sleep there, too."

"We don't know these people."

Later I realized that my mother could not give me a reason because she didn't know what it was herself. Her number-one instinct was for safety at all costs. She was motivated by fear. If I slept in someone else's home I was beyond her protection. *Things* could happen—scary, unknown things.

She didn't even like me eating in other homes. When I went to my friend Susan's house for dinner, my mother warned me: *If you don't know what it is, don't eat it. Just move it around on your plate and say you're not hungry. Or put a few pieces in a napkin and hide it in your pocket until later.*

Susan's family was Italian: They might serve trashy food, cheap food, tinny canned hams, or, worst of all, chopped meat from the supermarket. When I became an adult and found out that lots of people ate ground beef from the supermarket and not the ground beef the kosher butcher made from meat right in front of you, I was shocked. My mother told me that supermarket chopped meat was filled with all the things they couldn't sell: tails, gristle, cartilage, ears, and feet. It wasn't a matter of being kosher; we were not kosher. Eating in someone else's home was simply bad, dangerous, and *unsafe*.

Sometimes I wondered if my mother would have been less overprotective if I were not adopted. Perhaps being entrusted with this most valuable commodity—a child—turned her natural instinct for safety into a mania. Six years of waiting on a list for a baby, then two long years of weekly inspections: If something happened to me, she would not only have to answer to herself, my father, and her God, but to the agency, the social worker, the judge who finalized the adoption, the court system, the whole watching world. Did she feel she had to justify their approval of her as an adoptive mother by keeping us safe, always safe?

Friends were not safe. She told me over and over: Friends will turn on you; only family is there for you. "Blood is thicker than water," she said. But what did that mean? My blood and her blood had nothing in common; but somehow they were the same. What was this adoption magic that passed over our lives and made our blood identical?

I read my books, alone in my room, and wrote my stories. But my own story lay untouched, unquestioned. I rarely thought about the nice young couple who did the right thing for their baby. I never wondered about how I came to be reading book after book and writing story after story in a family that did not read, that did not write. I never asked myself or anyone around me: What are you born, and what do you become? How is the difference measured, and how does it matter?

7. BUNNY

WAITING

The Rembrandt light of memory,
finicky and magical and faithful at the same time,
as the cheaper tint of nostalgia never is.

IVAN DOIG
THE WHISTLING SEASON

I had no place to stay. I didn't want to go to my mother's; I would have been too helpless. Jake had given me the address of a woman he'd heard of in the Village, on Bank Street, who liked to take care of people. Maybe she'd let me stay with her until I found a place of my own.

She wanted to help me, she said. But she had put a man upstairs, and some girls in the other rooms, and she was already sharing her bedroom. So she let me stay on her couch, downstairs. When I woke up in the morning, I discovered somebody else had arrived after me, and had also been added to the household.

Years later, I found out that I had slept overnight in Auntie Mame's living room.

I went from there to our friends, Betty and Rick.

They lived on the Lower East Side, before it was the East Village, or Alphabet City, though they were between Avenues A and B. Betty was a small, elfin young woman with an open, sweet face circled by wisps of curly dark hair. Her body was fairly unbalanced by the enormity of her bosom. Her voice was soft, too, whispery, confiding, understanding. From Betty, sweet Betty, I learned how to use tampons, and I think she also told me about getting a diaphragm from the Margaret Sanger clinic. I had one; I just never used it.

Rick was an Antioch dropout, like Jake. He'd been drafted, too, but was a conscientious objector, a Quaker, and was working off his term of duty at Payne Whitney Hospital in Manhattan. He shared Betty with the world, but he worried about it. Now they both worried about me, on their couch, looking for a job, an apartment, a life. Staying in their apartment was like being in a warren, dark and quiet, the light barely penetrating through the endless rows of identical buildings, crowded and filthy.

Dinner at Betty and Rick's was an anachronism. Betty came home from work and made dishes like trout almondine. I set the table (the coffee table across from my couch), and we talked about Woody Guthrie, because he lived nearby, and photography and friends from Antioch and the awful new cars with huge fender fins, and poetry. At night, on the couch, I listened to their bedsprings creak and wanted to move.

Within a week, I found a day job, a night job, an apartment, a roommate, and a therapist, Alfred Ennis. He had been recommended by my psychology professor at Antioch. (In fact, a lot of Antiochians had an interlude with Ennis.) He wasn't much to look at: pallid, and tall and thin, shaped like an inverted numeral three, with rounded shoulders, and a stomach protruding slackly, triangularly, toward his toes.

After the first few visits, he explained his philosophy: "I once had a patient who was afraid of subways. I told her there was only one real solution, only one way to overcome her fear. She had to get used to subways. She had to take the subway.

"She tried it. It was difficult at first. We spent much time here talking about it. And she kept trying: uptown and downtown; the Seventh Avenue, the Independent, the BMT, and the Lexington. She kept trying.

"And when she got through, she wasn't afraid of subways."

I tried to look impressed, but I was mystified.

"But what should I do? I'm not afraid of subways. And I'm not afraid of Jake, either."

"No," he agreed. "But there is a problem here, isn't there?"

"I'm not happy," I said. "Jake is the problem. Why hasn't he written to me? How can I fix that?"

"Do you want him to write?"

"Of course I do."

"I wonder why you married Jake," he asked.

"Because we love each other." That seemed the obvious answer, still.

"Are you sure? Do you really love him?"

I had to think. "I'm not sure. But I've never felt that way about anybody else. Was that love? I don't know. I thought he was marvelous—I appreciated him."

"Maybe you married him because he asked you. Maybe you thought no one else would ever ask you?"

"I'm only nineteen, for heaven's sake."

"Ah! That's it exactly," he smiled. "I think you need more experience."

"But if Jake doesn't write me, how will I get it?"

"Screw around for a while."

It occurred to me that now we were getting to the subway idea.

"But I'm married." He waited. "And everybody I know knows that I'm married."

"Find someone new. Pick someone up."

I stopped thinking; I just listened.

"Go places where you can meet men—nice men, of course. Museums, galleries, libraries, coffee shops in the Village—places you like to be, wherever you think might be best. Pick out an interesting-looking man, look at him, and this is important: Make eye contact. Follow him if you have to. Be sure he notices you. Talk to him if you can. Ask for a match, or the time. Or say something about the weather, or whatever he's looking at. He'll take it from there. If he doesn't, try again with someone else.

"You need more confidence in yourself," he concluded. "Our time is up for today. We'll explore this further next time."

About two weeks after Jake left, I'd received a package from him, a large envelope containing daily newspapers from the transport ship he was on. They were legal-sized paper, folded in half, all about the voyage, and news gathered from the ship's radio: the weather, the speed of the ship. There was nothing personal, nothing from Jake.

My roommate, Sally, another friend from Antioch, was as puzzled by the package as I had been. We'd been friends from the very first day at Antioch, when she and Mary and I had taken a blanket out to the front lawn, in front of the campus's main building, and stayed up all night to watch the sun rise.

Now Sally was doing what my mother had wanted me to do: waiting. She was formally engaged to Leo, a soldier, drafted, like Jake—and now stationed in Georgia. She saw a rabbi several evenings a week, in the process of converting before the wedding, for Leo's mother.

Sally radiated patience and goodness and acceptance, all underlined by an ineffable aura of unhappiness, unease. She had the kind of face that belonged to a different time: She would have been a beautiful flapper. We shared a furnished studio apartment in Brooklyn Heights, beautiful Brooklyn Heights, where Long Island meets Manhattan, just below the Brooklyn Bridge. The Promenade, a long walk above the river, had one of the city's best views. Sally and I walked and gazed wistfully at the ships being loaded, getting ready to cross the ocean for South America, Africa, Asia, and Europe: the continents.

We were both saving money: Sally, for her wedding; me for the unknown future, and to pay Dr. Ennis. At home we ate hot dogs and sauerkraut for dinner. After dinner, we cooked hard-boiled eggs for breakfast in the morning, and we made sandwiches (sliced Spam and pickles, the cheapest thing we could think of) to take to work for lunch.

After we peeled the eggs, we'd lean against our windows and talk. Less than a year out of college, school was a very distant memory. We were caught between what we remembered, and what we were planning, the past and the future. Both of us lacked a present tense: Sally was waiting for Leo to come home for the wedding, and I was waiting for a letter from Jake. The simple fact of our friendship helped us both. Every so often, Leo appeared, and I disappeared. Our days were comfortable, and indistinguishable.

I spent my days working at Cinerama. Cinerama was a wide-screen multidimensional film effect with stereophonic sound, which supposedly brought the viewer into the action. A film using these new techniques was showing at a theater on Broadway. I remember a long sequence of roller-coaster rides, the viewer in the first car, careening up and down the rails, the sound track full of shrieks.

I sat all day in a narrow room, like a large horizontal closet, off the back of the auditorium, near the entrance. There were two or three telephones on a narrow table. On the wall behind the phones were lightbulbs that lit up when the phones rang. The chair in front of the table barely missed touching the door.

There I sat: "Yes, there are tickets for tomorrow's matinee." Or: "The evening showing begins at 8:30." I was the recorded announcement.

At night, I worked at Tavern on the Green as a cigarette girl, in a white blouse and a black skirt, with the cigarette and candy tray hung from a cord around my neck. "Cigarettes? Cigars? Candy?" We weren't supposed to accept tips, but each new girl was quickly initiated: You sewed or pinned a sock to the inside of your skirt's waistband, and dropped the tips into it as you went. By the end of the evening, on a good night you had a sock full of quarters, half-dollars, and even dollars, thudding against you as you walked.

I was saving money in the hope that I would go to Germany as soon as Jake wrote. Unfortunately, he didn't.

I tried following Dr. Ennis's therapeutic suggestions, but I was too timid. I called some young men I had known before; one took me to lunch at the Astor, where I was shocked to discover that the price of one cup of coffee would have kept Sally and me in sauerkraut for weeks. Another, now interning at Long Island Hospital, was more like me: We walked, sat on the Promenade and talked, and then had coffee with Sally in our room. Nothing came of any of this. Ennis never asked me how my adventures had gone and I never brought up the subject.

I continued to write to Jake via an APO address: short letters filled with dissertations about how the city renewed itself forever, discarding old, infirm buildings and reclaiming their tiny pieces of land for new roots; summer heat in New York bringing the city to its knees, humbling everybody, but thickening their ties to each other as they suffered together. I look back on those letters as filled with a nineteen-year-old's wonder, giving shiny significance to the world. This kind of seriousness must be as much a measure of youth as it is of unhappiness.

My mother worried about Jake's silence, but she said little about it other than asking me the occasional question: "Have you heard yet?"

On weekends when Leo displaced me, she was glad to see me, and she fed me properly. Until it was too chilly, my sister and I drove to the beach and lay on the sand while children played around us; their voices, their parents' radios, and the sound of the waves floating through the air. I felt full of the heat of the sun, watching the ocean, hearing the disembodied words. I can always face the world better after I've been to the beach, where nothing is a problem, because nothing exists—just sand, heat, the ocean, and me.

I lived that way for five months; but it was an endless, bottomless time, with very few landmarks. The mailbox anchored the days as they passed. A letter never came—or rather, a telegram came first.

"Sell the car. Come immediately. Letter follows. Love, Jake."

Nine words: Every one counted.

My mother was outraged. He hadn't written in five months. In all that time, my mother never said I told you so; she waited without comment, trying not to hurt my feelings.

"Come immediately! That's ridiculous!" she said. "How can you sell the car so fast? Why should you even sell it? How can you trust this man? Why didn't he write if he wants you to come immediately? Who does he think you are?"

With every question I felt more obstinate and more strongly that she was daring me to answer—when obviously there were no answers, certainly none that I could supply, or even bear to contemplate. My mother was protecting me from Jake in the most efficient way she knew, by demolishing me first herself. And the more negative she was, the more positive I had to become.

We agreed I would wait until a letter arrived.

"Don't run when he calls," my mother said. "'Let it be his turn to wait."

Ennis saw it differently.

"Why not go? It's a chance to see Europe, isn't it? Even if the marriage doesn't work out—and no sense fooling yourself, it probably won't—at least you'll have been to Paris. Don't deny yourself experiences."

I was happy; Jake wanted me to be with him. Sally was the only one who understood how I felt, though I suspect that she, too, felt sorry for me. Soon Leo would be back; he was expecting a transfer. They would be married, and she would only need the apartment a month or so longer. Sauerkraut had begun to lose its luster for both of us. She was sure I should go to Europe, immediately. I would find out what I needed to know there, not here.

My sister thought of other things, as she had when we decided to get married.

"Why don't you wait until he writes before you decide? He said he'd write. And then at least you'll know more. Now you don't even know where you'll be going—France, Germany, England, or where you'll be living. You don't know what you'll need. How long will you be there? Wait until he writes you and then decide. There isn't any point in making up your mind until you have all the facts. Sometimes not making a decision is a decision."

She was right; and besides, I had no choice but to wait. Jake's letters—two or three of them, fat pages, scrawled words, wonderful letters—arrived in a week.

Jake had been in Munich, beautiful, with Oktoberfest—beer and spitted lambs. He'd made his first joke in German. He had civilian friends. He'd sold his typewriter and bought some German clothes and only wore his uniform when the Army gave him no choice. As staff photographer for the post newspaper, he'd taken pictures of Gregory Peck. He was being transferred to Stuttgart, to Special Services. If I came, we could live off the post, wherever we wanted. Maybe we could buy a car. Everything was cheap or could be traded for. I should send him a cable to let him know when I was arriving, and he would borrow a car and meet me.

Even my mother agreed that I should go. I bought a ticket for an outside cabin, a single, on the *Ryndam,* a Holland America ship that was all one class. It was to sail in mid-November.

8. JIL
{ NINE
{ AND NEUROTIC

I really wanted to be a good Girl Scout, but I couldn't figure out how. It seemed as if everyone else had gotten instructions but me. I loved the forest-green uniform, the sash that draped from shoulder to hip, as if I were a Miss America contestant. I loved the badges I worked so hard to acquire: Basketry, Drawing and Painting, Music, Home Health, Sewing, Cooking, all with tiny embroidered pictures. I liked to follow rules. And I liked the scout troop meeting place, a long rectangular cabin built from actual logs, with a small bathroom at one end and a raised platform at the other, where we performed Indian chants, beating sticks to keep time, and practiced our oath and songs. I loved the oath itself, promising enthusiastically to be "clean in thought, word, and deed." It was the first time I ever wondered about the alternative.

I loved the *Girl Scout Handbook,* thick with what seemed to be all the advice anyone could ever need: how to survive in the woods, how to build a fire from twigs, how to be a good citizen. Surely somewhere in these hundreds of pages I would find the instructions for how to be the thing I most longed for: just like everyone else.

In June, after school ended, my entire troop went to Girl Scout Camp for five days. Amazingly, my mother gave me permission, despite her fear—her *horror*—of my eating and sleeping outside her dominion. The Girl Scouts were so wholesome, so *American,* that she couldn't summon up the will to resist my pleas.

The camp was scruffy and bare, a murky pond and a quartet of cold, damp cabins huddled around the dusty circle where we built our campfires and gathered in the evenings to roast marshmallows and sing songs. In between cooking breakfast on the rusty barbecue pits and the evening songfest there wasn't much to do; it was too cold to swim, and we quickly tired of hiking in the dark, piney woods. Without much purpose or order to our days, the group quickly devolved. There were tormentors and victims, just as there were in school; but here we had eight hours a day of unsupervised, unseen time.

Luckily for me, we had a new member, who was almost too good to be true. The new girl had a lisp, and a limp. She wore glasses; best of all, her name was Bertha. To my enormous relief, Bertha took some of the heat off me; she was my limping, lisping force field.

At nine years old, I had no decency or shame. If Bertha could become the new bottom rung of the ladder, maybe I could scurry up a couple of rungs while she drew fire. If she was "them," could I be "us"?

I bounced from group to group, girl to girl, trying to burrow my way into the social scene. By day two, Bertha recognized me as her most likely friend; but I rejected her soundly, ignoring her looks, her conversation, moving away when I saw her limping toward me, marshmallow stick aloft. I was not outwardly cruel, partly because I didn't have the courage, but mostly because I didn't know how. I'd been too busy trying not to get rejected to have had any experience with rejecting anyone myself. Mostly I ignored Bertha completely, until she caught on, and gave up pursuing my friendship.

By day three I had made some inroads with our social sovereign, Elizabeth, and her entourage. They let me sit at their picnic table for lunch, join their team at Sing. Maybe I've figured out the rules, I exulted. Maybe I could navigate this world.

On day five we packed up our sleeping bags and duffels and waited on the sandy shore of the pond for the bus to take us home. It was a chilly morning, so I wore the ugly green parka my mother insisted I bring, embarrassingly bulky and a hideous shade of iron-green, like the underside of old leaves. The hood hung down my back, trimmed with ratty fake fur that looked like it had been taken from an elderly German shepherd.

The girls were chatting, giggling; Elizabeth was whispering something to one of her lieutenants. I joined in whenever I could, happy just to be sitting there with them in the cool morning air.

"I want to ask you something," Elizabeth said, leaning toward me. Her Virginia lilt made "ask" into a two-syllable word. "Would you like to join our new club?"

I was stunned. I looked into her dark blue eyes. The color almost matched her thick navy pea coat, the coat all the girls in her group were wearing that year. She was so pretty, so long-limbed and supple, like a willow. I wanted to be her more than I'd ever wanted anything.

"It's going to be a different kind of club, an acting club," she said. "We're going to act out scenes from plays. Donna told me you can write stuff for us."

I nodded vigorously. "That would be great."

"Cool. We're going to call it the Shakespeare Club, but we're not going to use just Shakespeare."

I was thinking of the March girls in *Little Women*, putting on theatricals in the attic. I would be Jo!

"It's kind of cold today, you know?" she said, as she eyed my jacket: "That looks warm."

I stopped nodding.

"Why don't you put your hood up?" she asked. "You'd be warmer."

I wanted to believe she was being friendly. "I'm okay," I said.

"Go ahead," she said, her voice cold. "Put your hood up."

The other girls had stopped talking, and were all looking at me. Two of the girls stepped closer. Each took hold of one side of my hood, and then pulled it up and over my head, quickly, and the sand they'd packed into it poured down my face, in my eyes, my mouth, my hair, and down my shirt, where it ran cold and damp down my chest and back.

I was too stunned to cry. I ran to the cabin, shaking sand out of my hair and clothes, blinking hard, wiping it frantically from my ears and off my face. I flung open the door and there was Bertha, sitting cross-legged on a cot, reading a book. She didn't even ask me what happened.

That night, I told my mother about it, sitting on my bed in the pink-and-white bedroom that was my mother's candy-cane fantasy of a little girl's room. She didn't stop unfolding and folding my laundry when I started to cry.

"You don't need to bother with those girls," she said. "They're just jealous of you."

I didn't understand what she meant. I didn't "bother" with them; they were my classmates, they were the girls I saw every day in school, the girls I wanted to be friends with.

"They're not jealous of me," I said. "They hate me." This was the simple fact of my existence. They weren't jealous, they detested me. And they did so because there was something deeply, fundamentally *wrong* with me.

"They're jealous of you because you're beautiful and smart."

I knew I was fairly pretty, plump, sweet-faced, freckled. I wore funny-looking pink glasses with gold flecks in them. I was small and looked younger than my age. I was terribly innocent, even for a nine-year-old. I did believe I was smart, but Elizabeth and her friends would no more be jealous of my brainpower than they would my ability to collect stamps or conjugate verbs.

My mother was insistent: They were jealous because I was beautiful. I was brilliant. I was superior.

I knew none of these things were true. There was something at the heart of me that marked me as broken, something that made me different. I didn't know what it was, but the other girls could smell it, like jungle animals. I was *defective*.

"Don't bother with those girls," my mother repeated as she picked up the dirty laundry and headed for the basement. "They don't matter."

It was a denial of my reality so powerful that I decided then and there that I would never confide in her again.

I did not confide in my mother that fall, when I became convinced I was dying. I had strange pangs in my chest, twinges that stung when I took a deep breath. I was sure they were a heart attack. I lay in the dark at night, terrified of falling asleep, because I thought sleep was just like dying. Sleep was a lack of consciousness, which is what I feared in death. My solution was to delay sleep as long as possible.

I stayed awake reading later and later into the night. My mother tried to stop me. When she turned out the light; I read with a flashlight. She took away the flashlight; I sat by the window, using the faint glow from the streetlamp. She argued and demanded and ordered and nagged. In November, she took me to see Dr. Rosenberg, our fat, friendly pediatrician. Waving away clouds of smoke from his ever-present cigarette, Dr. Rosenberg asked my mother what was wrong. My mother told him I was up until one and two and three o'clock in the morning.

"Are you afraid of going to sleep, *shayna*?" Dr. Rosenberg asked.

I shook my head no.

"Are you afraid of dying in your sleep?" he asked.

I didn't have the words to explain it to him. In sleep I wasn't me; I wasn't anyone. And if I wasn't anyone, then what was I? *Dead.*

He did a quick examination, stethoscope in one hand, cigarette in the other, and then told my mother, "She's perfectly healthy. She'll sleep when she needs to. Ignore it."

But my mother couldn't ignore things; it wasn't in her nature. She nagged and argued, checking on me in the dark, hour after hour. She insisted that I stop reading by the window, which not only deprived me of sleep but also strained my eyes; so I lay in darkness, staring up at the ceiling. This made her skin crawl, so she bought me a television, thinking the sound would lull me to sleep.

My father set it up on top of my dresser, hooked to a timer so that once I was asleep, it would shut itself off. I disconnected the timer on the third night.

The black-and-white shadows flickered in my room: *The Late Show, The Late Late Show,* and sometimes, on really long nights, *The Early Show;* Fred and Ginger and Busby Berkeley, Esther Williams, James Cagney, Jimmy Stewart, and my favorite, Gary Cooper, always strong, always decent. Bette Davis was bug-eyed and powerful, compelling yet ugly; Katharine Hepburn was tough and witty, with a cold, confident intelligence I admired. I loved soft, beautiful Ingrid Bergman. Barbara Stanwick reminded me of my old Sunday comics favorite Brenda Starr, with her wavy brown hair and the smart twinkle in her eyes. The week I stayed home from school with measles I watched *The Thief of Baghdad* every day on *Million Dollar Movie,* and loved it more each day. I memorized all the words to Cole Porter and Irving Berlin musicals and I learned to love two things: old movies and the sleepless night.

That winter I spent a lot of time with my cousin Arlene, who was family, hence safe. Arlene's mother, Estelle, was my mother's first cousin, but she was raised with my mother and her brothers like a sister, because her father had died when Estelle was a baby. A year younger than me and sickly, Arlene often stayed home from school and couldn't be overstimulated. Arlene needed company, and I was it; but despite the fact that she had lots of toys and games, I couldn't stand her. She was dumb and drippy and she whined. I hated going there, but my mother made me.

"Poor Arlene," she would say, and I knew I would spend another overheated Saturday night in Arlene's stuffy bedroom, trying to ignore her sniffling while I played with her latest glitter paint set.

I always brought my Barbie, who was named Jessica, still my favorite name. Cousin Arlene didn't like playing with my Jessica Barbie; she liked watching television. We watched *Bonanza* and *Bewitched* and *Beverly Hillbillies.* I was most partial, however, to medical shows like *Marcus Welby, M.D.*

For all his wisdom, Dr. Welby was not a good man for me to consult. I went to bed after every episode with visions of rare blood-borne disorders dancing in my head. One week I even developed prostate cancer, despite my mother's insistence that this was not possible. She was so frustrated with my constant aches and pains that when I asked her, clutching first one side, then the other, where my appendix was, she replied, "In your head." I immediately developed a headache.

The twinge in my left side, just at the breastbone, was always worse at Arlene's house. At night, I lay very still, avoiding the deep breaths that made the hurt worse, my hand over my chest as if I were pledging allegiance to the flag, waiting for the heat of my palm to warm my sore heart and soothe the pain. I never told anyone about the fault line I was sure ran through my heart. But I lay there many nights, pledging allegiance, terrified, while my hand became wet with sweat and I waited to draw my last shallow breath.

When my mother took me to Arlene's house I could hear her and Aunt Estelle whispering in the kitchen. I grew up in a bath of whispers, piecing together stories from a shred and a hint. Horrors were whispered so as not to alarm the children. *Sha!* my mother would say to my father in the kitchen at night, *the kinder.*

Sometimes I wondered if I would hear something whispered about me—about my birth. I was terrified of this possibility, sure that whatever I heard would crack me in two and leave me sundered, near death. All the whispers fed my imagination, already overgrown. Adoptees grow up in a land of imagining, forced to create a truth: This is your mother, this is your family, and this is where you belong. I am a whisper, a secret; I am imagined.

Sha, the children can hear you.

At fifteen, I started three things simultaneously: high school, cigarettes, and drugs. I was a docile child, a good girl. I was not a docile teenager. My mother took me to see Dr. Rosenberg. He heard her out, then pulled out his prescription pad and wrote *Dr. J. Darling* and a phone number, and handed it to my mother.

"An adolescent psychiatrist," he explained.

"You think she needs a *psychiatrist?*"

"I think you both could use someone to talk to," Dr. Rosenberg said, and when he looked at me I swear I saw him wink.

My mother did not believe in psychiatrists. *Why would I want to go talk to a stranger about my problems?* She did not believe in unburdening herself even to friends. *Other people don't need to know my business.* When Linda's mom cried about her difficult daughter, already climbing out the window at night to meet boys in the woods, my mother said to my father in the kitchen after dinner, *She has no shame, washing her dirty laundry in public.*

But she trusted Dr. Rosenberg; and she didn't know what else to do. She was desperate.

I liked Dr. Darling right away. She was friendly and warm, and wore pants with long vests, like Maude on TV. We played Monopoly and Life in her cozy office, and she told me about growing up in North Carolina and how she babysat for James Taylor when she was in high school, which I thought was incredibly cool.

Dr. Darling and I met once a week; she met with my parents once a month. She arbitrated, usually on my side, in disputes. I wanted to go to a summer arts camp, which my parents were sure was a den of drug- and sex-addled iniquity. She convinced my parents to let me go. I wanted to change my name at school, to combine my dull first name, Jill, with my even duller middle name, Ann, to create one name, Jilann, which would be interesting and unique, and could be shortened to Jil, which I thought sophisticated and sharp. My mother was horrified: This was the name she gave me; I should not be allowed to alter it. She ridiculed my plan. *That's a dumb idea. What do you want to do something like that for? People will think you're nuts.*

Dr. Darling convinced her to let me do it. Not legally—that would be going too far—but I was allowed to change my name on school records and my working papers.

Dr. Darling often asked me how I felt about being adopted.

"I don't feel anything about it," I said.

"Do you ever think about your other parents?" she asked.

The question made me angry. "They're not my parents," I said. "My parents are my parents."

I parroted the words I had learned from my green book, *The Chosen Baby.*

"I was chosen," I said. "I know I was really wanted."

"You were wanted," she repeated. "What about your birth mother?"

"What about her?" I asked.

She looked at me. I wasn't making the connection. Adoptive parents/wanted. Birth mother/unwanted: In order to be chosen, you must first be rejected.

She tried another tack. "Do you know anything about your birth mother?"

I told her the story I had told myself so often it sounded unreal, like a fairy tale: young couple, unwanted pregnancy, a selfless plan to give the baby up. It felt like a story I'd read in a magazine. In my mind this "birth mother" was shrouded in fog, a tall, featureless woman, dark and shapeless.

Dr. Darling persisted. "Do you ever wonder about her? What her interests were? Where she came from?" She paused. "Why she gave you up?"

I was getting annoyed. "She couldn't raise a baby alone. She wanted to give it a better life. And I don't care about her. My problems with my mother have nothing to do with *her.*"

But I began to wonder if my problems with my mother might have something to do with being adopted. I never thought she loved me less because I wasn't biologically hers. I wondered, though, if she had the same sense of security about my love for her.

Dr. Darling was tactful. "I'm not saying your problems with your mother have anything to do with her. I'm just wondering what you know about her."

"Nothing," I said. "She was young. She was getting divorced. And she was Jewish."

"How do you know she was Jewish?"

"It was a Jewish adoption agency," I explained. "My parents wanted to make sure they got a Jewish baby."

"Couldn't they raise the baby Jewish no matter what?"

This was a new question for me. I didn't like not having an answer.

In the car on the way home, I steeled myself. Staring out at the road, I asked my mother, "Why did you go to a Jewish adoption agency to get me?"

There was a long pause: "Because we wanted a Jewish baby."

"But what difference does it make," I asked. "The baby would be whatever you raise it."

She glanced at me. "The baby has to be born to a Jewish woman to be Jewish."

"Why?"

My mother was not good at explaining things. She saw questions as challenges, and quickly became defensive. "What do you mean? So it would be Jewish."

"If you raise the baby Jewish, it will be Jewish."

Now she was really annoyed. "That's not the way it works. It has to be born that way."

"It's not like eye color or hair color, something in the chromosomes." I took biology in ninth grade. The teacher didn't tell us about a religion gene.

She was angry now, flushed red. "It's in the blood. Either you are or you aren't."

"What about people who convert?"

"That's not the same. They're not really Jews. They're converts."

"So Jewishness is something you're born with, like black skin or left-handedness?" I was making fun of her now.

"You don't know what you're talking about!" She was almost yelling. "You either are or you aren't."

She turned into the driveway and quickly got out of the car, slamming the door. I walked slowly behind, wondering. I had to be born Jewish, but I didn't have to be born *hers*. One thing is in the blood, the other is contingent. It's easier to convert to a new family, a new mother, than to a new religion.

That night she came to the door of my room while I was doing my English homework, an essay on *A Tale of Two Cities*. My grades were dropping in all subjects and I was cutting lots of classes. But I loved English and still did well in it.

She stood in the doorway and stared at me until I looked up. "What do you and Dr. Darling talk about?" she asked.

"Stuff," I said.

"Do you talk about adoption?" she asked quickly, looking at the wall over my head.

"Sometimes," I said, too surprised to lie. My mother had never brought up the subject of adoption. I knew she must have talked to me about it when I was very small, too little to ask questions. But as far back as I could remember, she had never mentioned the word.

"Does she think the reason you're having all these problems is because you're adopted?"

Standing there stiffly, arms folded, she seemed both angry and scared. Her discomfort made me nervous, and her question made me angry.

"I don't know. Maybe," I muttered. *All these problems? As if I'm the nutcase?* "Dr. Darling thinks it's your fault, anyway. She thinks you're the one with the problems."

"Oh?" she said, her voice cold. She turned and walked out of the room.

I never saw Dr. Darling again.

My best friend, Bonnie, and I tripped down the school stairs like giddy children, our 1940s Salvation Army dresses flapping in the breeze, loud, provocative, daring any adult to look at us.

Bonnie had been my best friend since the first week of high school. We met in gym class and were instant intimates. Almost without discussion, we immediately jumped into what we thought high school meant: cigarettes and drugs, Wild Turkey Bourbon and Boone's Farm apple wine, outlandish clothes and music, movies, books, and attitudes.

For the first time in my life I had a real friend, a friend who talked to me every night for hours on the phone, who wanted to be with me after school and on weekends. Together we flitted from role to role like hummingbirds. For a few months we only wore thrift shop dresses from the '40s, long skirts and platform shoes and hats with rakish feathers. We tried the hippie farmer look, in overalls and torn T-shirts with hiking boots. We even went Christian, reading our Bibles on the bus home from school. Every role felt equally real and equally false. Since I didn't have an identity of my own, switching from one to another was as easy as changing socks.

My mother and I spent most of my high school years fighting. We fought over my smoking. We fought over my friends. We fought over the clothes I wore, the drugs I took, the grades I got. Since my mother was an immovable object, and I was determined to get what I wanted, I soon found an easier method: I became a highly proficient liar. I lied about where I went and what I did and who was there when I did it.

I told her I was staying late for geometry help after school and got high and went driving, the car a smoke-filled box on wheels.

I told her I was going to school and I took the bus down Central Avenue to the number 4 subway at Bedford Park in the Bronx to Greenwich Village's Washington Square to get stoned and dance to the music of the long-haired boys with guitars and easy drugs.

I told her I was going over to Meg's house to study and Peter and I drove 90 miles an hour down the West Side Highway, past the George Washington Bridge shining like lit pearls over the Hudson while we raced, raced, raced away from boring suburbia, toward the city, toward life.

I loved the city, I hated the suburbs. I loved Herman Hesse and F. Scott Fitzgerald and J. D. Salinger. I memorized *The Little Prince* and every word to every song from *Cabaret* and *Man of La Mancha* and *Guys and Dolls.* My creative writing class wrote Kurt Vonnegut a letter, telling him how much we adored his books, and he invited us to visit his townhouse in Greenwich Village. Bonnie and I went to the bathroom, stopping to peek at his desk, where he wrote about Billy Pilgrim and Paul Proteus. The datebook was open. On the next day's listing, we read: *Lunch—John & Yoko.* We screamed silently.

Senior year came, and despite the fact that living together meant constant fighting, my mother insisted I only apply to commuter schools. The State University at Stony Brook on Long Island was her choice; she would buy me a car and I would drive back and forth each day.

I threw away the applications from any school within five hundred miles. My friend Ellie had gone to the University of Wisconsin in Madison the year before. She sent home reports of parties and politics, demonstrations every weekend for peace, gay rights, and feminism.

In May, I came home from school to find my mother at the kitchen table, the acceptance letter and contract in front of her. I wasn't surprised; she opened all my mail. My mother regularly went through my drawers, my purse, and my pockets.

"What is this?" she asked, waving the letter in front of me.

I knew what it was from the address on the big envelope that lay on the table. "I got in, great," I said, trying not to sound too excited.

"You're not going to *Wisconsin*," she said scornfully, as if I had applied to the University of Sodom.

"Fine," I said.

She was surprised. "You're going to Stony Brook," she said.

I leaned against the door frame casually. "I didn't apply to Stony Brook."

I had never calmly defied my mother before. I knew I had to match her power, or be steamrollered.

I took a breath. "I only applied to Wisconsin."

She gave me a long look. "You're not going to Wisconsin," she repeated.

"Okay," I said, shrugging. "That's fine. I didn't really want to go to college, anyway. I told Wendy that I would share an apartment with her in the city." Wendy produced extra disdain from my mother: She wasn't in any honors classes—and her family lived in an *apartment.*

My mother smiled sarcastically. "You're going to share an apartment? And how the hell are you going to pay the rent?"

"Wendy has a job, waitressing at the Café Metro. The owner told her I could have a job there, too. That's enough to pay the rent. She found an apartment in the Village that's big enough for two."

My mother hesitated. She was shaken. "You can't live in the city. Don't be ridiculous."

"I can and I will. If I don't go to Wisconsin, I don't go to college. I'll share an apartment with Wendy and be a waitress."

I went to Wisconsin.

9. BUNNY

WILKOMMEN

It is perhaps unfortunate that the existence of the incipient individual is still largely unnoticed and often unappreciated during the crucial weeks of the formation of the body.

GERALDINE LUX FLANAGAN
THE FIRST NINE MONTHS OF LIFE

Jake met the boat clutching an enormous bunch of flowers and smiling widely. The ship's crossing had been liberating, a genuine sea change: five days of belonging nowhere, of having no landmarks, no known territory beyond the confines of this gently rocking Dutch ship and the far horizon.

Each day was the same: morning bouillon and afternoon tea, bells heralding enormous meals: grilled fish, formed salads, sauced puddings. There were Dutchmen going home with tales of American cigarettes ("Do you *know* what we had to smoke during the war?"). There were silly games, a small library with good books, and a fast friend, Dieter, going home after his American year, engaged to a girl who would be waiting when we docked. It was a perfect interlude, restorative, filled with sun and spray and great peace.

Jake saw me before I saw him. He was wearing gold corduroy pants and a brown jacket, both of which looked baggy and comfortably old, and a scarf around his neck like a French schoolboy. He was happy to see me, and I was happy to see him. The flowers were wonderful; Rotterdam was wonderful. We walked all the rest of the day, looking at statues and buildings and parks with enormous piles of rubble from the German bombings.

Jake insisted that I buy Dutch boots and a new, warm coat to see me through the German winter. We shopped in strange stores, decorated for the Dutch Christmas—to be celebrated at the beginning of December—with dwarflike figures of St. Nicholas everywhere. There were crowds of Dutch housewives, with rose-splotched cheeks, so cheerful, so happy, so round: If they could mother the world, if we could live on Dutch cheese and pea soup and chocolate pudding...

Jake started to teach me German, though he warned me not to use the language in Holland: "They hate the Germans here, and if you speak German, they'll ignore you—or worse." We ate steak with strange mushrooms, as the proprietor of the restaurant beamed at us the way restaurateurs do when they think people are in love. Or it may simply have been that we looked American; Americans were warmly welcomed in Holland then.

Back in the room, where we had deposited my things, Jake took off my shoes and sat with my feet in his hands, rubbing them, telling me how much he had missed me, how glad he was that I'd arrived.

It was one of the best nights we ever spent together—one of the only times since we'd been married that we talked about loving each other, or that Jake showed tenderness toward me. It was one of the only times I felt loved, even wanted, by him. For the first time—since my first day at Marlboro, or maybe when my father died, and certainly for the first time with Jake—I felt real. In this strange place surrounded by differences—language, landscape, even teaspoons—for one night we existed without a past, with no expectations, no preconceived notions, and no reasonable knowledge of where we'd be tomorrow. Everything was new, everything was underlined, and everything was marvelous. This must be the way Jake had always seen the world.

In the morning, I asked him why he hadn't written.

"I tried. But so much was happening. All I really wanted to do was watch, and learn, and experience. I couldn't communicate yet, I couldn't explain, or tell you about it. I walked all around, every day, whenever I could. Munich was so beautiful! And the people! The faces! I took so many pictures. I had to learn German. In the beginning, the Army was worse than in the States—until I bought the clothes. They hate soldiers in Germany; no one would talk to me when I was in uniform. You can tell a soldier right away, even if he's not wearing khaki. You can tell an American, even just by the shoes. I didn't feel free until I bought clothes here. Now they don't know who I am, until I start to talk."

That's why he hadn't written.

We had a continental breakfast, my first (America had not yet imported continental breakfasts). Everything was perfect: a perfect roll, perfect butter, perfect jam, and a perfect cup of coffee with perfect cream. Nothing had ever tasted like this before.

We left Rotterdam amid a sea of bicycles. The car Jake had borrowed was a low sports car, a two-seater, with an open top and a canvas cover in case of rain. It was cold, so we used the cover, and drove through Holland in two days and a night.

I remember herring stands and an incredibly beautiful church, modern, perhaps by Le Corbusier, and filled with the presence of God—built with such strong conviction and faith and so much beauty, that it was a witness to God.

I remember market squares filled with wheelbarrows and wagons holding flowers and vegetables and bits and pieces essential to life. I bought a beautiful wooden spoon for only pennies. There were rows of cypress trees, and tiny stores tucked in at the bottom of old houses on small streets. We slept under an enormous feather bed, on the top of a mattress filled with feathers, and in the morning ate another continental breakfast. Then we came to the border, at Aachen, and saw bullet holes in the sides of the buildings.

On the next evening, we reached the outskirts of Stuttgart. Jake drove too fast down the road on the side of a steep hill leading into the city; he was going to be late getting the car back.

"After the war, they cleared away the debris, and piled it all up in one place, this mountain of rubble. It's incredible! Most of the city has been rebuilt—you'll see the difference right away between the new part and the part they call the *alte Stadt*." He turned sharply around a curve. "You tired?"

"Who could be tired?" I said. "I'm scared stiff." We were going very fast.

"I wondered if you were." Jake smiled, pointing out the sights: an art gallery, the main trolley station, the Army club. "That's the railroad station, *der Bahnhof.* That's the first sentence the Army teaches GIs in Germany: *Wo ist der Bahnhof?* So they can always get home."

"Or get away," I said.

"Yes," Jake answered. "Or get away. So you learn it, too. *Wo ist der Bahnhof, bitte?* You can buy great sausage there."

Our hotel was, in fact, a restaurant with rooms upstairs. We met the landlord, drank some welcoming brandy, and went to inspect our room. It was small. There were twin beds set at right angles to each other, a desk and chair, and a closet. Everything was immaculately clean. There was hot water in the bathroom (in the hall); the owner said it twice.

In the morning, Jake took me to the camp, the *Caserne*, a short walk from the hotel. The guards at the gate checked my passport. Inside was a grassy field with cannons at one side. To the left, there was a large, rectangular building with a small shop (a PX, Post Exchange, for buying American cigarettes and other goods), a lounge, a coffee shop, and a library. There were barracks, garages, mess halls, and other buildings scattered around—and men in fatigues everywhere. Fatigues have the advantage of every uniform: Faces emerge so clearly without the distraction of individually chosen clothes. There's so much you don't know about somebody wearing a uniform; he could be anybody. He hasn't made any choices yet.

The *Caserne* was a world within a world in concentric circles. Outside its gates, everything was different. Inside the gates, there was meant to be an echo of home, but it was Army, and still unfamiliar. Away from the *Caserne*, everything seemed free, unregimented. Inside became neither here nor there, just a place to be. Home was very far away.

Jake's friend Quint quickly became my friend, too. He said we were his ménage à trois, just what he'd always wanted; the three of us had read the same books. But what I'd always wanted when I got to Europe was not a ménage à trois, but to drink calvados and look at the Arc de Triomphe in a trench coat with the collar turned up.

I liked Quint's face. Where Jake's face was hard and angular, Quint's was rounder and softer, containing sweetness. He had a way of looking that was both piercing and gentle. The world he watched amused him; it made him sad; but it didn't amaze him. Jake was the discoverer; Quint kept the journal.

We were together much of the time, laughing, singing, joking, admiring each other and the new world we were in. Quint was funny and smart and horny, very horny. He talked about German girls who lifted up their skirts and sat with bare bottoms on wooden chairs; he talked about German prostitutes, all named Ilse—behind-the-couch Ilse, quickie Ilse, the captain's Ilse. He wrote Jake and me funny letters, and left them for us at the hotel, pretending to be an anonymous correspondent who thought I should know my husband was sexually depraved. He had been found screaming on the Autobahn: "*Wo ist der gonads???*"

"I love my wife," he quoted Jake as saying, but "Oh! you *Fraulein!*"

College humor? We were recently out of college, and we loved it.

At Christmas, we went to Paris together on a three-day pass, taking the fabled *Orient Express*, now like everything else in Germany, old, gray, dirty, and shabby. At every station middle-aged men carrying pails of hot water filled with sausages peddled their wares; when you bought a sausage, it was given to you on a small paper plate with a dab of mustard and a hard roll. The sausage was always delicious; the men were always angry as they cringed, bowed, and served, but not happily. Before the war, they had probably been lawyers. During the war, they had certainly been soldiers.

Just after Heidelberg, a young woman opened the door to our compartment and asked if there was room. She was pretty, tall, obviously American. Maybe a Christmas present for Quint, I thought.

"*Willkommen*," Jake said. "What's your name?"

She mumbled something. Later, Quint and I discovered we both thought she had said, "Oh, really." We called her Rilly.

She told us she'd been waiting at the *Bahnhof* for the train, and had stood too close to the stove. "Look," she said, turning around to show us a round hole with charred edges in the back of her skirt. She was tall, silent, strange, distant, and not quite there; yet she was clearly taking our measure. She stayed with us until Paris, where Jake insisted we all have a drink together first thing, though it was morning, early morning. Quint and I had calvados, Jake and Rilly cognac. We toasted Paris, ourselves, each other.

Rilly didn't have a place to stay in Paris, so we found rooms together, a double and two singles, at the Hotel Odéon. The hotel was large and dark, with a single bulb in the ceiling of each floor lighting the hallways; you pressed a button and the light went on. It stayed on for a minute or so, and then went off until the button—or the one on the next floor—was pressed again. There was one bathroom, a water closet, on each floor; stuck on a nail next to the toilet were squares of newspaper. Alternate floors had a bath in a large closet at one end of the hallway. We paid $2 a night for our double room in the hotel, just off the Avenue Saint Michel, down the street from the *Comédie-Francaise*.

We set off to explore, walking along the Seine. I remember Sacre Coeur, and all the steps, and Montparnasse, and the bridges over the Seine. Paris was not the City of Lights then; the big streetlights had not been turned on since the war. The streets were gray and dirty, and every so often you'd see bullet holes in the side of a building. But it was as beautiful as it had been described in every book we'd ever read.

I remember an acrobat with a chain across his chest, just as in *La Strada*, which hadn't been filmed yet; and a man selling a magic peeler-shredder-slicer kitchen implement, as well as one making crêpes. We stopped to watch. I sifted through my purse to find some money, and then when Quint and I turned around Jake and Rilly had disappeared.

"They've probably gone ahead," I said. We walked on for a block or two; but they weren't there.

"Maybe they're waiting for us back at that corner," Quint said. They weren't.

We stood at the corner for several minutes, thinking that if we'd missed them, they'd look for us there. After a while, we went into a café near the corner and sat at a table near the window, drinking *chocolat* and watching the street. Finally, a long time later, we took the Métro back to the hotel.

Jake and Rilly were stretched out on our bed with a bottle of wine, two glasses, and a deck of cards, with a few cards scattered between them on the rumpled bedspread. They didn't look surprised, or worried. Rilly looked smug; Jake looked guilty.

"Where were you?" Jake sounded faintly accusatory, as if he were exploring the possibility of accusing me of having done something wrong. "We couldn't find you anywhere! We figured if we came back here, you'd turn up eventually. What happened to you?"

Rilly smiled.

When she left the room, she left the hotel. We never saw her again—at least I didn't.

We only had one day left: I have no memory of what we did. I know the three of us went back to Stuttgart together on the *Orient Express*. Wives then had a certain advantage in this kind of situation—the only advantage I was to discover. They were expected to go along with their husbands. I don't think Jake and I talked about what had happened; I don't think I expressed anger or hurt or dismay. I went along with the pretense: Nothing had happened.

For our first wedding anniversary, Jake bought me a beautiful pair of earrings. I bought him a German cigarette lighter.

We liked our presents, but we weren't terribly enthusiastic about the occasion. On we went, messing up our impeccably neat German hotel room, eating doughnuts for lunch at the *Caserne,* which was in Vaihingen, a suburb of Stuttgart, connected by an old wooden trolley, with seats reserved in the front for the *Schwerferwundet,* wounded veterans of the war. After dinner we made friends with ex-Nazis in the hotel restaurant, where we had great, simplistic conversations: *"Krieg ist schlecht,"* I said: War is bad. None of them had ever fought against Americans; they had all been on the Russian front. Hitler wasn't a bad man; he just made some mistakes.

One of the men went to great pains to explain that he would drink with me, but not with Jake, because Jake was a soldier. It still amazes me that I was willing to accept what he said and drink with him. Didn't I have the faintest idea of who

I was, of who I had a right to be? With Jake, I was still looking for happy endings. But I wasn't willing to create them, or to make them happen, because I simply didn't know how. I thought he was a happy ending; but he turned out to be another unhappy beginning.

For Americans after the war, everything was cheap and easy. For Germans, it was the opposite. American cigarettes, American coffee, and American dollars were prized. Those who held them were coveted and cosseted—and despised.

When we first arrived in Stuttgart, the unit was preparing a Christmas play to be presented to local children, German as well as children of the soldiers stationed there. It was based on James Thurber's *Many Moons,* in an adaptation Quint had written.

Many Moons is about a princess who is pining away, terribly unhappy because although she can have anything she wants, the only thing she wants is the moon. The king can't figure out how to give it to her. The court mathematician is consulted, and the king's philosopher is asked. Even the wise man doesn't know what to do. The king offers her hand in marriage to anyone who can resolve this apparently insoluble problem. Finally, on a dark, moonless night, the court jester presents her with a paper cutout of the moon, big, round, and golden, on a stick. She's thrilled—the moon, at last!

When the king, unable to believe that anything so simple could be the solution, asks her what will happen now that the moon is hers, no longer in the sky, she explains, sweetly and simply, that there are several moons: Each one comes and shines for a few days, and then slowly leaves, and after several dark days, another one comes to take its place. Her moon is just one of many—happy ending.

Quint wrote and directed the play, and Jake took photographs. I was the princess. After the first performance, the cast joined the children for punch and cookies. Some of the awestruck children looked at me as if there were stars over my head as well as a paper moon in my hand. It was a beautiful princess costume.

After Christmas, when we came back from Paris, our ménage à trois changed. Quint was finding other friends. He joined a German-American club, in hopes of making out with a non-Ilse *Fräulein,* and, indeed, he did meet a sweet young thing. The four of us went one night for *Kuchen* and *Kaffee mit Schlag;* she told me, in response to something one of us had said, that you could always tell who was Jewish because Jews wear long coats, and carry bags full of money. All the men have dirty tangled beards. We won the war, I thought, but that was all.

Quint was working on the next Special Services play; but for the rest of us, there wasn't much to do. The days were short and cold, with quick, damp bursts of snow and ice. Sometime in late January the owner of the restaurant asked us, very nicely, to leave. I think we'd tried the patience of the chambermaid: We left clothes tossed on the chair, and piles of papers and books on the floor. We didn't make the beds. Every day, she straightened everything: The clothes were hung up or folded and put away, the books and papers neatly arranged on the desk, and the bed linen straight and taut. It was a conflict of cultures, and more: We were careless and young, barely postadolescent.

It wasn't difficult to find another a room, a *Zimmer*, in a house down the road. I think our room had been the master bedroom. The furniture was big, heavy, and dark, but the room was comfortable. We gave the landlady a pound of coffee after we'd been there a while. She was thrilled. Since she didn't make the room up every day, that source of conflict was eliminated.

Sometime in February, Jake was sent to the hospital. Though this is where I should remember the most, it is the beginning of remembering the least. I don't want to say I've forgotten, because that would imply there was something to be found, retrieved, and eventually restored. What I have instead is blankness: In places, there is simply nothing there. It's as if there never had been anything there.

10. JIL

MADISON

The drive to Madison was one long, straight, flat road through cornfields, or at least it seemed that way from the backseat, where my brother and I dozed and argued and stared out the window for endless hours.

I was going to Wisconsin because the alternative, living in the city with Wendy, was even more unacceptable to my mother. And maybe there was a part of her that was relieved to get me out of the house, away from the constant struggle our relationship had become.

Driving down Johnson Street to Witte Hall, my cinder-block freshman dorm, we passed sidewalks chockablock with gorgeous, ragged, long-haired boys unpacking guitars, milk crates of record albums, and the complete works of Herman Hesse. Girls stood smoking in groups, wearing overalls and dirty sneakers, T-shirts tie-dyed pink and purple, straight long hair sliding down their backs. To me, it looked like heaven in torn denim and fringe.

We pulled up in front of Witte and I jumped out, hoping to be shed of my family before anyone saw me. I wanted to slip into a new version of myself: a Joni Mitchell sound-tracked, pot-stoked, patchouli-oiled hippie chick, shoeless, rule-less, family-free.

I pulled out my box of record albums, which I had refused to entrust to the trunk shipped two weeks earlier. Behind us three scruffy, bushy-haired guys were unpacking a blue VW van.

"We gotta score today," one of them said. "Shouldn't be hard."

My father appeared at my side, upset. "Watch out for those boys," he said. "They're looking to take advantage of you girls."

I didn't know if telling him they wanted to score drugs would make him feel better or worse, so I just nodded. At least half my conversations with my father revolved around maintaining my virginity until marriage.

"Why buy the cow when you can get the milk for free?" was his favorite saying. "There's only one thing men want" ran a close second. I had the feeling that, to my father, I was a carefully guarded hymen wrapped in a thin coating of flesh and denim.

Preserving my purity was his number-one objective. Losing it was mine.

Second only to having sex was making friends. Third was having fun, however that worked out. Somewhere down the list were things like going to class, getting decent grades, figuring out what I wanted to be when I grew up.

To my amazement and joy, making friends was easy. I loved my roommate, a frizzy-haired, highly focused girl from Cleveland. Janey was a lot straighter than I was: She listened to the Jackson Five (*so juvenile!*) and slept with her hair tightly wrapped around empty frozen juice containers in an effort to straighten her curls; but she was friendly and warm, and willing to be my immediate best friend. She didn't know I was the high school weirdo, the dork who sat alone on the bleachers and wrote sad poetry. She knew the exuberant, new and improved me.

Down the hall were Annie, Tory, and Debra. With them, Janey and I formed a fierce fivesome who went everywhere together in a wild clump of energetic youth, intense and dramatic. There were at least a half-dozen film societies on campus; many films were free, none cost more than $2. Our first semester, Janey and I saw forty-two movies from Labor Day weekend to Christmas break. We went dancing and to concerts: Bette Midler! Joni Mitchell! Roberta Flack! We ate matzo ball soup at Ella's Deli, and demonstrated against the war in Vietnam. We petitioned for George McGovern and sat at the Memorial Union in a great loud laughing herd, and talked and talked and talked all night.

I was a colorful college butterfly instead of a lumpy high school worm.

I was having a great time.

What I was *not* having was sex. I went to student health the first week of the semester and got my little plastic circles of birth control pills; but it seemed that I was taking them for no reason.

Notwithstanding my father's constant "Why buy the cow" clang, there turned out to be plenty of guys who were allergic to free milk in Madison, Wisconsin, despite its reputation as the dairy state.

Guy #1: Lyle, a Wisconsin native as sweet as the name of his hometown: Appleton. A blond-haired, blue-eyed junior, Lyle was madly in love with my RA, another Appletonian. He'd gotten Melinda pregnant in high school. She'd had an abortion, which so traumatized her that she broke up with him, and so traumatized him that he couldn't—or wouldn't—have sex with anyone, including me, no matter how many times I expounded on the infallibility of birth control pills. Our sexual activity was like a movie that went forward and backward in fast motion. Lyle would open my shirt, then close it again, take off his shirt, put it back on, always terrified of causing another disaster.

When Lyle talked about Melinda, he wept. In October, she gave him another chance, and I moved on.

Guy #2: Daniel, a nice Jewish boy from New York—someone I should have dated in high school. But until I became a butterfly I would never have had the nerve to speak to him. Daniel was smart and driven, knew old movie musicals, and was already planning where he would attend law school and how long he'd practice law before entering politics. He knew all the words to every song from *Guys and Dolls* and could recite both Gene Kelly's and Debbie Reynolds's lines from *Singin' in the Rain*. Daniel was funny and handsome. But he'd recently had a large mole removed from his penis and was not allowed to enjoy any sexual activity for a month. In college years, a month is the equivalent of half a decade. I dropped him.

Guy #3: Steve, a dark-haired, leather-jacketed rebel from Chicago who rarely talked and always seemed to be alone, even when I was with him. Steve was gorgeous, Steve was willing, and Steve had no known skin disorders or former girlfriends haunting the halls. What Steve did have, strangely, were scruples. Steve would not deflower a virgin. Steve would not even kiss me, since kissing might lead to a loss of control. I metaphorically kissed him good-bye.

Guy #4: Talal was a tall, slender, caramel-colored sophomore from Kuwait. He was gorgeous, a catlike, raven-haired god with high cheekbones, charm, money, and a car. Talal also had a penis the diameter of a large soup can. It took several hours, several joints, and several shots of bourbon but, finally, the weekend I turned eighteen, the messy deed was done . . . with an *Arab*. My mother would have died.

I started spending much of my free time at Talal's apartment off campus, where he lived with several other students from the Middle East, another Kuwaiti, a Saudi, and a Lebanese. All of them had generous government scholarships that included cars and the cash for nice apartments, even a woman who came in to clean once a week. The only requirement was that they maintain a B average and major in engineering. None of them particularly liked engineering, but it was a good deal, and they loved Madison. They loved eager, easygoing American girls; they loved their cars and their apartments. Soon, most of my friends were hanging around their apartment, too. These guys had a nicer place, better drugs, and more food than any of us could afford. And they were exotic, interesting, and fun.

"What are you going to do for the break?" Janey asked the group one night in early December. We were draped around the living room, listening to music, reading, doing homework, getting high.

I was going home: All the girls were going home, to New York, Chicago, Ohio, and Michigan.

"I don't know," Talal said. "Maybe we'll stay here, or maybe we'll go on a trip. Maybe we'll come visit you," he nudged my head, lying in his lap.

"Yeah, my mother would love that," I laughed. Nice Jewish girl goes to college and brings home Arab god. That apartment in the city with Wendy might suddenly look good.

"Your mother wouldn't like me?" he asked innocently.

"I don't think so," I said, chuckling as I imagined her reaction. "Why, would *your* mother like me?"

"My mother is no longer alive," he said.

We'd been together a good three weeks, and I didn't know this!

"She died two years ago. But I have a picture of her." In a minute he was back with a crumpled photo of a lovely-looking woman in a long tunic and head scarf.

"She's beautiful," I said, as the rest of the group gathered around to look.

"You look like her," Janey said, and I agreed. She had the same wide cat's eyes, the same long, slender face, and the same full lips.

"Do you have a picture of your mother?" Talal asked me.

I laughed. "No, I didn't bring one." I couldn't imagine the kind of relationship with my mother that would lead me to stand her photo on my bedside table.

"Do you look like her?" he asked.

"No, not at all," I said. "I'm adopted."

Talal looked at me. "You're what?"

"Adopted," I said. "You know, like born to one person, raised by another."

"So you're an orphan? Your parents died?"

I'd never had to explain this before. "No, they didn't die. They gave me up."

He looked confused. So did his roommates; in fact, so did my girlfriends. They were all looking at me, waiting for an explanation.

Janey stepped in. "Jil's parents couldn't take care of her, so they gave her away."

"Well, they didn't really *give me away*," I said. "They put me up for adoption."

Ahmad spoke up. "You were like an orphan, only no one died."

Annie asked, "So you were a foster child?"

"No," I said. "It's completely different."

"Do you know who your real parents are?" Tory asked.

"My *real* parents are the people who raised me," I said.

"Your foster parents?" Annie asked.

"They're not my foster parents. They're my parents!"

"But how can they be your parents if you're not related to them?" Talal asked.

Everyone was looking at me wonderingly, waiting for me to explain. But suddenly it all seemed complicated and inexplicable. I knew that I was just like them, with *real* parents, not two sets of parents with adjectives attached; but I couldn't find the right words to make them understand.

"They're my parents—take my word for it." I got up and went into the kitchen to refill my glass. When I came back everyone had turned their attention to the new Bob Dylan album and I was off the hook.

But my face burned: Why didn't they understand? Why did they think my story was any different than theirs? Tongue-tied, disturbed, and confused, I decided I would never again tell anyone that I was adopted. That way I could pretend to be just like everyone else.

11. BUNNY

{ PARIS }

A baby begins life as a single cell, smaller than the period at the end
of this sentence, and would be only barely visible to the naked eye.
This cell is created by the union of two parent cells:
the female egg cell or ovum, and the male sperm cell.

GERALDINE LUX FLANAGAN
THE FIRST NINE MONTHS OF LIFE

Jake was in the hospital for a month, at first with a high fever and a swelling
on his neck. Twenty-four hours later, the fever was down and the swelling had
disappeared. The Army doctors began a series of tests to determine what had
caused the fever and swelling. Each day's tests came back negative; nothing was
wrong. More tests were scheduled.

He was in a large, light room; his was the only occupied bed. He seemed to
love being there; nothing was expected of him, nothing was asked, nothing was
required. He was not in pain. The nurses were attractive and cheerful. He was
young, good-looking, mysteriously ill, but relatively healthy, and charming, with
that wide and crooked smile, that happy aura of delight.

The Army hospital was in another suburb of Stuttgart, across the city and
diagonally opposite Vaihingen, a long, double trolley ride away. When I visited, I
brought him books and magazines, cigarettes and fruit. I must have gone every day
at first, and then every few days.

While Jack was in the hospital, I occasionally went to the clubs with our friends.
It was *Fasching*, a kind of German equivalent to Mardi Gras, celebrated sometime in
February and involving masks and much beer. There were a few clubs in downtown
Stuttgart we frequented: We liked the ease with which everybody—the girls, the
waiters, and the musicians—presented themselves to us for the taking. Though it
was all on the surface—their lives cannot have been easy—that surface was very

appealing. It seemed much more real than the earnestness and anger of the sausage men on the train, or the dangerous darkness of the men who hung around the Bahnhof, hawking black-market cigarettes, offering to change money at unofficial rates. This was the other side of sophistication: Have another beer—or a glass of wine—champagne, *bitte*? Germany was still good at making a cabaret.

Sometimes in the afternoon I'd walk with Quint across empty stretches in downtown Stuttgart. I think he felt responsible for me; in any case, I very much needed him—his friendship, his steady reserve, simply his presence. . . .

Quint was a little removed; he watched, but he didn't quite participate. His cool reserve was the opposite of Jake's romanticism. He saw things the way they were, perhaps with a bit of cynicism, certainly with humor, and always with goodwill. He was quiet and funny and very good company.

Was I attracted to him from the beginning? I don't think so. I think I came to need him, to rely on him, to value him; with him, I felt real. And then I realized I cared about him. It wasn't a matter of vindictiveness or revenge; my feelings for Quint had nothing to do with Jake.

The turning point came when I went to visit Jake at the hospital sometime in the fourth week he was there.

"I've been thinking," Jake said, after we had been talking for a while. "As long as I'm here, and as long as the Army is paying for it, I think it would be a good idea to ask to be circumcised."

I was astounded.

"I've always thought it would be better to be circumcised. It's supposed to be much healthier for a man. It's cleaner. And I'm here, anyway."

"You'd want the Army to do it?"

"There's good care here. And it would be free."

"It would still be painful," I said.

I could not believe he meant what he was saying.

"Well, at first. But it'd be okay after that."

"You'd have to stay longer."

"I wouldn't mind that. Would you mind that very much?"

"You've already been here for a month."

"Well, I'll think about it." Jake was ready to change the subject.

I was stunned. There were two things I couldn't imagine: The first was staying in the hospital a minute longer than was absolutely necessary. Had this been a four-week vacation? The second was letting Army doctors—any doctors, really—operate on his penis if that operation didn't need to be done. How could he do that voluntarily? Why not have his appendix out, while he was there, or his tonsils? The answer is obvious: He didn't have appendicitis or tonsillitis. Foreskins don't have to be infected to be removed. They just have to be there. Other meanings were more obscure.

I would like to justify myself. I would like to say that you can't betray a betrayer. I'd like to remind you of Jake's disappearances, of the five months with not a single letter, and the trip to Paris with Rilly. I'd like to say I hadn't recovered from my father's death; that the last years of his life had been traumatic, and astonishing, and that he'd died of a brain tumor, which had affected his behavior for a very long time before it was diagnosed. I was thirteen when it started, almost eighteen when it ended—and nineteen when I met Jake.

But of course, you can betray a betrayer. Jake left me many times while we were together, but he always came back. He didn't give me what I needed, but, at the beginning, he told me he loved me, and he offered me a way to escape from Marlboro and from my mother. I was wounded, certainly, when he met me; but so was he, though I was too young to recognize it.

He was dishonest: He said he'd never had sex with anyone else after we met, not even with Rilly. I didn't believe him. I didn't want to fool around, or draw lines in the sand about what constituted honest behavior, and what didn't.

In the end, though it wasn't quite the end yet, I betrayed him when I asked Quint to go to bed with me. I didn't seduce him—I wouldn't have known how—except through our friendship, through my presence, and through my loneliness. Nor did he seduce me. We were both very innocent, for betrayers. We didn't need to be seduced; what we needed was each other.

I remember sweetness.

I remember making Picasso faces nose to nose. I remember exploring Quint's face with my fingers as if what I had always wanted to do was touch him. Across the bridge of his nose, there was a soft brown birthmark. That's important. I remember teasing him about his name, and stopping the moment he told me to. He cupped his fingers together and tried to show me how to make body noises. I couldn't, though I tried hard. I remember watching him; it gave me pleasure just to watch him.

I remember walking with him, afterward, in Stuttgart, and wanting to put my arm through his, wanting to be close to him in a public place.

"If we were still just friends," I said, "I wouldn't think twice about putting my arm through yours; it would seem so natural. That means that if I don't put my arm through yours, I'm doing something wrong."

We walked, arm in arm.

After that, everything is blurred. The next time I visited Jake in the hospital, he knew immediately that something had happened, that I was different. He says that Quint and I came to see him together. I don't know. In any case, Jake was released from the hospital the following day.

He and I sat in the *Zimmer,* our room full of dark, heavy, wooden furniture, and agreed that I could not stay in Stuttgart. I would go to Paris to look for work. We would let the days unroll, and give ourselves time to wait to see what happened and how we felt.

I must have said good-bye to Quint, but is it possible that I didn't? I must have been alone on the *Orient Express* to Paris. I do remember going back to the Hotel Odéon, to another room like the first, with a large bed, an armoire, a small desk and chair, for $2 a night. Every morning, the chambermaid strapped a pair of wet brushes on over her shoes and shuffled back and forth across the floor. I spent hours in that room, lying on the bed reading, dreaming, sleeping, and waiting.

I also spent hours in a record store on the Champs Elysée, in the listening booth. When it was crowded, the clerks would tap on the door after I'd been there for a while to let me know that it was someone else's turn. If it wasn't crowded, they let me stay as long as I wanted. When I asked if they had work, they said they'd let me know. I went to the USO and looked at the bulletin board; I went to the movies, where I discovered that the usher expected a tip, that there were advertisements to sit through before the feature film began, and that you could buy ice cream without leaving your seat. I think I saw *Moulin Rouge* and *Hellzapoppin* and *The Beggar's Opera.* I went in and out of stores, looking for work. I checked the ads in the *International Herald Tribune,* and its office. But there was no work.

Jake forwarded my dependent's check, but it wasn't very large. I ate hard-boiled eggs I bought at bars from baskets on the zinc counters. At a restaurant near the hotel, there were free baskets of bread and little jars of mustard on every table, and I ate bread with mustard on it and paid for a cup of coffee. Sometimes at night, I'd go early to a restaurant and order something cheap and delicious—an *omelette fines herbes,* for instance.

I'd sit at outdoor tables in the afternoon and sip my *chocolat,* or coffee, or wine, and feel as if I had been submerged into a pool of unhappiness. Voices floated by me speaking in sounds and tones I couldn't understand—slightly muffled, slightly dampened, all fast and jumbled together, high-pitched, no pauses, no periods, no commas. But I was in Paris, and it was beautiful. I remember thinking that I was desperately unhappy in a place I'd never been unhappy in before. This was different from being unhappy in New York City or at Antioch. This was surreal: enormous unhappiness, surrounded by strangeness and by a beauty that itself was a kind of happiness.

I had almost no associations with anything in the city; I'd never been to any of these places before. I didn't belong anywhere. I was very much alone.

At first, I didn't realize that my period was late. But gradually, I knew my body felt different. I went to the American Hospital. I think of myself in that Paris suburb walking down a leafy street, as if in a dream, floating an inch or two above the sidewalk, but slowly and inevitably getting closer to the hospital, as if drawn by a magnet. A doctor examined me and told me, yes, I was pregnant.

I had no idea what to do. I simply went through the days as if they would go on forever. I didn't even try to imagine the future.

The next time I needed to change money, I went, as always, to Pierre's Coca Cola Bar on the Rue du Roi de Sicile. Pierre changed money on the black market. He wore a long, dark jacket with many pockets on the inside, where he kept different denominations. You'd give him your dollars, and he'd ask you what you wanted back, and how you wanted it.

We always talked for a few minutes; I'd buy a coffee, a requirement, and sit alone at one of the tiny round tables, watching him pirouette and strut his stuff, wrapping his jacket around himself, and then letting it flare ever so slightly.

This time Pierre apparently watched me, because after I had been there for several minutes, he came back to my table. We had already completed our financial arrangements, and there were no other customers.

"*Q'est-ce que c'est?* You are not happy?"

To me, Pierre was part of Paris—a sweet uncle, perhaps, foreign, but familiar. I had to agree with his estimate.

"*C'est l'amour?* Eet's love? You have trouble wiz a man?"

I smiled. "No, everything's okay."

"Ah! Of course! I know it! You are *enceinte*, no? How you say—with baby? Pregnant? Yes, of course, you are."

Having Pierre confirm the doctor's diagnosis was devastating. It was much more real. Could everybody tell just by looking at me?

"Wait," he said. "I come right back."

He disappeared for a moment, and when he returned, he sat down next to me.

"I can help," he said, quite kindly. "I know people. Places you can go, cheap. I know good man. Yes? I arrange? Fix for you? We make you happy again."

In my mind, I saw the dark alley I'd read about, and the doom it held. I could see myself being taken silently through a door and placed on a table in a barely furnished room. I thanked Pierre, my only friend in Paris; but I didn't accept his offer.

There is more and more I don't remember. It frightens me even to try. I can feel tears ready to form, and my body braces itself; it knows that remembering will be painful. But nothing happens. I don't remember; and I don't cry.

When Quint arrived in Paris, he came with a friend. That's all I remember of his visit—simply that he was there. And the feeling that he was not there for me, that he had brought a friend as a buffer, in order to defend himself, to be sure that he kept a safe distance.

I know I received letters from Jake, thick letters, telling me what was happening in Stuttgart. There had been a dance at the *Caserne,* he told me, and Quint danced with George, which everybody thought was very funny. The paragraph was full of innuendo, but I took it no further than words on the page in Jake's artfully formed handwriting. There were phone calls—from Jake? Quint? Finally, Jake came to Paris on a weekend pass.

I remember two things about that weekend: One, eating perfectly peeled tangerines that Jake bought at a street market. Two, telling him I was pregnant. We were in bed.

"That's wonderful!"

Neither of us said anything for a minute.

"Of course, you'll have an abortion."

When we went back to Germany together, I felt as if the pieces of my life had been swept up and packed along with my clothes; I'd been drifting through the days by myself, finding no work, no answers; now I was being offered a chance to put my life back together.

Jake had a long pass coming, and we took it, leaving Stuttgart. We went to Switzerland and Italy, Zurich, Bern, and Lucerne, hitchhiking from Milan to Venice. In Bremerhaven, Germany, before we shipped out, I used the last of my marks to buy a beautiful hammered silver ring.

Then the Army ship home, arriving back in New York City, and realizing what a jumble my country was after the extraordinary neatness of Germany and Switzerland, and the luscious beauty of Italy. My life was no less in disarray.

12. JIL

WEDDING

I was nineteen and three-quarters, in my parents' living room, chilly with central air conditioning on a hot August day. I was waiting for the man I was about to marry.

My mother was so happy she was giddy without benefit of champagne. My father was a little unsure; but given that my mother made all his decisions for him—what to wear, where to live, who and when his children should marry—he was nervously pleased. My soon-to-be-husband's family was there, too, waiting tensely: We'd been making increasingly desperate conversation for more than half an hour. The groom was late.

I sat on the sofa arm, wearing a long white cotton dress with colorful embroidered flowers along the side. It was my compromise wedding dress, white but hippie-ish, like a dress for a Woodstock wedding. I should have been angry at the groom for being so late, but I was more scared than angry.

The night before, the phone rang just as I was getting ready for bed. It was Janey, calling from Wisconsin, where all my friends had stayed for the summer. I hadn't seen her since May, when I left Madison for a job in New York. I had already been accepted to NYU Film School, which I was scheduled to start in a few weeks.

Janey was blunt. "You don't have to do this," she said, for the tenth or twentieth or thirtieth time. "You can just live with him. Why don't you just live with him?"

"I want to get married." We had been around this for the last three weeks, ever since I announced that Lenny and I were marrying in a couple of weeks, so we could be settled in a new apartment before school started.

"You're nineteen, for God's sake! You're too young to get married." My friends took turns calling in their objections, night after night, but they all said the same thing and none of it changed my mind: *You're too young, you hardly know him, just live together. You should wait, and think about it—what's the rush? No one gets married at nineteen anymore. You don't live in a trailer park!*

Sometimes they altered their objections, from *You are too young* to *He is too old*. Lenny was twenty-nine, exactly ten years older than me. He was a lawyer. He owned—and wore—*suits*. To my friends this was as exotic as if he wore a kilt or a dhoti. They thought he was old, and square, and very not-for-me. He read the *New York Times, which doesn't even have comics,* my friends whined. *He plays golf,* they said, as if he disemboweled chickens. I couldn't explain it to them because I couldn't explain it to myself. If it doesn't work out, I thought (but never articulated, even in my own head), I'll just get divorced. I'm young enough. Even if we're married five years, I'll still be only twenty-four when I'm single again. I was getting married to Lenny, despite my friends' pleas, despite my age, despite my mother's blatant joy, which was the one thing that made me hesitate.

I was certainly not getting married to escape Madison. My first two years of college had been wonderful. Freedom, friends, days at my disposal, nights to enjoy; it was bliss. Even the misery, the overwhelming, powerful, dramatic adolescent misery, was wonderful, because it was *my* misery, *my* drama. I was having—at long last—a life.

I loved Madison, the flat, scruffy, friendly campus, the lakes that anchored the town, the old stone buildings climbing Bascom Hill. I loved ugly cinder-block Witte Hall, and Janey, my roommate, and I loved the dilapidated red house on Chandler Street, where I lived sophomore year with four other women. We pulled straws for the room choices and I won an L-shaped corner room that overlooked an overgrown patch of rhubarb that we picked and cooked for hours with massive amounts of raw sugar into a sticky pulp that hurt our teeth when we spread it on the wheat bread we bought from the food co-op. We lived on grainy, thick bread and cheese—cheese was cheap in Wisconsin—baked potatoes with cheese, pasta with cheese, and sometimes a stray vegetable or fruit.

We *ate* those things. We *lived* on romance, and books we read and reread, and loud music and pot and dancing in the living room to Bette Midler till 2:00 a.m., and boys with guitars and Cat Stevens scruff who looked sad because they knew it made them look sexy. We convinced ourselves—through our tears, our sleepless nights, and our pain—that without the lows there would never be highs: that the pain was essential to the pleasure.

Even though I loved the roller coaster, there was a part of me that was always watching, always judging. I decided this was because I was a writer. *The theory of the one-third,* I called it, the belief that part of me was always observing and recording. It was the same old emptiness, really; I'd just learned how to dress it up in fancy ideas.

I'd met Lenny a year before in the legal department of the company my friend
Linda worked for. I was a secretary for the summer, wearing dresses I borrowed
from my mother, and pantyhose that itched in the heat. The job felt pretend, but
I liked making money, and I liked the people there, who were older and seemed
glamorous. They went to Puerto Rico for long weekends and after work gathered at
a bar for drinks, instead of someone's dorm room to pass a joint. Lenny and I didn't
go out, alone, until the very end of the summer, just a week or two before I went
back to school. He invited me to a Judy Collins concert in Central Park, and dinner
beforehand at a restaurant near Lincoln Center. He lived in a brownstone just off
Central Park West, right where I had always wanted to live.

He seemed as different from the boys I knew at school as a Manhattan
skyscraper is from a clothing-optional commune. He was confident and strong. He
made me feel safe. He made me feel grown-up. He made me feel *real*.

In my parents' living room nearly an hour had passed, and the judge was tipsy.
I had asked him two things: to please say "love and honor" instead of "love and
obey" and to say "husband and wife" instead of "man and wife." I was pretty sure
he had forgotten, and made a mental note to remind him—if the groom ever
arrived.

My mother refilled glasses and put out more cheese and crackers. She was
so nervous she spilled a few drops of champagne onto the beige shag rug. My
wedding, clearly, was more important to her than it was to me. Linda's father had
come to take pictures of the ceremony, and my mother sent him away. "Lenny's
been delayed," she said, as if we'd heard some news of him.

Lenny's brother and "little sister," as he called her, even though she was a
year older than me, talked quietly on the couch. They were weighing the odds, I
thought—was he backing out? Had he changed his mind? His mother was wearing
a long dress, even though we were in someone's living room, not a church, and
going out to dinner at a local restaurant afterward, not to a hotel ballroom.

My mother wanted the hotel ballroom and the long dress. She wanted two
hundred people and a rabbi and a cantor and piles of presents from everyone whose
children she had given presents to over the years. But she tossed it all away with
hardly a whimper, because the fact that I was getting married—to a nice guy, to a
grown-up, to a *lawyer*—made up for all of it.

Three weeks earlier when we made our announcement, my mother had gone
into overdrive. She pulled out a guest list that she'd been working on for years,
maybe since I was adopted. She booked the temple and started calling hotels to see

which function rooms were free. She spent a day at Kleinfeld in Brooklyn, scouting wedding gowns.

A few days later, we held the first meeting of the parents at the Jaeger House, an old-fashioned German restaurant my father liked in Manhattan's Yorkville, then a German neighborhood. Lenny's parents were early. Mine were earlier. Everyone was nervous. His parents were Italian Catholics, and mine were Russian/Austrian Jews. But that was the only difference. They were both comfortably middle-class, striving, self-conscious immigrant families. By the time Lenny and I arrived, his father and mine had discovered they had served in the same regiment in Europe. Everyone was old friends, until the subject of who would perform the wedding ceremony came up.

"A rabbi," my mother said, as if there could not be other options.

"A priest," Lenny's father said. "The men in my family have been married by Catholic priests for a thousand years." Lenny's father was nearly as proud of his Italian heritage as my mother was of her Jewish one, although she couldn't claim roots that went back to the Roman Empire, as he often did.

My mother, to whom a priest was one step removed from a shaman with a bleeding sheep's entrails in his hands, looked at him as if he had suggested a moon man.

"My daughter should be married by a rabbi," she said.

"My son will be married by a priest," Lenny's father said.

Lenny and I looked at each other. "Actually," he said into the silence. "We want to be married by a judge."

No one was pleased by this idea.

"We could have a priest *and* a rabbi," Lenny's father said, "if we could find a priest who's willing."

My mother bristled. *Willing? A priest should be honored!*

Before she could speak, I opened my mouth. "We were thinking about eloping," I said. "This seems like too big a deal. Eloping will be much easier."

Suddenly everyone was in agreement.

"Eloping? No, no, that's not a good idea," my mother said.

"A judge isn't so bad," his father said. "My brother can do it, he's a judge."

"I know a judge in White Plains," my mother said. She gave up her rabbi, but she wasn't allowing in more of his family.

"Fine, fine," his father said, and everyone drank happily. We would be married by my mother's judge from White Plains in her living room, in front of just the immediate family, and Lenny's two roommates.

In the living room, Lenny's roommates had not yet arrived; they were driving up with the groom. Lenny's father began to pace. He disguised it as best as he could, picking up a handful of nuts from one table, then checking out the fireplace at the other end of the room. After an hour, my future brother-in-law and sister-in-law fell silent, and even my mother's Herculean efforts to keep the conversation aloft started to fail her.

Sitting in my corner of the brown sofa, my stomach ached with fear. I had worked so hard, but he'd figured it out. I'd held my breath for months. I had asked him— *asked him*—to marry me. ("I think we should get married," I'd said to him three weeks earlier, in his parents' living room. "It'll be good to be settled before school starts." "Okay," he answered. *Okay.*) I had convinced him, somehow, to love me. I had made him believe that I was sane and normal and real—*just like everyone else.*

People, I realized much later, marry for right reasons as well as wrong ones. The right reasons are simple: You love him, he loves you; he supports your goals and dreams. You share the same values. He makes you happy. He makes you feel whole.

I knew my right reasons. I loved Lenny: I loved the way he made me feel. I loved his generosity, his dependability, his decency. I loved that he understood movies better than I did, even though I was the film student; that he swam like a fish; that he loved good food and travel and was always willing to give someone a second chance. I loved his remarkable confidence, I loved that he loved me.

But the wrong reasons often remain subterranean, sometimes for a lifetime. Maybe your wrong reason was a repetition of the past. Your father drank; you marry a druggie. Your mother's a narcissist; your wife is unloving. Your father was distant; your husband cheats.

I knew, without really knowing, that I was in search of a replacement for my often absent father. But I had no idea why else I was marrying, what my wrong reasons were.

"Do you have anything in common? Do you want the same things?" Janey asked me. "Of course we do!" I huffed. But I had no idea what my values were, what I wanted, or who I was. My wrong reasons were so far beneath the surface that it took me years to even recognize their existence.

The judge's eyes were starting to close. My brother had gone off to watch television; my mother stood nervously at the window. She started to turn away, probably to finally say what we were all thinking, when a little green Fiat pulled into the driveway.

Lenny got out of the backseat, where he'd been lying down. His two roommates helped him to the front door. Apparently, the bachelor party had gotten a little out of hand, and all three had been sick for hours. No one said anything about how late they were. Though Lenny was drawn and looked exhausted, he managed to stand through the short ceremony. The judge slurred our names and forgot the two things I asked him to say. I could barely look at Lenny, who was greenish-gray and swaying.

The judge pronounced us "man and wife" and we kissed, barely. My new sister-in-law and brother-in-law hugged us, but my mother pushed them aside. She threw her arms around Lenny, tears in her eyes for the first time I could remember.

"Thank God!" she said to him. "She's your problem now!"

I was too stunned by everything to react. *Doesn't matter,* I thought to myself. *I'm married now, I'm an adult. I've drawn the line between my mother and me. This is the end of something and the beginning of something else.*

What's the rush? my friends asked. *Live with him a while, see how it works out.* But I had to marry him now, fast, before he changed his mind, before he found out the truth, before he got past the surface that I spiffed and polished just for him— before he saw underneath and discovered the real me. Though I wasn't sure who she was, I knew she definitely was not someone anyone would ever want to marry.

13. Bunny

WITH CHILD

[Menstruation] has been called the weeping of a disappointed uterus.
When the uterus is not disappointed, menstruation is suppressed
through a change in the maternal hormone balance,
and the spongy lining continues to build up throughout pregnancy
to maintain a hospitable environment for the baby.

GERALDINE LUX FLANAGAN
THE FIRST NINE MONTHS OF LIFE

B ack in New York, I made an appointment for Jake and me to see Dr. Ennis together. In his office, at his behest, we did the math: The baby had been conceived in February or March. This was July. An abortion was out of the question; it was too late. He reminded us that abortion was legal in various countries in Europe. Why hadn't we done that? Now it was too late: We were here.

He suggested adoption, and gave us the name of a lawyer who could arrange it for us. We could be paid for the baby. We went to see the lawyer, and after a long conversation, he turned us down because, he said, I would never go through with it. He could tell by my face.

In retrospect, what happened seems inevitable. When you travel without a map, your path may seem accidental; but sometimes when you arrive at your destination and look back, you can see that every turning brought you closer to where you wanted to be. When you don't know where you're going, my professor at Antioch had said, in a different way, any road will take you there.

It was in that way that I found the Louise Wise Planning Service for Jewish Young Women, in the Yellow Pages under "Adoption."

Jake and I each saw a counselor at the agency once a week. We explored the issues of adoption, and the procedures we would be going through. The baby would spend the first few months with a foster mother, to be sure it was healthy and doing well before it was adopted. The foster mother would be as carefully chosen as the adoptive parents. We could name the baby; the adopting parents would change its name, but they would keep the initial. We would be given some broad, general information about the couple who adopted the baby.

Neither Jake nor I believed the baby to be his. "You need to explore this," the counselor told each of us separately. "If you're going to stay together, you should examine this question. Why are you both so unwilling to think the baby might be Jake's?"

We didn't have an answer, and we didn't want to explore the question and find one. It was not something either of us felt safe enough to talk about. It had never been mentioned between us at any point—in Paris, or now. We both assumed the baby was Quint's, and we never talked about it. I still find it hard to talk about. For Jake, it must have been even harder.

Why did he stay with me through all this if he believed the baby wasn't his? He has said he stayed because that made him—finally—the good guy in our story.

I think it was more complicated than that. There's always a payoff, and there's always a price. I'm certain the price was high, but I don't know what the payoff was for Jake. His own answer must be part of the reason, but there must also be more. Perhaps he simply wanted to help me; perhaps he wanted to act as if—or even, in a way, to believe—the baby were the child of his own conceiving. Perhaps there was a bit of adventure for him in what we were going through. Perhaps it was more comfortable than leaving and starting over; perhaps he really did love me or need me; or perhaps he thought that he did. I think there's more that I didn't understand then and can't know now, because whoever Jake is or may have been, he is almost as far beyond my understanding and knowledge now, when I no longer know him or need him, as he was then, when I thought I knew him so well and believed that I needed him so much.

It seemed to me then that he was not much interested in the baby, and that he was only slightly interested in me. Maybe he was staying because it was convenient. In that case, we were together because we were together. My hope was that things would get better. Hope, Emily Dickinson said, is a thing with feathers, and it hadn't flown away yet.

Four months before the baby was due, Jake found an apartment with four rooms, parquet floors, a skylight in the bathroom, a working fireplace, in a walk-up on the fourth and top floor of a small building on Second Avenue between 25th and 26th Streets. The rent was $69 a month.

Jake bought a flush door for a desk, another for a table, a wrought-iron frame with a foam rubber slab for a couch, a bed, and two wicker chairs. He found a cat, a beautiful gray kitten we named Hollis, because her mother's owner was the daughter of Admiral Holly, whose statue stands in Washington Square Park. I registered with a temporary work agency. Jake started looking for a job.

For prenatal care, I went to an outpatient clinic at New York Hospital. The expectant mothers learned exercises and relaxation techniques, and were told about the stages of labor. We waddled through the halls, looking at the labor rooms and the delivery rooms. I liked being with all these women who were not hiding their pregnancies, who were happy about their babies, whose husbands were proud.

I remember taking the bus up First Avenue to the hospital. I sat in the waiting room at the clinic, listening for my name to be called, and, when it was, I undressed in a little cubicle like the bathhouse lockers at Jones Beach, or a fitting room in an old department store: a square space with a bench across the back, hooks on the wall, and a curtain for privacy. I remember having my pelvis measured—ample!—and a series of young doctors leaning over me, a different one at each visit, to listen to my baby's heartbeat.

I remember being alone in the apartment on Second Avenue, standing in front of the floor-length mirror. From the front, I looked the same. Sideways, my body bubbled out into an awesome bulge.

I don't remember the baby moving or kicking. I don't remember discomfort. I don't remember whether the birth was early or late. I don't remember my water breaking, or feeling contractions and going into labor, or getting to the hospital. I only remember those few things—the times when I was alone, or at the hospital, when it was all right to be pregnant, when I could look at my body and watch it change, or when I could hand my body over to its caretakers and have them measure it, and listen to it, and tell me it was all right.

In those weeks and months just before the baby was born, I came no closer, even with the help of the agency counselor, to knowing why this had happened. I had a diaphragm; why hadn't I used it? The easiest answer is to say that the idea of having a baby had never occurred to me. It wasn't something that could happen to me. It was an idea that had no reality. I was not stupid, but I never made the personal connection between having sex and having a baby. Like when you acknowledge that everybody dies, but you certainly don't really believe—can't imagine—that you yourself will turn out as everybody else does: dead. That's the surface. Of course there had to be more.

Later, with the support of a very good psychiatrist, I would finally be able to shake off that awful numbness and passivity and begin my life. In the process, I came to believe that this baby was wanted—not in any healthy way, but because, like those teenagers today who become pregnant because they want someone to love, I wanted this baby.

I didn't want to have an abortion. I wanted the baby to grow; I wanted it to be safe inside my body; I wanted it to be born.

I certainly didn't want to sell my baby on the black market, as if it were a carton of cigarettes or a pound of coffee. I didn't want to be part of a babies-for-profit corporation, with parents chosen because they could afford to pay the price. I didn't want my body to be part of a lawyer's production line: That's what Ennis's lawyer had seen in my face. I wanted my baby to be brought up by people who had been chosen, checked and double-checked, not handed to someone in exchange for a bundle of money.

I wanted this baby to have what I couldn't give it—a chance better than my own. I didn't want another me, another passive and numb soul, drifting through life.

I can't pretend all this was logical, commendable, or rational. It's simply what was. I didn't expect to be pregnant; but once I was, I wanted to have the baby.

And I wanted to have it by myself. The counselor at the agency urged me to talk to my mother, to tell her that I was pregnant; but I couldn't. She would not have allowed me to give the baby away. However she did it, she would have stopped me. I couldn't take care of a baby. Most obviously, I had no money; I didn't even have a job. There was no day care then. Jake would not have stayed with me: He'd told me that plainly and clearly. Single mothers were shunned then. It never occurred to me to go on welfare. I don't even know if there was welfare for single mothers at that time.

And even if I could have managed somehow, how could I be a mother? I could barely take care of myself. If my mother knew about the baby, she would have kept it; that's the only way it could have been managed, and the baby would have been hers. The baby would have been another me, and I didn't want another me.

I also believed that if my mother had known what I planned to do, if I had done it with her knowledge, her heart would have been broken. I thought she would die—surely, literally, die—just as my father had if she knew what I was doing. I couldn't tell her. I didn't tell her.

I did try to do what was best for the baby; given everything else, the baby was real, no matter how unreal it all seemed. The adoption agency was a good one;

everything seemed to be done with care and thought. I believed the baby would be loved, would be safe. I thought adoption was the best possible solution. I also wanted to keep this baby, with all my heart. But I couldn't put it all together, and so I went through the motions, one by one, each one as it came along.

Almost no one knew I was going to have a baby. In Europe, Pierre knew, period. In America, only Ennis, his lawyer, and the adoption agency knew—not my friends, not my sister, not my mother.

We told my mother that Jake had found a temporary job in Cleveland, to last until just after Thanksgiving. A friend of Jake's lived in Cleveland; we wrote letters to my mother and mailed them inside addressed and stamped envelopes to Bobby; he mailed them to her and then forwarded her answers to us.

We disappeared. To the middle of New York City, where no one knew we were.

14. JIL
LOSS

Because I didn't have the wedding she'd been planning since the adoption agency called and said, "We have a baby girl for you," my mother hosted a big party for us a few weeks after we were married.

On a wet morning in August a big tent went up in the backyard, with music and dancing, a bar and buffet. It rained so hard that the ground under the temporary wooden floor was soft, and the boards of the dance floor bounced gently beneath our feet like long sponges. Dozens of people came, all my aunts and uncles and cousins; there were seven first cousins on my mother's side, and twenty or more on my father's, I could never count them all. We rarely saw my father's family: My mother called them "common," a term that covered everything from *uneducated* to *drinks too much* to *scratches himself in public.*

But we were very close to my mother's two brothers and their wives, despite the fact that my mother disliked her sisters-in-law. Despised them, actually, with a fury so intense it was sometimes hard to be around. After each visit—every Rosh Hashanah and Thanksgiving and long weekend—we'd be trapped in the long car ride home with her furious litany. Aunt Cynthia was a snob, she said, a show-off. She had gone to college and to Europe on vacations with my Uncle Bernie. She liked to talk about books and magazines and went on *Jeopardy!* when I was in second grade, and won. *Who the hell does she think she is,* my mother would spit. *She grew up in the Bronx—same as me.*

Her other sister-in-law was a bad wife and mother. Aunt Michelle was twelve years younger than my Uncle Sam, my mother's twin brother, and loved to cook exotic meals and decorate her beautiful homes. *Did you see those poor kids, the little one doesn't even have clothes that fit,* nebbuch, *and the girls run around like wild animals, and she doesn't give a damn.*

I loved my uncles and my aunts. I loved my cousins, too, especially my cousin Neil, a year younger than me, smart and irreverent. His was the first penis I ever saw, breathless under the blankets of our makeshift bed in my parents' den, playing "I'll-show-you-mine-if-you-show-me-yours" while the grown-ups drank cocktails upstairs and Neil and I nearly wet ourselves giggling while the flashlight bounced from our laughing red faces to his fishy-looking little member.

Neil organized my first séance, in the loft of Uncle Sam's unused barn upstate. Using candles he swiped from Aunt Michelle's party supply, we nearly burned the place down trying to contact the spirits with my battered Ouija board. Neil scared me silly and made me laugh. He went to tennis camp and boarding school, both faintly gentile and completely alien endeavors that I admired. He made a joke of everything, but somehow managed to get through cutting classes and smoking pot without ever getting caught. There was a lucky charm on Neil's head, and it made him a joy to be with, and a pleasure to love. *He's going to be the first Jewish president,* his mother said. In spite of her jealousy, my mother agreed.

At my wedding party, Uncle Bernie cracked bad jokes and made funny faces for the camera. Aunt Cynthia was elegant and reserved. Neil's younger brother, my sweet cousin Jon, hung out with my brother. But Neil was driving cross-country before heading back east to start college at Williams. Two weeks later, he was dead.

I don't remember who told me—it must have been my mother. But I do remember knocking on my grandmother's door in the Bronx, and how her face looked when she opened it. We never paid unexpected visits in my family; she knew immediately that this had to be very bad news.

The next day, we rode in near silence the four hours to my aunt and uncle's home in Massachusetts: my parents, my brother, my new husband, my grandmother, and me.

"I don't understand," my grandmother said. Mema, we all called her, had become an old lady overnight. In two weeks she had gone from the wedding of one grandchild to the funeral of another.

My mother said all she knew. "It was a robbery. He picked up a hitchhiker on the road. And..."

She couldn't say it again. They camped somewhere along the way, in Colorado. In the middle of the night the hitchhiker shot Neil and stole his car. That was all we knew.

"I don't understand," Mema said. She looked shriveled and worn.

I was terrified. Sitting in the backseat, sandwiched between my husband and my grandmother, I could not imagine what I would say to my aunt or my uncle. I could not imagine how they would survive. This was a world I had no words for.

We struggled up the walk of their home like the survivors of some horrific disaster, too afraid to go on, too tired to go back. Inside the house, several of my aunt and uncle's friends sat scattered on the Swedish modern furniture, which seemed too spare and low-slung for such a grave occasion. Their hands were clasped in front of them, their voices a furry hush, their eyes darting, confused. They seemed desperate, as if they were looking for a way out—a way not to feel guilty that this had not happened to them. Perhaps they wondered, hoped, that this would insulate them. My aunt and uncle had generously absorbed all the bad fortune for the entire community.

My mother gave her brother a stiff hug, her sister-in-law an even stiffer one. We sat down, absorbed into the mourning mass. Small talk sputtered around us. *How was the drive? Did you hit traffic? Are you hungry?* I had expected a rending of garments, or furious hot tears. This quiet buzz was strange; I was very afraid of what lay under it.

A few minutes later, Uncle Sam and Aunt Michelle arrived. Sam shook hands with his older brother, unable to look him in the eye. My two uncles seemed like people who had long ago survived a terrible disaster and never quite recovered, but weren't really sure what to say to each other.

Aunt Cynthia spoke, her voice raspy. "Why don't you hug your brother?" she asked Sam. "He needs it." She started to cry quietly.

Both men stared at her in silence.

"He doesn't have to hug him," my mother said, her voice loud in the hushed room. "Bernie knows what we feel." She turned her head away and whispered loudly to my grandmother, "Idiot."

Later that day, Uncle Sam flew to Colorado to identify the body and bring my poor torn cousin home. I never saw either of my uncles cry. My mother seemed to channel her misery into hating Cynthia, despising her tears, her scenes. *She has no shame,* she said. *She has to make a big show in front of everyone. She should shut up and pay attention to my brother.* My mother hated her for what she saw as weakness, for her tears and her red nose—for her mess.

"There's something wrong with your uncle," my mother said on the phone. Two years had passed since my cousin's death. I had graduated from college and was working in advertising. "It's very bad."

I knew what that meant: the one unnamable thing—cancer.

Once again we drove in silence to Massachusetts, a drive that seemed to grow longer, because of the pain we were in, and at the same time, shorter, because I longed never to arrive—to have this road that led to awful darkness go on forever, leading nowhere.

My mother and grandmother and I went to see my uncle several times during the long, slow course of his illness. I was freelancing then, and could come and go when I wanted, and my mother would take a day or two off from her job as a saleswoman at a local department store, a job she started when I went to college. Each time we saw him, my uncle was thinner and paler, until he seemed to become transparent, his blood pulsing a weak blue beneath his skin. He still laughed and made bad jokes, but quieter and slower, as if he couldn't concentrate. He was trying to be himself, the son his mother adored, the older brother the twins worshipped, the funny uncle, the beloved father and husband. But he was slipping away from himself.

On our awful, painful visits, my mother and Mema and I stayed at a nearby motel. My aunt didn't want us at the house, and my uncle was too sick to insist that she play host to us. I understood, and was glad to have someplace to go that wasn't surrounded by death and dying, a place where I didn't have to wait tensely for things to erupt between my mother and my aunt.

At our last visit, when it was clear that it was all almost over, my mother and grandmother and I sat in the hospital's waiting room. It was gray and a little worn out, just like we were, and dimly lit, a protective darkness that helped us keep our pain to ourselves. A strange woman entered, holding a clipboard. She had professional warmth and shrewd eyes.

"Excuse me. Are you Bernie's sister?" she said to my mother with a slight Boston accent.

My mother stood up. "Yes?" she said, shaking hands.

"I'm Joanne Rubin, the hospice ward's social worker," she said, extending her hand to my grandmother. "I've been spending some time with Bernie and Cynthia and Jon. I'm here to help you through this very difficult time."

I could see my mother's back stiffen. "We don't need any help," she said. "Thank you. We're fine."

Joanne smiled gently. Clearly, this was not unexpected. "A lot of people say that. But this is a very hard time for all of you." She shook her head sadly from side to side. "And I'm sure it would help to have someone to talk to."

"We don't need anyone to talk to," my mother said. "No offense intended."

"None taken," Joanne smiled, not dissuaded. "Many people feel that way at first." It felt a little like a recitation, a performance. "But it does help to talk, to cry, and to share your feelings with someone outside the family. It's a safe place to open up."

A little more steel crept into my mother's voice. "We're fine," she said. "Thank you."

It was a dismissal, but Joanne didn't pick up her cue. Uneasily, I backed away; I always got nervous when my mother's voice chilled. I'd read that before a cyclone touches down, the air gets still and metallic. When my mother's voice sounded that way, it meant some haggard supermarket cashier was about to be dressed down for overcharging on the frozen peas, or the unfortunate man who forgot to clean the windshield in the gas station was about to be told how little he knew about doing a good job. My mother's trigger was always ready to be pulled, and I hated to be a bystander for the bloodletting.

"Sometimes people have a hard time saying good-bye," Joanne said gently to my mother. "For example, I think it might be a good idea for you to tell your brother that you love him."

There was a pause, like the silence before a thunderclap.

"How dare you," my mother said, moving closer to Joanne, who flinched as my mother's face came right up to hers. "My sister-in-law told you to say this to me, didn't she?" Her spittle was landing on Joanne's cheeks, which were red. "That bitch. Do you think my brother doesn't know how I feel about him? Do you think he doesn't know how his mother feels about him?"

"Hush…" my grandmother whispered. But my mother didn't hear it.

Her chest was heaving. "My brother knows I love him. I don't have to make a goddamn fool of myself in front of him. I don't have to listen to that pig."

She had Joanne backed up against the door. "Get the hell out of here."

Joanne reached behind her to open the door.

"And tell my sister-in-law that my brother knows what I feel and she can go to hell."

Joanne yanked the door open behind her and slid out without a word. My mother stood there for a moment, staring through the glass, breathing hard. When she turned around, there were tears in her eyes, but her teeth were gritted. "That bitch," she said, blinking hard. "She'll be married again in a year. But I'll never get another brother."

She was wrong: Aunt Cynthia did not get married again, in a year or ever. Elegant Cynthia, the smart one, the college-educated one, the one who took her children to Broadway shows and trips to Europe, who sent her boys to tennis camp and boarding schools, slowly crept into darkness and death while my sweet cousin Jon went to college in North Carolina.

Only one year behind him was my brother, my smart, offbeat, funny brother, who had never seemed quite real to me despite growing up in the room next door.

Kenny was happy his first year at college, happy to be on his own, away from home. He made friends, he told us, something that hadn't been easy for him. All through childhood he had trouble connecting with other kids, playing with the children on the circle in the afternoons, but rarely meeting up with a friend from school. He was smarter than the other kids in his class. In elementary school I overheard my mother telling Mema that the children had taken IQ tests and Kenny's teacher said his score was the highest she had seen in twenty years of teaching.

In junior high Kenny started creating his own artwork out of scrap metal and junk. My father bought him an arc welder, and later an acetylene torch, and on weekends and after school Kenny would hole up in the garage, a huge pair of bug-eyed goggles across his face, and create strange, elaborate works of art that jiggled and danced. He liked cars, engines, anything with moving parts and metal, *Mad* magazine, Frank Zappa, Superman comics, and slot-car racing.

In high school, Kenny decided he wanted to be on the football team. This was a stroke of remarkable perverseness. Up until then he had never expressed the slightest interest in football. I'd never seen him watch a game; I wasn't sure he even knew how it was played. Plus, Kenny was about 5-foot-6 and weighed maybe 135 pounds soaking wet.

Football—the game itself, much less playing it—was beyond my mother's comprehension. Football was dangerous, it was foreign, and it was pointless. Football was for big, dumb *goyim*, who were never going to college, not for her smart, short, skinny son.

"You have to talk to him," she said on the phone. She called me every night and sometimes during the day to repeat her pleas.

I couldn't understand it myself: Was Kenny trying to make friends—to rebel? Silently I cheered him on. For the first time, he was on my side of the family divide, fighting with my mother.

"He's not going to listen to me," I protested.

"He's too little. He'll get hurt. It takes up too much time. His grades will suffer." My mother had so many objections she didn't know where to begin.

Kenny had set up weights in his room, and worked them obsessively, until lumps and bumps of muscles appeared all over his skinny body like pads under the skin. He drank raw eggs for breakfast, puréeing them in the blender with milk, and ate steak for dinner. He ran up and down the streets after school, red and wet with sweat, wearing sweatshirts and pants he bought with money he earned himself. My mother would not contribute to this misbegotten effort.

"He won't listen to anything I say," my mother said, nearly yelling. "He's being an idiot."

In my mother's language, that meant he wasn't doing what she wanted. For the first time in his life, he set himself against her, and ignored her yelling and nagging and badgering. But she was relentless. She had spent a lifetime guarding him, protecting him, pulling the food from his throat with her fingers when he choked, and a pigskin ball and a bunch of overmuscled louts weren't going to get in her way.

Kenny didn't fight back, or yell. But he tried out for the football team and somehow, amazingly, he made it. The coach said he would probably sit on the bench most of the season. But even making the bench was an astounding accomplishment, especially if you were 5-foot-6 and skinny as a stick.

"It'll interfere with your studies," my mother screamed. When she found out about five-times-a-week practices and two weeks of football camp, she escalated her campaign. "You won't get into a good college. You'll be a bum your whole life because of stupid football."

She came at him relentlessly, day and night, from all angles.

"You'll get hurt."

"You won't be able to go to school if you get injured."

"You'll have permanent damage."

"You'll ruin your life."

"It's a stupid game."

"You're too *smart* to care about football."

"You don't care about me. If you cared about me you wouldn't put me through all of this."

Then she pulled out the biggest weapon of all.

"You're killing your father. He's so upset about this he doesn't sleep at night. He can't concentrate on his work. He's miserable with worry. I've seen him *cry*."

But my brother held firm. He attended practices religiously, working hard to bulk up, warming the bench with devotion, always at the ready, always, fully, there.

And then he wasn't. He quit the team without warning or explanation.

I was stunned; he wouldn't say why. My mother didn't dare question him.

Football was Kenny's one and only rebellion. He let it go, and then left for college a year later—a good college, where he would major in engineering, as my mother told him to. Her husband would never be an engineer; he would always be an electrician (an "electrical contractor" she told us to write on our school forms; it sounded classier). But her son would be.

Kenny didn't much like engineering, but he didn't complain. After football he went back to being his compliant self. He liked physics and philosophy, but my mother couldn't see what good those subjects would do him.

He seemed to like college. He wrote me strange, quirky letters in his jagged, slanting print, letters filled with offbeat observations, silly sketches, and quotes from things he read, lines from poems or songs. He often ended them with cryptic phrases I didn't really get, like "The most important thing in life is underpants," or "The universe is a salami."

The summer after his junior year, he spent a lot of time in the city, hanging out with Lenny and me. He liked Lenny, who accepted all his oddities. They skied together in the winter, went to the beach together in the summer. And his closeness to Lenny brought him closer to me. We weren't good friends yet, but we were working on it.

One night in late August, shortly before he was to head back to school for senior year, we went to see Devo in Central Park. The opening act was a magician whose tricks couldn't be seen past the first few rows of seats. The audience booed him mercilessly.

"This is stupid," I said. "I have no idea what he's doing. Nobody does."

Kenny grinned. "It's a metaphor," he said.

I thought about it: "A metaphor for what?"

He looked at me. Up close he looked tired, maybe from working construction all summer. "For everything," he said. "He's up there, pretending to do something that isn't real, and we can't even see him do it. What does it matter if we can or can't see it? We know it isn't real, anyway."

"But it's pointless," I said.

"That's the point," he said, grinning.

I didn't get Devo either, the jerky movements and tiered plastic helmets. But Kenny loved them, and I was willing to like them for the sake of what was slowly becoming a friendship.

Walking up Columbus Avenue later, Kenny said he had a headache.

"No surprise," I said. "That music would give anyone a headache."

"No, it's not from the music," he said, rubbing his forehead. "I've had it for a while."

"How long?" I asked.

"Six weeks."

I turned to him in shock. "You've had a headache for six weeks, and you didn't say anything about it?"

"I've had it off and on for a few months. It's no big deal."

"Did you tell Mom?" I asked.

He laughed. "Are you nuts? She'll get all crazy."

It was true. My mother thought every headache was a brain tumor, every cough, pneumonia.

"It's nothing," he said.

He went back to college in a week and visited the doctor at the campus health center. Perfectly fine physical specimen, Kenny wrote me in his nearly illegible scrawl. He enclosed a cutout of Clark Kent from an old *Superman* comic, prying his jacket apart to reveal the bright yellow "S" against the red costume. Kenny had glued a yellow plastic Devo helmet on him. "Invincible," he wrote across tier one. "Omnipotent," was on the next tier.

His letters to me got stranger. He never wrote about classes or friends or activities, just odd fragments of things he'd been reading, or a quote from a song. When he came home for the holidays, the change was shocking. He was very thin, and only ate strange combinations of foods, which couldn't be altered in any way. Breakfast was one-half of a baked potato with a peeled apple, or a raw egg with one quarter of a banana. None of it made any sense, but the rules were inflexible. If there was a scrap of peel on the apple or part of the banana was brown, he would throw it all out and start over, calmly, deliberately, like a scientist focused on a very difficult task. When he talked to me, he stared somewhere over my shoulder. When he did look at me, I felt frightened. There didn't seem to be anyone behind his eyes.

Another shock arrived when we received his grades. He'd taken incompletes in most of his courses that semester. Handwritten notes came from his professors. They wanted to give him good grades, they said; they could tell he was capable. But at some point during the semester he had stopped doing the work, and then stopped coming to class.

He started seeing a chiropractor, who recommended certain nutrients, particular foods, exercises, and frequent visits. Kenny was already eating according to a rigid standard that eliminated 90 percent of the foods in the world. Now he got rid of an additional 5 percent.

My mother was petrified, so frightened that she became incapable of movement, or decision. In frantic phone calls the same questions went around and around. *What's wrong with him? What do you think we should do? Should we take him to see a doctor? Will he go? Can you ask him? Should we take him to a psychiatrist? Will he go? Can you ask him?*

But Kenny was adamant: no doctors, no psychiatrists—just the chiropractor, and his strange nutritional regimen.

After he returned to college in January, we waited, worried, hoping that this was just a bump, that somehow normal life would kick in, and he would go back to the way he'd been before.

His letters became fewer, and then stopped. Phone calls failed to reach him. He was living alone in an apartment off campus, and we didn't know any of his friends. There was no one we could call for help.

His midterm grades arrived: incompletes in every class. In April, terrified, my parents flew down, and brought him home.

He was emaciated, hollow-eyed. His moods shifted suddenly from silence to fury. He went back to the chiropractor, eating almost nothing, sometimes staying in his room all day. He was obsessed with germs, with illness and cleanliness, with cleaning the kitchen counter over and over, ten times or more, before he would peel his apple or pour a glass of water. Sometimes he spent hours in the bathroom, scrubbing his flesh raw, or, even worse, giving himself enemas once, twice, sometimes three or more times a day. It was my mother's obsession with germs, her focus on food and digestion and safety times ten, times a hundred, times infinity.

Every few days I would catch a glimpse of my funny, smart, silly brother inside this sickly shadow.

Walking down the block in early July, steaming in the summer heat, Kenny wearing a sweatshirt because he was cold now all the time, he said, "I'm thinking of starting a T-shirt business, personalized shirts, with funny sayings like 'Everything is relative—especially your relatives.'"

I laughed: *There's my brother!*

But most of the time we circled around him warily. Everything Kenny said and did was analyzed. My mother, who had spent years running the show, giving orders, was frozen, which scared me almost more than anything. I was twenty-six years old, and had no idea what to suggest, or do.

In July my parents forced Kenny to see a psychiatrist, a customer of my father's electrical contracting business. The doctor met with my parents and then with my brother, then with my parents again. He told them he needed to see Kenny several times a week. Kenny saw him once more, and then refused to return.

"He's an asshole," he said. "He has no idea what the fuck he's doing."

My mother begged; she ordered. But he refused.

By the end of July, Kenny would only talk to my cousin Susie, who was close to him in age, and shared a cynical worldview and a wicked sense of humor. She told me later they talked about comic books, superheroes, Roman warriors, knights in armor, and samurai. Kenny admired the Romans and the samurai, because they were men of honor, willing to fall on their swords, to not only die in battle at the hands of another, but to die by their own hand if they were defeated.

On August 10 he sat at the kitchen table and had a fight with my mother, a fight about going to the chiropractor or eating a raw potato for breakfast or washing his hands twelve times with Ajax until they nearly bled, or any one of the dozens of things that we argued with him about. He yelled at her, "Go fuck yourself," and my mother got in her car and went to work. She stopped to run an errand, and half an hour later, when she heard sirens and saw a police car racing past her in the opposite direction, she turned the car around and went home. Kenny wasn't there. She sat by the window in the empty house and waited for the police to come tell her what she already knew had happened.

After their fight, Kenny had driven to a nearby building, one of the very few apartment buildings in our suburban town. He parked in the lot in front, and went up to the roof. Later the police told us two girls saw him sitting there, on the edge, his legs dangling, sometimes swinging, as he surveyed the scene from sixteen stories up. At some point, he wrote his name and address and phone number on a piece of paper in his spiky print and put it in his pocket. Then he wrote five words on a torn piece of paper, tucked it into another pocket, and let himself fall.

I barely remember the next few days. My uncle Sam went to the county medical center to identify Kenny's body. Somehow I ended up with the death certificate, which said, "massive internal injuries" as the cause of death, not suicide, or madness. I remember going with my uncle to bring my brother's car home from the lot in front of the building where he died.

I remember, and I wish I didn't, going with my husband to tell my grandmother that she had lost another grandchild. When she saw us at her front door, unannounced, uninvited, she knew, and her legs gave way. When we told her, sitting in her art-filled living room, my tiny grandmother shrank a little. She trembled, then steeled herself. "Oh my," she said softly. She didn't cry.

My mother wept quietly at the small hasty funeral. There were a few family members there, a few family friends, but no friends of Kenny's. He had lost touch with them by the time he died.

The second night we were sitting shiva—the traditional seven-day Jewish mourning period—the psychiatrist who had seen my brother came to call, and asked to speak to my parents and me alone. Sitting downstairs in the chilly den, he told us that he'd diagnosed my brother as schizophrenic, although he never told my brother of his diagnosis. In his opinion, this meant Kenny was doomed.

"Many researchers now believe that schizophrenia is an inherited condition," he said, his gaze traveling carefully from my mother to my father to me. "It's a condition that cannot be corrected."

My mother and father nodded at him.

"Perhaps your son's birth father or mother was schizophrenic," he said. "I understand you know very little about them." My mother nodded.

The doctor continued. "Schizophrenics often spend their entire lives heavily medicated or institutionalized. I think Kenny understood enough of what was happening to him to make a different choice."

The night before, I'd gone into Kenny's room, a small room with a dresser, a desk and a bed. Amid the mess of papers and books, clothes and magazines and record albums, I found several library books on mental illness. One had a bookmark at the chapter on schizophrenia. Did Kenny diagnose his own mental illness without the doctor even telling him? Was suicide his self-prescribed treatment?

It all worked out so neatly, I thought, gazing at this pompous doctor's smile of comfort, watching as he patted my mother's thin, shaky hand. I didn't need to worry—it was a condition caused by an inheritance Kenny and I didn't share. My parents didn't need to feel guilty because it wasn't their fault. It had nothing to do with bad mothering, absent fathering, or lousy sistering. How convenient.

I should have asked the doctor why, if he had diagnosed my brother with this serious mental illness, he'd never informed my parents. At the time, I didn't think of it; I never saw the doctor again.

I'd imagined so many endings to the story, but this was one I did not, could not, have thought up. Maybe if I had, I could have rewritten the ending. I'll never know. I have lived a long time without my brother, and there are days and days that go by without my thinking of him, which seems the saddest ending of all. When I summon Kenny in my mind, I see the photographs in my albums: Kenny at age three, wearing red shorts and suspenders, his head buried in my mother's lap, refusing to be part of the formal family portrait. I see him as a floppy-haired thirteen-year-old in a chocolate brown suit, holding open the door to the country club in the last photo in his Bar Mitzvah album. I see him at fifteen, leaning on a tree branch, grinning, big crooked teeth smiling at the camera. I see him taller and skinnier, a mop of brown curls atop his head, in corduroy bell bottoms with a little brown scarf tied around his neck like an ascot, going out to dinner with all of us to celebrate his high school graduation.

I don't see him much after that. I don't see his college graduation picture, his wedding photo, heading off to a job interview in a suit and tie. I don't see him holding my first baby, born a year and a half after Kenny died. I don't see him becoming an uncle, a husband, a father.

I miss him more now as a sibling than as the person he was. I don't want to be an only child, the only person who has my memories, my parents, and my history. I want to be able to turn to someone and say, "Remember that stupid *Here Come the Brides* show we used to watch on Tuesday nights? Remember you used to tease me about how much I loved Bobby Sherman? Remember when Dad used to take us slot-car racing and we'd always fight over who got the red car? Remember when we went to Lake Placid and you got scared by Santa Claus and yelled at him, 'I'm Jewish! Leave me alone!?' Remember? Remember? Remember?"

At the end of our week of sitting shiva, my uncle Sam took me aside and handed me an envelope from the county medical examiner's office. "I thought you might want to keep these," he said. Inside were Kenny's birth certificate and the contents of his wallet, a driver's license, a library card. There was the piece of paper on which he had thoughtfully written his name, address, and phone number for the police he knew would come. And there was the other little torn scrap of paper, with five words in my brother's slanty, spiky, almost illegible handwriting.

"The universe is a salami," it said.

The universe is a salami.

15. BUNNY

BIRTH

[The baby's] eyes will have no tears, no functioning tear ducts,
for several weeks. The first cries are always tearless ones.

GERALDINE LUX FLANAGAN
THE FIRST NINE MONTHS OF LIFE

I'd like to write at great length about the birth—paragraphs upon paragraphs. I don't want to leave "The Baby" behind on the page as I did at the adoption agency. As long as I'm writing, she's still mine.

But even before I *have* to stop, I don't want to write about how she was born, how difficult the labor was, how afterward I looked at her and fed her and touched her. Writing about that means leaving it behind again, just as stopping writing does. The closer I come to the long labor, the delivery, the four days in the hospital, the harder it is to write. The closer I come to the birth, the less I remember. These are the cold spots where there are no memories. They turn from the air, from the light; they suck up energy in the form of darkness.

Somehow I was at the hospital, in labor. In her book about pregnancy and birth, Geraldine Lux Flanagan quotes Dr. Samuel Reynolds, a biologist who has studied the mechanics of labor, as saying that there are three Ps in the process of laboring to give birth: the Passage, the Passenger, and the Power. Ms. Flanagan adds another: Psychology. "Certainly," she writes, "attitudes are involved in the progress of birth. The length of labor, the welfare of the passenger and mother will depend on these three, and perhaps four, Ps."

The labor was a long one. Finally the doctor, one of the ones who'd bent over me and listened to the heartbeat and told me all was well, used forceps to pull the baby out, away from me, and into the world. The nurse said, "It's as if your body doesn't want to let the baby go. You're working and working, but your body doesn't seem to want to let the baby come out."

I asked the nurse whether the baby was a boy or a girl.

"Your baby is a beautiful little girl," she said.

I began to cry.

"Did you want a boy so badly?" she asked, sounding amused.

"No," I said. "I wanted a girl." That's why I was crying.

There were four women—mothers—to a room. Because I was allowed to give my baby her bottle, the other women may not have known I wasn't going to keep her. The nurses knew; it must have been on my chart. I remember being visited by a hospital social worker who discussed the adoption with me. She was concerned about me. I remember a nurse who told me to sleep on my stomach so my breasts wouldn't hurt so much. I remember sympathy and kindness.

The baby was perfect. Her face was beautiful, and she had a soft brown birthmark across the bridge of her nose. When I held her, I had the feeling that she was given to me first and taken away last, as if the nurses knew this was all I was going to have of her. I wanted to hold her all day, every day. I wanted to hold her forever.

When we left the hospital, the social worker gave me a blanket to wrap the baby in; I think she bought it herself. Jake says that in the elevator, leaving the hospital, I told him I wanted to keep the baby. I don't remember saying that then. I do remember telling him that at other times. But I recall exactly what his reply was whenever the subject came up: He would leave me immediately if I kept the baby.

Everything else is blank. We must have taken a taxi from the hospital to the adoption agency, from the Upper East Side to the Upper West. I have an image of the foster mother waiting in a room on one side of a wide corridor, and our being taken into a room on the other side. I must have signed papers.

I named the baby Jessica. I'd been told her adoptive parents lived in Westchester, that they were Jewish, that they were Democrats, and that her father was an engineer. They would change her name, but keep the initial J. She was their first baby. They hoped to adopt another.

I want to remember more. I want to remember holding the baby in the taxi; I want to remember whom I gave her to; I want to remember what I felt. I want to remember how she looked. I want to remember everything. I want to remember being pregnant, and giving birth, and being in the hospital. But when I gave away The Baby, I lost the memories, too. I don't think I would have survived otherwise.

I look inside. I blank everything else out. I notice the tears forming in my eyes, without being aware of them until they're there, but then I ignore them. I reassure myself—it's safe now, I can bear it now, truly I can. I want to remember, I even need to remember. I focus on the glassy surface of my memory and I push, as if I were giving birth to memories.

I wait.

Nothing happens. Nothing comes.

The next thing I remember is standing on the corner of Third Avenue and 23rd Street, unable to move.

16. JIL

BIRTH

In the spring of 1981, a few weeks before my shrunken, changed brother came home from college, I awoke in the predawn darkness, a searing pain on the right side of my stomach. I couldn't sit up, I couldn't bend, I could barely breathe.

"Len," I whispered. I had trouble turning my head toward him. "There's something wrong."

He helped me dress and took me to the emergency room in a taxi, where a sonogram revealed that I had a cyst in my right ovary.

"The size of a peach," my gynecologist said cheerfully when he showed up a couple of hours later. "It's a dermoid," he continued, while I tried to focus. I was light-headed from taking only shallow breaths for several hours.

"What's a dermoid?" I whispered.

"It's sort of an egg cell that begins to reproduce without fertilization. It's fascinating, actually." He tapped the sonogram. "It can develop hair, bones, nerve tissue. Look," he said as he pointed to a small, white fuzz: "Here's a tooth."

"Kind of like the immaculate conception," I wheezed. He laughed.

The next morning I had surgery to remove the cyst, which turned out to be more of a grapefruit than a peach. The operation went well, and when I awoke from the anesthesia a few hours later in my bright, sunny room, my mother was sitting next to my bed, a magazine in her lap.

"I've been waiting for you to wake up," she said. "The doctor said everything went fine. Lenny went to get something to eat."

She looked as if she'd been sitting there for days, like a woman whose train has failed to come, but she has nowhere else to go.

I wasn't sorry to see my mother there. Since I was a little girl, I always liked my mother more when I was sick; it was the only time she was tender with me, the only time she touched me—to feel my forehead for a fever, to stroke my arms with watery rubbing alcohol, to smooth my sweaty hair or clean my face with a warm washcloth. Hospitals were her milieu. At home, there was always too much of her. But all that energy, all that pugnacity, made her the perfect person to have on your side in a crisis. If you needed a shield, a guard dog, you needed her. The best defense, I knew from experience, was my mother.

When I was in fifth grade, I brought home a report card that contained, for the first time in my life, a B; in fact, several of them. My mother was horrified. I told her what my plump, prissy teacher had explained to the class: Miss Barr believed that giving straight As didn't leave students with anything "to strive for."

The next morning, my mother drove me to school, a rare occurrence. We got there early, before any other kids arrived. In the empty classroom, I sat down at my desk nervously. My mother calmly explained to Miss Barr that there was something wrong with my grades. Miss Barr calmly explained her belief that children needed something to reach for.

"My daughter reached for As," my mother said. "And she got them."

I could see the veins on her neck tighten. I could tell that Miss Barr could see them, too.

"Is there anything wrong with my daughter's work?" She leveled a look at Miss Barr that resembled the gaze a cheetah directs at a downed antelope.

"Is there anything wrong with my daughter's work?" she repeated, louder this time. I held my breath.

Miss Barr shook her head. "Her work is excellent," she said.

"Then you should give her the grades she deserves for excellent work," my mother said. She stood up and put out her hand. "Thank you."

The following marking period I received straight As.

That sunny morning in the hospital, I knew my painkillers would never be late, my hot meals would be hot, and my cold drinks would be cold. I knew the nurses would come when I buzzed and the doctors would be asked all the right questions. I would get excellent care, and, best of all, I would be spared her harsh words, prying questions, and punishing criticism. She would treat me gently and lovingly and direct her anger at someone else.

I turned my head on the pillow to look at her. She was staring out the window onto East End Avenue. Her face looked pinched and pale.

"I want to tell you something," she said. For a moment I thought there was some bad news. But then I realized that my mother did not look sad. She looked scared and still, like someone who has made a terrible, painful decision.

She didn't look at me but began to speak to the pale green wall eight feet away.

"I got my period for the first time when I was fourteen," she said. "I was terrified; I didn't know what it was. Nobody talked to me about it. Your grandmother could never talk about things like that."

Why was she telling me this now? I wanted to stop her, but the drugs in my system were powerful, and her voice was a monotone, lulling me.

"My mother sent me to a nurse at the clinic in the neighborhood to tell me what it was. It wasn't bad at first. But every month it got worse. When I was fifteen, I had to stay home from school for a week every month, sometimes more. The bleeding was awful, like a hemorrhage. I missed so much school I was falling behind, and I was a very good student until then. By the time I was sixteen, nothing could stop the pain. I would heat up an iron and put it on my skin with just a thin cloth in between. I still have the burn marks on my stomach."

She paused to draw a long breath. "Finally, my parents took me to some local doctor. I don't even think he was a gynecologist. My mother could barely explain to him what was wrong, she was so embarrassed. He didn't even examine me. He just put me in the hospital and operated. I wasn't even sure what he was doing. No one told me anything."

She sighed, looked out the window again. "When I left the hospital two weeks later, I didn't have the pain anymore—but I couldn't have children. I don't remember who told me that: I was sixteen, and I could never have children."

She turned, finally, toward me, looking drained, and drawn. "We wanted you so much," she said. "We waited six years for you, four more for your brother—a very long time."

Then she turned away and stared out the window. The drugs were pulling me under and she was blurring, the sunny window was fading. I fell asleep and when I woke up the magazine was on the chair, but she was gone.

My gynecologist said that the operation was a success. My right ovary was intact, and it should have no effect on my ability to have children. He was right. Less than a year later, just a few months after Kenny died, I was pregnant.

At my first visit to the Maternity Center on the Upper East Side, the midwife asked me for my family history.

"I don't have one," I said. "I'm adopted." The midwife, a thin, warm, older woman, looked up.

"No information at all?" she asked with a heavy Kentucky accent.

"No." I wondered if this was a problem.

"So this will be your first blood relative," she said, smiling.

I was confused. I had so disconnected myself from the concept of blood that even becoming a mother didn't make me think about the woman who had given birth to me for a minute.

"You'll have a blood connection to someone," she said.

I still didn't seem to be getting it.

"The baby—someone will look like you, and maybe have your talents or interests, or your health issues. A *real* relation."

It was like explaining God to an atheist: Why does it matter what God looks like or what his powers are, if you don't believe in him?

I nodded to please her, and tried to sound more enthusiastic. "Yeah… I guess I hadn't thought of it that way."

I loved being pregnant. I was growing a new life! And I was good at it—the baby grew and grew without my doing a thing. I read every book I could find on pregnancy. I took a class on labor and delivery, breast-feeding, and child care. At my seven-month checkup, the midwife checked my vitals and told me I was made for childbearing and should consider a large family. I felt like an earth mother, huge and womanly. I felt, for once, that I was good at something important, that I understood the rules, that I was *normal.*

It never occurred to me that the one thing I was good at was the one thing my mother could never do. Although I didn't understand why, I knew she was treating me differently. Unlike every other event in my life, she now had no advice and no criticisms. Other than the infrequent secondhand suggestion ("Estelle says you shouldn't eat garlic when you're pregnant; it's bad for the baby"), she didn't have much to say, and she even occasionally asked *my* opinion ("I heard about these amnio-something tests—are you thinking of having one?"). It was a revelation. I felt more like her equal, more like an adult, than I ever had before.

The arrival of a grandchild gave everyone something positive to focus on after the death of my brother. It pointed us toward the future. Although my mother never spoke of my brother, and removed every picture of him from the house, closing the door to his room the day he died and, as far as I knew, never opening it again, his death was a long, dark shadow. This baby lifted the darkness, and moved us away from the past.

My marriage, which had seemed shaky for several years, was secured by the pregnancy. Although we hadn't been trying, we also hadn't been actively avoiding pregnancy, leaving it mostly to chance. We'd been married nine years, and seemed incapable of making a major decision: Stay married? Split up? Have a baby? When the accident happened, we were thrilled. Although a baby seemed absurd, it also seemed exciting and wonderful—a new reason to be a grown-up.

On a cold day in February, my first son was born. Damien looked like a combination of Winston Churchill and Alfred Hitchcock, with blue eyes, pink skin, and a round, bald head to match his round, bald belly. From the first moment, he was strong-willed, stubborn, and extremely focused.

I wish I could say I took to motherhood the way I took to pregnancy. I wish I could say how much I loved it, how much I loved mothering my baby. I wish it more than I have ever wished anything in my life.

Damien was a cranky baby, not colicky, but demanding. He rarely slept, and getting him to fall asleep required lengthy, elaborate combinations of walking and rocking and nursing. He ate every two hours around the clock, and each nursing session took about forty-five minutes, which meant I spent about nine hours of every day with a baby hanging from my nipples. I never slept more than an hour and a half at a time, and rarely more than three or four hours a day.

Most of my friends were working, and I missed work almost as much as I missed sleep. But most of all, I was terribly ashamed of how much I hated being trapped at home with this baby. I resented his intrusion into my life, his endless demands. I resented having to put his needs ahead of mine. And I felt embarrassed for feeling that way. I was lonely and sad and nearly crippled by a sense of failure.

I had fantasies of giving him away to childless strangers who would be so much better at this than I was. I felt rage, fear, and tremendous, overwhelming shame.

Years later, I read that many female adoptees get pregnant early, often as teens. Some experts think it's an unconscious attempt to imitate their birth mothers. Like abused children who grow up to become abusers, the statistics for adoptees who abandon their children are higher than normal.

I did not give my baby up for adoption. But there are other ways to abandon a child.

In the mornings, my husband left for work and dread bloomed in my stomach like a dark flower. It was the end of a cold, wet winter that led into a cold, wet spring. We lived in a small apartment in an old brownstone. In the cold and the rain that never stopped, I rarely left those two rooms, rarely showered or dressed, and almost never saw other people.

I remember standing over his crib while he writhed, awake and fussy, still in my nightgown in midafternoon, still unwashed, running on two hours' sleep. I remember looking down at him in fury, fantasies running through my head of closing the door behind me and leaving him to cry while I walked away alone and in silence.

I begged him. "Please be quiet. Please go to sleep. Please, please." I was angry and afraid to tell anyone about my anger—afraid of the judgments, the condemnation, the recognition of my failure.

I loved him fiercely, powerfully, and inadequately. Love was not something I doubted. I often thought of how much my mother loved me, how smotheringly, how wrongly. And now here I was, a child in emotional development if not in fact, a child with a child, with a love that sometimes knocked me off my feet, and only made me feel more ashamed of how poorly I showed that love.

When spring finally took root, I put him in the stroller and walked through Central Park for miles, the only time he was quiet and peaceful. Sometimes I stopped in a playground or on a park bench. If another mother talked to me, I pretended. I acted the way I thought a new mother was supposed to act. Nervous and terrified that someone would see through me and realize what a failure I was, I pretended to be happy and confident.

It took years for me to feel like a mother. It took years before I was comfortable with my child, before I found the joy, the wondrous intimacy and pleasure of motherhood.

I wish I could say that I took myself to a good therapist and worked my way through my problems so that I could be a better mother to him. But I was not courageous. I judged myself and feared the judgment of others. I was terrified of someone else saying to me what I said to myself: I was not normal.

If I could do anything over in my life it would be my first son's early years, so I could love him and be with him in the way that he deserved. I think he has forgiven me for what he didn't get, for what I was unable to give him. I often think he is a better son than I deserve. I am still working on forgiving myself.

A little while after going back to work when Damien was a few months old, I went to a luncheon with a new client. There were five of us in the magazine's elegant dining room, four from the magazine, and Steve, the client, a sweet-faced man about my age. I had never met him before.

Before we finished our appetizers, Steve started telling us a story that had nothing to do with the conversation; the words just tumbled out of him as if he couldn't possibly talk about anything else.

"I'm adopted," he said. "I always knew I was adopted; it was never a big deal."

I put down my fork halfway to my mouth. I had never heard anyone announce this before; I had never met another adult who had been adopted.

"I love my parents," Steve continued. "They're my parents, no question. I wasn't unhappy growing up. But I always wondered about that other mother out there. Not the father so much, but the mother—who she was, where she was living..." He paused. "Why she did what she did—why she gave me up."

My face felt hot and red, as if he were telling my dirty secrets in public. I tried to concentrate on my plate. But no one was eating; they were all staring at Steve. Now I felt embarrassed for him, too.

"A couple of years ago, I decided to look for her. I knew where I was born, and the date: November 15, 1954."

I dropped my fork; that was my birthday. Everyone looked at me. "Sorry," I said.

Steve went on quickly, in a rush to get it out. "The adoption agency wouldn't give me any information. I went there—Louise Wise, it's called. I even met with the same social worker my parents had when I was born, who still worked there, a Mrs. Tanner."

My head jerked. I felt slapped.

"Mrs. Tanner?" I asked.

Steve looked at me. "Yeah, why?"

I had never told anyone I worked with that I was adopted. I hadn't told anyone in years, since college. But Steve had been born on the same day as me, adopted through the same agency, with the same social worker. Could he be my twin?

"Nothing," I said. "Where were you born?"

"Staten Island," he said.

I breathed. At least he wasn't my twin brother; I knew I'd been born in Manhattan, though I didn't know how I knew.

"I hired a private detective," Steve said. "He bribed someone and got the hospital records. They had my mother's last name, a German name, a pretty unusual name. I went through the old Staten Island phone books at the library, but she wasn't in them. The detective said maybe she was living with someone else at the time and didn't have her own listing, which made sense if she was poor. She had to be poor, to give her baby away like that."

He was filling in the cracks, sewing his story together like patchwork. He had his fantasies too, I thought.

"It took me a year to find her. Since I couldn't afford a lot of the detective's time, I went through newspapers and synagogue bulletins. Finally, the detective found her name in immigration records from the early fifties. Turned out she had been brought over after the war to work for a rich family as a maid. He helped me run some ads in German-language newspapers, asking if anyone knew anything about a woman with that name who had come to the United States in the early fifties. I ran the ads for months, in every big city, and then I got a call from a woman in the Bronx. It was her sister—my aunt—and she gave me my mother's name and phone number. She had a different last name because she had been married, but now she was a widow, who'd never had any kids." He paused to correct himself: "Any *other* kids."

We had all put down our forks and knives and were just listening. Steve was leaning over his plate, his eyes shining with intensity. His hand, still holding an unused fork, was trembling.

"I got her address and went to see her. I couldn't call; I couldn't talk to her on the phone. I had to do it in person. I just went to her apartment one night, in this really old, run-down building in the Bronx. I knocked on the door and she opened it. She looked old, even though she's younger than my mom, my *adopted* mom. She's had a harder life, I guess."

Everyone was staring at Steve.

"She knew who I was," he went on. "Her sister had told her about talking to me, and she was just waiting for me to show up. She looked at me, and she knew. I didn't have to say anything."

"How did she react?" someone asked.

Steve thought for a minute. My mind raced. How does someone react when her abandoned baby shows up thirty years later—with horror, fear, terror, dismay? I had been raised to think that once the baby is given up for adoption, it's over. The birth mother walks away as if it never happened. The baby goes on to live a happy life with new parents. It's a second cutting of the umbilical cord: Sign the paper, and the old connection is no more.

"She was overjoyed, I guess," Steve said, and smiled a little, then sighed. "She started crying. She took my hand and pulled me into the apartment and started hugging me and kissing me. She wouldn't let go of my hand; she was holding it and stroking it the whole time I was there."

"Did she tell you why she gave you up?" I asked.

"Later she did. She was ashamed to tell me at first. She got pregnant by the son of the family she was living with, the family that brought her over to work for them. She was only seventeen, and he was sixteen. They kicked her out. She had nowhere to go, no place to live, and no way to support a baby. The agency put her up at some facility they ran for unmarried pregnant women. After she had the baby and gave it away, she found another job. But she didn't tell me that the first time I met her. She just kept crying and patting me, saying, "*Mein Sohn, mein baby.*" She made tea, gave me cookies. I couldn't even eat; I was totally freaked out, and didn't know what to do, or say. I hadn't really thought it all the way through; I just wanted to find her."

"Do you look like her?" someone asked.

He shook his head. "Not really. We have the same eyes, which was kind of weird, because both my parents have really dark eyes and mine are blue, like hers." He paused, looked down at his plate.

"How come she never had other kids?" I asked.

"It just didn't happen," he said. "She worked for a while as a housekeeper for a rich family in Riverdale. A lot later, she married a man who worked in a bakery. They weren't married all that long when he died. And now she works in a bakery and lives by herself. Even though she's only in her forties, she looks old. She still has a pretty heavy accent. She told me she had been waiting for me my whole life."

Steve looked down and spoke more softly. "Thirty years. She said she thought about me every single day and was sure that someday I would find her."

"Didn't she ever try to find you?" someone asked.

"When I asked her that, she just cried and shook her head and said that she didn't have the right. I don't know if she meant that she didn't have the right legally because she'd given me up, or if she felt she didn't have the right to be the one who searched. I don't know."

"How often do you see her?" I asked.

Steve didn't answer right away. "I don't," he said finally. "I don't see her anymore."

We all asked at once: "Why not?"

There was a long pause. "I... I couldn't take it," he said, his voice low. "At first, I saw her a lot; I really wanted to get to know her. She wanted to see me all the time, too. It was intense, it was almost—"

He searched the ceiling for the right word: "It was passionate. She'd been alone, I guess, for most of her life. And she wanted a child so much."

When he looked at me, there were tears in his eyes. "I felt terrible. She loved me so much. But I felt... nothing."

"Nothing?" I repeated.

He shook his head slowly. "She wanted to be my mother. But she isn't my mother. She wasn't even a family member. I have a family. I *tried* to feel something. I kept seeing her, probably more than I should have—sometimes three or four times a week, for months. I don't even see my girlfriend that much," Steve laughed ruefully. "She wanted to meet my girlfriend. She wanted to meet my parents, my sister. I thought that if I kept seeing her I would find a connection, I would see something in her that was in me. But I didn't."

There was a long silence.

"So what did you do?" I asked.

He looked at me. "I ended it."

He smiled, embarrassed. "I didn't know what else to do. She wanted me to be her son; but I'm not. She called every day, sometimes two or three times a day. She wanted me to help her pay her bills, to fix her shower. One time she called me to come kill a bug in her kitchen. She wanted me to love her. But I just couldn't. She's not my mother."

He looked around the room, checking to see if we understood, or disapproved.

"I told her I couldn't see her anymore. I felt horrible. She didn't understand; she kept calling me. Finally, I told her that I was going to change my number if she didn't stop. I felt like a monster. I mean, what's wrong with me that I couldn't feel something for this woman who gave birth to me?"

He felt it, too. There was something missing, something damaged. He knew we were defective.

I thought about Steve's story for weeks. I took it as a warning not to open the door: *Leave it alone,* the warning said. Let it lie; don't take the risk. You don't know what you'll find.

17. Bunny

The End and the Beginning

That we cannot remember such things, that our memory,
which is our self, is tiny, limited and fallible,
is also one of those important things about us,
like our inwardness and our reason.
Indeed it is the very essence of both.

IRIS MURDOCH
THE SEA, THE SEA

The Baby was born in November. Jake and I separated in May, on Mother's Day, as life would have it. The six months in between were predictably unhappy.

The world didn't stop turning as I stood paralyzed on the corner of Third Avenue and 23rd Street. Everything went on as it had before, except that I was no longer pregnant. Now the only way I could see to atone for having given up The Baby was to stay married to Jake. I was wrong.

I found a temporary job from December until March at a magazine that documented the social season for New York's well-to-do, with stories and photographs of the goings-on at resorts in Florida and Virginia, and articles about travel and things to buy. What could have been further from my life? The editor was a man who seemed terribly old to me, though he was undoubtedly younger than I am now. He was having an affair with the assistant editor; she, too, was what I thought of as elderly.

At first, I didn't realize they were having an affair; it didn't take much to fool me. And I assumed they were too old. I typed up stories, ran errands, and took dictation from a Dictaphone, a strange machine that involved a disk and a foot pedal and earphones. It was clunky, but then so was I. There was another

secretary. The magazine came out every few weeks during "the season," and my
name was one of the four on the masthead.

Like my boss at the society magazine, Jake was having an affair—with
Anna, a young woman he'd met when she was going out with his friend Craig.
We'd known Craig at Antioch. He was the school poet; not quite a mascot,
but almost. The first time I saw him, he was leaning, not terribly steadily, over
a jukebox at the bar, his straight blond hair falling down over his forehead as
he muttered things to himself, all of which, since they were unheard, seemed
enormously poetic.

Craig visited us several times at the Second Avenue apartment. When he and
Anna decided to get married, he apologized for not being able to invite us to the
wedding. Under the circumstances, he explained, he couldn't.

Jake wasn't home often. Of course, the less available Jake was, the more I
wanted him to be there. But, in truth, I wasn't happy either way.

On Mother's Day, Jake refused to go with me to visit my mother. He just
didn't want to. I went without him but before I left, I told him I didn't want to live
with him anymore. When I got back that night, he was gone. After all that, after
two years, after the pregnancy, after the loss of The Baby, after all my dependence
on Jake for everything I needed, good and bad, it was me who said, "Enough." Just
like that, it all came to an end.

Reaching bottom has two related advantages. First, something solid is finally
under your feet; I had floated down through a misty, foggy sorrow for so long. At
last, there is something to push against; the first weak surge upward can begin.

Now there was just Hollis, the little gray cat, and me. Amazingly, we were
enough. Hollis had been mine from the beginning, even though it was Jake who
found her. I've had many cats since then, cats who loved me and that I loved, but
I've never had one who was mine the way Hollis was, or who knew me as well as
she did. She was always next to me when I needed her; I needed her often.

She was a wonderful cat: She stayed with me throughout the day when I
was home; she slept in the crook of my elbow; and she never complained about
anything. She played with everything, including shadows on the floor, and
sometimes she looked as if she were smiling at me. She didn't like many of my
friends. She preferred a more solitary life and liked things best when we were
alone.

In that apartment with Hollis, I grew up. I finally wept for my father there;
I learned to be alone and to love it; I learned to cook; I learned to squeeze the
toothpaste tube from the bottom; I learned to be painfully unhappy and filled

with joy, and to feel every minute of both. I learned about sex—that it has to be learned and not just experienced. And I fell in love more than once.

After the society magazine's publishing period ended for the year in March, I found a job at Harper & Brothers, now HarperCollins. Working there was perfect. I was in the children's book department, working for Ursula Nordstorm, a gifted and wonderful editor. I loved the books: the Ruth Krauss books illustrated by Maurice Sendak, Tomi Ungerer's first books, Margaret Wise Brown's books, *Harold and the Purple Crayon, Stuart Little, Charlotte's Web, Goodnight Moon,* the *Little Bear* books, and the first of Maurice Sendak's own books. It was another way to grow up—through books, and the people who made them.

For the first time, I understood what the *idea* of a book meant: its permanence, its importance, its feel in the hand, its weight, its substance, the look and feel of its pages. For a while, I was first reader, reading manuscripts that were "unsolicited," having arrived without benefit of an agent or a contact. They landed on my desk in great quantities. I read them and wrote very brief reports on each; the ones I liked went on to the second reader. In the process, I learned the difference between a nice, passable story and something that could become a book. I learned to know what I thought, and how to state those thoughts succinctly and clearly. I learned how to search inside myself for words. Later, I was an editorial assistant, and later still, director of publicity for the department.

For the first time in a very long time, I was doing something that mattered to me; it was definable, important, and fun, and I was doing it well.

I think that was a large part of why I was able to tell Jake I no longer wanted to live with him. I think that's why the rest of my life could begin again—on Mother's Day.

18. JIL

THE SECOND TIME

A few years after Steve's warning convinced me that I should never, ever consider looking for my birth parents, I found myself wondering, often, about them—more specifically, about *her*.

What changed? A lot: A new baby, a new job, a new home, and then, a new friend.

The new home was perfect, two floors of an old brownstone on Manhattan's Upper West Side, with a garden and a wall of windows. It was just where I'd wanted to live my whole life.

The new job was not perfect. I was working at Time Inc., but I hated it. Compared to the ad agencies and small magazines I was used to, Time was a bland, bloodless corporate machine, where every day I felt loud, bushy-haired, and *ethnic*. I had a colleague who had never met anyone whose parents weren't born in this country. Another fellow told me he thought the Star of David a friend of mine wore around her neck was a Christmas tree decoration. And when I asked if we could buy just one roll of holiday gift wrap that didn't have wreaths and reindeers on it, the associate publisher said, sneering, "Why, for our *Jewish* friends? I don't have any Jewish friends!"

"What's this?" my boss asked one night, fingering the line of colored folders taped to my office door.

"They're color-coded," I said. "Because I'm always in meetings or out of town, no one can ever get time with me. So each person has their own folder and can leave me stuff to review or sign. Then I leave it in the folder for them to pick up. I got the idea from my son's nursery school class."

My boss's look was icy. I knew he didn't think much of me; I wasn't the Harvard MBA-type manager he wanted. I took my staff to picnics and potlucks and celebrated birthdays with homemade cakes. We had the best morale of any department, the lowest turnover, and did great work. But I couldn't configure a budget to save my life, and five-year plans were about four and a half years beyond my ability to project. He wanted a number cruncher, and I was a granola cruncher.

He grabbed the topmost folder, bright blue for our special events coordinator, and plucked it off the door. "Get rid of this nonsense," he said, thrusting it at me. "This is not a nursery school."

"But it works," I said. "It makes everything go more smoothly."

"I don't care if it flies to the moon," he spat as he stalked away. "It's idiotic."

I pulled the folders off the door one by one and piled them on a chair, fighting tears. The only reason I'd stayed in this job I hated was for the benefits. I'd been pregnant, had a miscarriage, and then tried to get pregnant again. I'd finally decided that, benefits or no benefits, I was out by June 1. But now, six weeks ahead of my deadline, I was pretty sure I was finally, *finally*, pregnant.

The next morning, a sunny April day, I walked through the park on my way to the doctor to confirm my suspicions. There were police cars on the park drive, clusters of cops, official vehicles off to the sides. I learned later it was the night of the infamous Central Park jogger attack—New York at its lowest and most vicious.

But *my* New York was bright and happy. "It's positive," my doctor said. "You're pregnant."

I almost wept with relief. We'd been trying so long, since Damien was three. Now he was six and would be nearly seven before his sibling arrived.

"Let's talk about stress," the doctor continued. "You know, there's a good chance the miscarriage was blood pressure–related. I don't want you in any stressful situations, physically or emotionally. Are there any major stressors in your life right now?"

Did crying nearly every day count as stress? Did being continuously criticized and demeaned count as stress? "Yes," I said. "My job."

"How do you feel about going out on disability?"

I looked at him like he was Santa Claus and the Lone Ranger wrapped up in one. "That would be great."

I spent the next seven months relaxing. Some mornings I took Damien to school, some mornings Lenny did. Usually I stopped on the way home to pick up something to make for dinner. Then I read, or watched television. Sometimes I knitted a little, or wrote. Occasionally a friend came over. Most days, I had an afternoon nap. Sometimes our nice babysitter picked Damien up to bring him home, or to an after-school program, or on a playdate; but sometimes I did. It was heaven.

The spring passed, then the summer. In the fall, Damien started first grade. I was better at being a mother now, especially without the drag of work pulling me away, tiring me out. But I still wasn't great. I felt like every other mom had gotten a neat little brochure, called something like "Mothering: What You Need to Know." I was a stranger in a strange land, fumbling my way through.

In December, Alex arrived. It was an easy labor after an easy pregnancy. He was a placid baby who smiled a lot and slept a lot and was content to sit in his infant chair and watch the world go by.

It was so simple: I loved him, I took care of him; I was good at it.

Why was this so much easier?

Isn't everything easier the second time around? Or lovelier, or whatever the song says? I was fairly confident. I was in a bigger, more comfortable home, not trapped in two small rooms in a walk-up apartment. I was no longer isolated. Lenny worked at home, and I'd met a lot of moms and kids at Damien's school. More of my friends had children. In fact, I was almost never alone. I had a community, a village—something to do every day, people to do it with.

When Damien was born, I had a job I loved, and my social life revolved around it. I missed work terribly and felt trapped by the baby. But Alex's birth rescued me from a job I hated, and a boss who made me miserable. I was grateful.

But the biggest difference was probably the passage of time. I was nearly seven years older, and calmer, and maybe a little smarter. I had prepared myself, joined a new mothers' group, signed up for infant massage class, infant music class, infant exercise class. I knew I couldn't be trapped in the house again, unshowered, in my pajamas all day.

I loved my life, my family. I loved my children so much that sometimes I wondered how anyone could give a baby away. There was a strange disconnect: I had learned about my adoption as if the birth mother was no more than a womb, a vehicle. There was never a mention of her difficulty, her pain. She did the right thing, and she did it easily.

The story of my birth parents was a shadow, like a house I lived in before I was old enough to remember it clearly: two young people, a precipitous marriage, a decision to separate, a baby that could not be cared for. But now I could not imagine doing it. And trying to imagine it led me to thinking about how someone had done that to me.

Then I met Maureen, the mother of a child in Damien's elementary school, a little older than me, a journalist, and a birth mother. After we became friends, she told me the story of how she'd gotten pregnant by her high school boyfriend, and was sent to a home for unwed mothers before anyone in their small town realized she was pregnant. She gave birth to her son in secret, and gave the baby up for adoption. Her son was now thirty, and for three decades she had mourned the loss, and felt that she was missing a piece of herself. She had searched for him for years.

This was not the birth mother of my imagination, the clutching, grasping immigrant birth mother of Steve's story, or the weepy teenage simps of the stories in the women's magazines. Maureen was smart and funny. She lived on the Upper West Side and volunteered on the school board and loved books and theater. She was a lot like me.

A tiny window opened inside of me. Maureen made me think: Maybe my birth mother would be okay. Maybe meeting her would be a good thing.

"Your birth mother will welcome you," Maureen said, over coffee at a sidewalk café on Columbus Avenue. "I know it. She'll like you and you'll like her."

"How can you be so positive?" I asked.

"That's how it is. That's how it always is. I know it."

I never questioned how invested she was in my situation, how important it was to her that *all* adoptees want to meet their birth parents. But I was drawn to what she was saying, and the more I was drawn to her, the closer I got to actually doing something.

In the fall of 1995, with Maureen's encouragement, I decided to get some basic information about my adoption—just a few facts. I wrote a letter to the Louise Wise adoption agency, requesting information on my parentage: medical history, ethnic background, anything they might be able to tell me. I was humble and nervous. I felt like a bank robber asking permission to visit the vault. It didn't occur to me that I had any right to information about my identity. I had been brainwashed well.

What I got was nothing: no phone call, no return letter.

A couple of months later, I sent another letter, enclosing a copy of the earlier request—but no response.

By the time the New Year rolled around, I had been waiting three months, and was getting annoyed. I still wasn't completely positive that I wanted to know any of this—just the thought of it made my stomach clench. But now I was invested, and tired of being ignored. I got the name of the agency's president and wrote him a letter personally, enclosing copies of the two prior letters.

On January 25, 1996, I finally received a response. Ruth Hubbard, the agency's supervisor of postadoption services, wrote to apologize for the delay and enclosed a brochure and application for the New York State Adoption Registry. She asked me to complete and notarize the form and return it to her, along with a check and a copy of my amended birth certificate—the only birth certificate I had—which every adoptee in New York State receives when he or she is legally adopted .

I showed the brochure to Lenny once the kids were asleep. I felt as if I were showing him pornography. I was nervous, excited, scared—of what, I didn't know.

"It says there are two types of information," I explained. "Nonidentifying and identifying: Nonidentifying is all they can give me if the birth parents haven't signed up for the registry."

"Like what?" he asked.

I read the list. "Like ethnic and religious background, education, age, occupations, hobbies, health history... even general appearance. And circumstances related to the adoption."

"What does that mean?"

"I don't know, I guess why they were giving up the baby."

Lenny looked at the brochure. "So what's the *identifying* information?"

"Names and addresses. *Their* names and addresses. But that can only be released with the permission of *both* birth parents." That seemed incredibly improbable to me, which I liked. It felt safer.

I looked the form over. *Check Box A*, it said, *if you are requesting nonidentifying information. Check Box B if you are requesting identifying information.*

I hesitated. I thought about it. I hesitated some more.

It seemed completely unreal. The fact of my birth parents' existence felt nothing like fact to me. I knew they existed, but only theoretically. I had no sense of actually being *born* to someone.

"How much do you want to know?" Lenny asked. This whole thing made him nervous, too, I knew. He expended a lot of effort keeping my relationship with my mother from boiling over, and I could see that he viewed this as potential trouble.

It was a hard question to answer, like a riddle. Since I couldn't believe that the information existed, I couldn't imagine knowing it.

"Just a little," I said. "I want a medical history, ethnic background. I mean, I know they're Jewish, but where they were from. Maybe that's it."

But I was getting curious. If the information existed, how could I *not* know? If some government agency knew the identity of my birth parents, it only seemed right that I should know it, too. Didn't it?

I looked over the form again. "Do you know how unlikely it is that both of my birth parents would have signed up with the registry?" I asked. "I mean, they were splitting up when I was born. How likely is it that they would be in touch with each other, or even know how to find each other, much less agree to register."

Mentally hedging my bets, sure that (1) they didn't exist and (2) if they did exist they would never have jointly signed the registry, I checked both boxes A and B, requesting identifying and nonidentifying information. I mailed the form off with my check for $20.

Then I waited some more. Once every week or so, I would wonder if my form had gotten lost. I wasn't sure if I wanted it to be lost or not.

Finally, over the summer, I got a confidential letter from the Director of Vital Records at the State Department of Health. *Your mother is not registered at this time,* he wrote. What did he mean "your mother"? My mother was up in Westchester, where I grew up. *When she registers*—not "if she registers"; how could they be so sure?—*we will request your consent to release your current name and address. She will be asked for a similar consent. When both consents are received, current names will be exchanged.* Like bodily fluids, only way scarier. *We are not allowed to search for your mother and do not know when she will register.* No surprise.

The letter went on to explain that since the program was confidential, they could only respond to questions in writing. What did one thing have to do with another? Were telephone calls too revealing? Could they only be discreet on paper? He pointed out, helpfully, that I might want to consider a private registry, such as Soundex, and provided the registry's address and phone number.

Was he kidding? I was so relieved that the information wasn't there that I almost kissed the official State Department of Health stationery.

The registry notified Louise Wise Services that I had signed up for both identifying and nonidentifying information, and had paid my fee, giving the agency permission to release the nonidentifying information to me.

Was it strange to me that I had to sign forms to find out whether or not my grandmother had blue eyes? Was I angry that I didn't know where my father was born, or whether or not there was a family history of diabetes? I am almost ashamed to say no. The fact that some agency knew more about me than I knew about myself made sense to me. Besides, those birth parents were all imaginary anyway. It was just a story. Not knowing the details about something that wasn't real was fine with me, like not knowing the Tooth Fairy's dress size or Santa Claus's zip code.

In early August, Ruth Hubbartt, the supervisor of postadoption services at Louise Wise, called. We made an appointment for the following week for me to come in and receive my nonidentifying information.

Suddenly, it felt real: agencies, services, information.

"I'm not sure I want to do it," I said to Maureen that night on the phone.

"Why? Why would you not want to do it?" her voice was strident. "You have the right to know. It's your life."

"I know that, it's just..." but I didn't know what it was. It was both scary and unreal, like the monster in the closet you know isn't there, but you're scared of anyway.

"You have to do it," she said.

Though I wasn't sure if she was seeing me, or the son she'd given up so long ago, she was convincing.

"All right," I said. "I'll do it."

19. Bunny

The Second Time

Betrayal can only happen if you love.

John le Carré

A Perfect Spy

I was still living on Second Avenue when I met my second husband several years later.

By then, I had left Harper to become director of publicity at a small children's book publishing house. After that, I took some time off because I wanted to write, and thought time was what I needed. Finally, discouraged, I started over at RCA Victor Records.

At the office Christmas party, a few months after I'd begun working there, a slim, handsome man asked me who my favorite composers were. I said Mozart, Beethoven, Bach, Verdi, and Wagner. It was Wagner that got him. If I'd said Bruckner, he'd have wanted to move in with me that very night. As it was, he waited from Christmas until the middle of June. The April after that, we were married, a year and a half later—not quite as fast as the first time around.

We've been married a long time. We have two grown children.

After a year or two, we moved from Second Avenue to an apartment in Brooklyn Heights, just a short walk from where I'd lived with Sally, eating sauerkraut night after night, in those empty, sad days so long ago. The past was gone; it happened when I was someone else.

I never told my children about The Baby. When they were little, I thought they'd think I might give them away, too.

But later there was never a right time, never a moment in which I could say that I'd given away my first child.

I should have told them, and now I wish I had. I thought I would when they were old enough, but old enough was never the age they were. I paid a penalty for not telling them.

I didn't ever decide *not* to tell them; I never found the moment for talking about The Baby, and so I never did. And in a more important way, The Baby gradually ceased to exist. I imagine the process was like that of having a limb amputated: I remembered pain, and sometimes I felt pain, but in a place that was no longer there.

I did count her years; I watched her birthdays go by. She's ten now; she's seventeen; she's thirty. I might sit next to her at the movies, even talk to her at a meeting, or sit near her at a restaurant table. Would I know who she was? Would I recognize her? Would *she* know me? But none of that was real, because on another level, she stayed The Baby, the warm infant I carried from one place to another and then lost forever.

It was a loss that I closed off. I couldn't live with it for all those years in any other way. Even on the fourth day—the day she was four days old, the day I gave her away, lost her, began to be without that baby forever—the pain was so paralyzing that when I felt it, I couldn't move from the street corner where I stood, immobile. After that, after she was gone, after I had allowed her to be gone, I stayed on the edge of numbness for such a long time: the long passive stillness was like a cloud I moved through. I put pain at a distance, because I was afraid that if I allowed myself to feel it, I would be unable to move at all.

I didn't do that deliberately, close off the place in my mind where The Baby was, but that's what happened. Even after considerable therapy, those emotions stayed there, alone, seemingly safely hidden beneath the surface. But emotions don't leave when your mind pretends they're not there. If they can't reach light in one direction, they turn, and in a photosynthesis of the soul, they try to find it in another. They don't go away; instead, unacknowledged—in fact, even more so because of that—they affect the way life is lived.

For me, those feelings burst open at moments when they were least expected. All of a sudden they were there, their power enormous. That was the most surprising thing about the pain of missing The Baby—it never went away, but became an underground part of me, hiding there, to leap out suddenly and attack—always when I was alone, most often when I was driving in the car, perhaps because I could cry in the car without anyone seeing. I would be listening to music on the radio, daydreaming as I drove, and find myself suddenly in pain and in tears. And then it would slowly stop, and I would forget again.

During all these years, The Baby's birth, even on the conscious and deliberate level, became my great secret. I was ashamed, but I'm not sure why, because the adoption, I believed, was the best thing I could have done. But I was ashamed of having been pregnant, and no matter what was best, ashamed of the loss. Talking about it was difficult, much too intimate. At first, I *needed* to talk about it, because talking was a way to dilute the emotions I had been left with. Later, with the gift of therapy, it meant talking about another person, the one I had been, so that the connections could be well understood and then severed. Soon it was impossible, and I never talked about it at all. My husband was the last person I told.

The birth of The Baby, and her loss, certainly affected the kind of mother I became: over-protective, full of the fear, without identifying it, that I would lose another child, that the baby would be taken from me.

I couldn't have loved my children more. I thought they were perfect. I didn't look at them when they were infants, the way I'd gazed at The Baby, trying to memorize her face, to keep it unchanged, in my mind. When I looked at my daughter as an infant, I looked into her eyes to see who she was. When she looked back at me, I felt we recognized each other.

I also thought I was a perfect mother. I learned how to breast-feed, in a perfect rocking chair: I loved being the mother of this beautiful child. I sang to her, rocked her, played with her, held her, and adored her. She was mine, no one else's—just perhaps her father's, too.

She was almost three when my son was born. I prepared incredibly detailed instructions for her care while I was in the hospital (still a stay of four or five days then after a birth). Several pages long, the list included her favorite dessert, the music she liked to listen to at bedtime, in what order she liked to get dressed in the morning, as well as approximate times for naps.

I didn't recognize my son in the same way, but I adored him, too. When we came home from the hospital, his sister refused to acknowledge us.

The first time I felt that fear, the terror of loss, had to do with a babysitter. I had to leave for an afternoon to do some freelance work. Though I trusted the babysitter, I didn't want her to leave our apartment, even to go to the playground. The playground was nearby, and it was a beautiful spot, near the harbor and with a view of downtown Manhattan, She knew that both children would be happy to be there. But I was afraid: Leaving the children inside the apartment was one thing. Knowing that they'd be gone was another, and I couldn't deal with it.

Worse, from the babysitter's point of view, was that I couldn't explain my
reluctance to let the children out of the apartment. *I* could leave *them*—but the
idea of them leaving me (and being taken from the apartment) was impossible.
I barely recognized the fear; it was simply there. Clearly hurt and puzzled, the
babysitter did as I asked; they stayed inside until I got home. But she never agreed
to work for me again. She thought I didn't trust her. It was life I didn't trust.

That didn't change after we left the city and moved to a small town in the
Hudson Valley, to a house with a lot of grass, on a very quiet street. The children
grew older, but my fears remained the same. A friend's parent wanted to take his
son and mine to Coney Island for the son's birthday—impossible.

Why not? my son begged.

It's not a good idea, I said, explaining nothing. It happened over and over—
with variations. I didn't approve of this, and said no to that.

On another level, I made deals with fate. If I don't do this—whatever it was—
they'd be safe. And they always were. The deals worked. But I never articulated
my fears to my children, or to anyone else. I moderated them as they got older, but
I was still haunted by unspoken—and worse, unknown—fear.

This was one kind of betrayal: not a sweet and helpless one, like leaving
my daughter so that my son could be born. This was insidious, because I never
allowed it to surface—at least not deliberately—and I chose not to investigate or
understand it. In my mind, that would be harmful to these two children I loved
so much.

There were other betrayals—there always are. Every mother betrays her
children, as all children betray their mothers.

I only betrayed The Baby once, when I gave her away. I betrayed my other
children more times than I can bear to think of. I wasn't the perfect mother
I thought I was. I did a lot of things I regret, and there are things I didn't do
that I regret. But for the woman I still thought of as The Baby, the betrayal was
primal: I gave her away.

I didn't hold her hand on the way to nursery school. I didn't take her
temperature when she was sick. I didn't play the piano while she sang, or write
down her words when she told me a story. I didn't comfort her after a bad day
at school, and I didn't watch her while she learned to swim. I wasn't there for
the good times. I wasn't there for the bad times. I wasn't there, period. Yes,
somebody else was; but I wasn't. I was exactly what my label says: I carried her
for nine months, and then went into labor: I was her birth mother.

I was much less of a mother than the woman who adopted her, who was there for all those things, who picked her clothes up off the floor, and taught her to say "Please" and "Thank you" and who sang lullabies at night. I hoped she sang lullabies.

But if love counts—and it must, at least a little—then I am also her mother, because I loved her. I loved her for four days, and for forty-two years, and forever.

20. JIL

MEETING RUTH

Louise Wise Services looked as if it had seen better days. The building, on Manhattan's Upper East Side, had most likely been a private home, a mansion built for a Carnegie or a Vanderbilt. But the white stone façade had faded to gray, and the marble steps bowed in the middle where thousands of pregnant women and hopeful couples had walked nervously into their futures.

I was nervous myself as I climbed the well-worn steps. I felt as if I were walking into darkness, maybe trouble, and I half-hoped Ruth Hubbartt would tell me my records had been lost in a fire or washed away in a flood.

She met me in the reception room and walked me up a flight of carpeted stairs to her office. Dark-haired and fiftyish, she had a professionally pleasant, sympathetic manner.

Her small, narrow office was packed with floor-to-ceiling file cabinets. A long window at one end spilled August sunlight onto a desk piled with papers and folders. Did each folder represent one adult adoptee, I wondered? I wondered, too, if Ms. Hubbartt spent every day meeting with the people those folders represented. Because of legalized abortion and better contraception, there were no more adoptable Jewish babies for Louise Wise to manage. Maybe all that was left for them to do was answer questions about what they had done in the past, moving forward by looking back.

Nervously I sat down in an old wooden chair next to her cluttered desk. She pulled a thick folder from the pile and put it on her lap.

"I have regards for you from someone," she said.

Who could we possibly have in common?

"Mrs. Tanner," she said.

Mrs. Tanner? I was shocked. The caseworker who had handled my and my brother's adoptions seemed like an old woman way back in the sixties. I tried to think of a polite way to say, "How could she possibly be alive?"

Ms. Hubbartt smiled. "She finally retired last year. She's in her seventies now. But she remembers you and your brother. I still talk to her often. She wanted me to be sure to send you her regards, and find out how you and your brother are doing."

I shifted uncomfortably in my seat. It hadn't occurred to me that she wouldn't know about Kenny's death.

"My brother died in 1981," I said, and her smile vanished. I wanted to forestall further questions. "He killed himself."

"Oh, I'm so sorry," she said gently. "That explains something."

She opened the folder. "There are calls from your mother throughout the years," she ran a finger down a sheet of paper, "letting us know how you and Kenny were doing. Let's see: 1972, your brother's Bar Mitzvah, your high school graduation; 1974, your marriage, 1976, your college graduation. It looks like the last call was in—" she flipped a page, "1977, your brother's graduation from high school."

"My mother called you?" She kept in touch with Louise Wise? It was like finding out that my mother had had an affair. I felt as if I'd been secretly shadowed, reported on, by spies.

Ruth looked through the folder more carefully. "Yes," she said. "It looks like she called fairly regularly, sometimes with questions, sometimes to tell us something. When you were a teenager, I guess you two were having some problems. She called to ask advice."

My mother didn't ask advice; she gave orders. She never shared family problems with anyone—even her closest friends. She'd called the agency and asked for help? How exalted, how wondrous and wise they must have seemed to her at Louise Wise.

Ruth continued to flip through the pages. "A lot of adoptive parents keep us informed about the babies' lives. But she never called to tell us that your brother had died." She looked up at me. "Had he been ill?"

"For about a year," I said. "One doctor diagnosed him as schizophrenic. He said it was often hereditary."

Ruth nodded. "I'm so sorry."

Then she got down to business. She took some stapled sheets from the folder and put them in front of her on the desk. "Let me give you some information about your adoption," she said.

I took a deep breath. This felt really frightening, like opening the door to a dark, forbidden room. But Ruth's voice was completely calm, as if she were giving me driving directions.

"Your birth parents met in college," she half-read, half-talked. "They got married after only knowing each other for a month—that was in February 1953. Your birth father left for Army duty a little while after they married, and soon after that they realized the marriage wasn't going to last. Right about the time they decided to divorce, your birth mother found out she was pregnant. So they agreed to put the baby up for adoption."

So far, this was pretty much the story I knew. But finding out it was real was, to my surprise, shocking, like finding out that a recurring dream you'd had all your life wasn't a dream at all, but reality.

"It looks like they came in for some counseling throughout the pregnancy," Ruth went on. "Your birth mother was depressed and confused, unsure about what to do. There isn't much here about your birth father." She handed me several sheets of paper. They were forms, the official documents of nonidentifying information. The first two pages were about the birth mother. "Age: 21," it read. "Race: Caucasian. Religion: Jewish. Marital status: Married (discussing separation). Occupation: Part-time typist. Interests: Piano, guitar, reading. Education: Two years college." The physical description said only, "Brown hair, hazel eyes." And then it added, "Intelligent, confused, unhappy, and depressed."

I stared at the paper in shock. *She was real.* I realized that I was sweating. My head felt light. *She was real?*

Ruth filled in a few more details: My birth mother was from a Russian-Jewish family. ("Like us," my mother had said all those years ago. She *was* like us.) Her father, a pharmacist, had died of a brain tumor four years before my birth. Her mother ("dark hair, blue eyes, olive complexion," the sheet said) was a housewife. She had an older sister, with "brown hair, hazel eyes."

Page three was about the birth father. He also had two years of college. An "unemployed photographer," his interests were writing and acting. Writing and acting? Those were *my* interests. His description: "Six feet, dark hair, dark eyes, intelligent." His mother, a college graduate, was a chemist; his father, described as "tall and dark," was an advertising executive. His parents had divorced when he was ten, and both had several subsequent marriages. His older sister died in a tobogganing accident at the age of sixteen.

Bunny at the window of her apartment on Second Avenue around the time Jil was born.
(Courtesy of Jill Picariello)

TOP: Jil and her mother, shortly after she was adopted.
BOTTOM: Jil in the backyard with her mother.
(Courtesy of Jil Picariello)

TOP: Jil at about twelve, visiting her Uncle Sam in the Catskills, in upstate New York.
BOTTOM: Jil at seventeen, with her brother at his bar mitzvah.
(Courtesy of Jil Picariello)

Jil leaving her parents' house with her new husband after their wedding.
(Courtesy of Jil Picariello)

TOP: Jil's son Damien as a baby.
BOTTOM: Jil's son Alex as a baby.
(Courtesy of Jil Picariello)

Jil cruising the Danube with Lenny.
(Courtesy of Jil Picariello)

TOP: Jake with his camera, photographed by Bunny.
BOTTOM LEFT: Bunny, about two years old.
BOTTOM RIGHT: Bunny and her mother, with the same rascally glint in their eyes.
(Courtesy of Bunny Crumpacker)

TOP: Bunny, fourteen, at the beach—her favorite place in the world—making castles in the sand.

ABOVE LEFT: Bunny and Jake with their red 1938 Ford sedan convertible.

RIGHT: Bunny and Chick at their wedding, April 1961.

(Courtesy of Bunny Crumpacker)

"What's this?" I asked, pointing to a line that said the birth father's mother was half-Jewish, his father was Protestant, and he had been raised Protestant. "I thought you only took Jewish babies?"

"Babies born of Jewish mothers are Jewish," Ruth said.

I knew that, of course: But how could I only be a little more than half Jewish?

I couldn't make these pieces come together. I quickly turned the page, headed "Adoptee." The baby: weight at birth, date of admission to the agency, weight at admission, even the time, developmental milestones, date of placement.

"What's date of placement?" I asked, pointing to the line.

"The date you were placed in foster care," she said.

"Foster care?"

"From the agency you were placed into foster care until the time you were handed over to your parents."

"When did that happen?" I asked.

Ruth ran her finger down the page. "April 6, 1955."

I calculated. I was five months old before I went to live with my parents? What about my story about the rows and rows of little bassinettes? "We'll take that one," they say. "This is *our* chosen baby." I am lifted out and placed into their arms. Ruth's papers told another story.

My reality was not real, Ruth's papers were telling me. The past I believed was mine was not. A piece of my puzzle had been taken away, and now a new piece needed to be forced into place.

Ruth continued. "The pregnancy was full term and normal, labor was fourteen hours and eighteen minutes, forceps delivery. The baby was placed with a foster mother in Queens until placement was decided. Apparently she was a little overzealous. It says she fed the baby too often. The agency's doctor had to instruct her not to feed the baby so much." Ruth pointed to the agency checkup report for March of 1955, when the baby was four months old. "Relaxed baby," it read: "Responsive, bright-normal range."

Ruth said the baby was healthy. The baby had regular checkups. The baby, the papers told her, was alert and attentive.

The baby was me.

None of this made sense. How could these papers know things about me I had no knowledge of? It was like finding out I had done amazing, incredible things while sleepwalking or hypnotized.

I took a deep breath. "I'm having trouble believing you're talking about me," I said, sounding crazy even to my own ears.

Ruth chuckled. "Everyone says that," she said. "It's hard to put this information into any context."

Hard—how about impossible, insane, inconceivable?

I couldn't even decide which piece was the most improbable. My birth father wasn't Jewish? But being Jewish was part of my identity: How could it not be part of my DNA? It was like finding out I was half-black, or Asian. I was shocked, and shocked again at how shocked I was.

I was in foster care for the first five months of my life? Suddenly I remembered an odd comment my father made when Damien was just a few weeks old, and I put his first grandchild into his nervous arms. "I've never held a baby this small," he said. "You weren't this little when we got you." He's confused, I thought. Maybe he'd forgotten how small I once was, or maybe I never seemed small to him. Now I knew what he meant.

I looked at my birth parents' interests, listed on the form: reading, writing, acting, photography, theater, music. Though I grew up in a home without books, as far back as I could remember, I read and wrote constantly. My parents rarely listened to music, never went to the theater, and hardly ever even watched a movie. But from early childhood I adored movies, especially musicals. I took acting classes all through high school, and auditioned for acting school in college with a hilariously inappropriate monologue from *The Effect of Gamma Rays on Man-in-the-Moon Marigolds*. I didn't get in, but later, in film school, I loved acting in other people's films.

As a teenager I went to every Broadway show I could. I kept a journal of poetry I wrote, and one of poetry I loved: Millay and Dickinson and Eliot. I memorized entire scenes from Shakespeare, and longed to play Juliet and Beatrice and Shylock, who had the best lines.

I thought I had cooked myself up from scratch, invented myself from thin air and wishes. Listening to Ruth in her overheated office, I started to wonder if that were true. It made complete sense, yet no sense at all. It made me sad. Sad because of what I had missed; and sad because I didn't even know the story of my life. The pieces fit and yet couldn't possibly go together. I was Jewish but I wasn't. I had made my own way to books and music, but really they had been there before me, pointing the way, these people I didn't know, didn't understand, didn't even really believe existed. I'd always felt I didn't fit in—and believed it was my fault. But maybe I wasn't meant to fit in.

Then Ruth handed me another new puzzle piece.

"Did you parents ever tell you your birth name?"

I stared at her.

"The name on your original birth certificate?"

I realized I had to be called something during those first five months in foster care. I knew I was born with another *last* name—my birth father's last name, I assumed. But in my story of the babies in long rows of white bassinettes, I didn't have a first name until my parents stopped and picked me up. "This is *our* chosen baby," they said in the movie in my mind. "This is Jil."

But a secret identity I wasn't even aware of? It was as if Superman didn't know Clark Kent existed. Is this what people with multiple personalities feel like?

"They never told me," I said. "What was the baby's name?" I asked. "*My* name," I quickly corrected. The pronoun was nearly impossible to choke out.

"I'm sorry," Ruth said. "I'm not allowed to tell you that. But you'd be surprised how often an adult adoptee's favorite name is her birth name. Often it's the name she gives her own children."

"My favorite name as a child was Jessica," I said.

She didn't respond.

"But I also like Christina, and Emily. And biblical names like Rachel and Rebecca."

"I can't tell you what it was," she said, ending the guessing game.

I was disappointed. "Is there anything else you can tell me? Where they lived or where they grew up?"

She shook her head. "I can't say—just that it was in the New York area."

I must have looked downcast.

"Well, I can tell you one more thing," Ruth said. "I'm not supposed to, but… In New York State a person's birth certificate number doesn't change, even after an adoption. The number on your amended birth certificate—the one that was issued when your adoption was finalized in—" she looked down at her papers.

"1956," I said. I had a hazy memory of a huge, wood-paneled room and a scary but friendly man behind a big high desk.

"Yes, 1956," she confirmed. "The number of the amended certificate you got that day is the same number as on your original birth certificate."

She looked at me expectantly as I struggled to put two and two together. Much as I'd never thought I had a name before I was adopted, it never occurred to me that I had another birth certificate. I know that every baby gets one at birth, and I knew my amended birth certificate was dated two years after I was born. But I'd never questioned what record existed of my birth for the first two years of my life. I wondered if all adoptees just accepted what they were given without asking questions; or was I unusually lacking in curiosity? I didn't know what I didn't know, and I didn't think to ask.

Ruth was still waiting for me to get to where she was leading me.

"So the original…?" I finally asked.

"Is in the birth records at the public library," she said.

"And it has my birth name on it?"

"Yes. I don't know if it will lead anywhere. But it's something."

I thanked her and stood up.

"If you want more information," she said, "or if you would like to know about support groups for adoptees or search groups, please get back in touch with me."

I already had more information than I could comprehend, more than I ever dreamed existed. I had no intention of looking any further. This was it, done, *finito*.

Before the door of the agency closed behind me I was already planning my visit to the library.

21. Bunny

HOPE

Hope is the thing with feathers—
that perches in the soul—
and sings the tunes without the words—
and never stops—at all—

POEM 254

Dear Mrs. Crumpacker: As per our conversation, a caseworker at Louise Wise Services wrote me on August 31, 1983, *I have checked our records and can now assure you that your birth daughter has not contacted us requesting a reunion.*

That's the whole note. The letterhead gave an address on East 94th Street; I remembered the agency as being on the Upper West Side, but I wasn't sure my memory was correct. I could almost see the front door in my mind, but certainly not the street sign. And it was no longer the Louise Wise Service for Jewish Young Women but simply Louise Wise Services. No mention of religion or age, though undoubtedly the clients were all premenopausal.

I folded the letter and kept it in its envelope.

I think that was the first time I tried to find The Baby. I also asked that the agency's records indicate that I wanted to be found, should The Baby ever search; but the letter from Louise Wise didn't note my request.

My attempts to search were hesitant; I took one tiny step after another, and there were great intervals between each one. I learned later that my slow pace is not unusual; it's the halting gait of many birth mothers who begin searching for their children. Everything that made our babies' births a secret is at stake.

I wanted to find The Baby, to know that she was healthy, that she had survived unscarred; even that she might be happy, but at least that she was still in this world, and that she was well. And I wanted to let her know I was hoping she'd want to meet me. But the very possibility of finding her brought fears. I assumed that she'd want to know something about her heritage, a family medical history at the very least. Beyond that, I might have wondered what she'd be like, and whether we'd like each other. It never occurred to me that I wouldn't like her, even if I ever reached the point where I could differentiate between *like* and *love*. How could we not like each other? No, what was involved was the peril of secrecy lost, and the touching—and opening—of those dangerous emotions. It was pain, revelation, shame, and risk. It was immensely frightening.

I went very slowly.

I registered with several of the agencies that help birth parents and adopted children find each other. The agencies maintain directories, listing as much information as they've been given. In theory, those who are searching can find each other by recognizing birth information in the directory, especially birth dates and places of birth.

I have so many tattered clippings: a small one, first, that lists "how natural parents can trace their children—and vice versa." It notes three places to contact: Adoptees' Liberty Movement Association (ALMA), Concerned United Birthparents (CUB), and Origins, with addresses for each. It adds only, "Enclose a stamped, self-addressed, legal-sized envelope." The last is an e-mail, dated May 1, 1995 (twelve years after the letter from Louise Wise), from a woman I found on the Web, who wrote that most of her experience was helping adoptees find their birth parents; she was glad to hear from a birth mother who was searching for her child.

"Making yourself easy to find is a good step," she wrote, though a paragraph later she went on to say, "In general, the laws on records access are even more restrictive for birth parents wishing to search than for adoptees." She didn't know where I lived, but suggested that my state might have a registry that simplified the search process; but only if both birth parents and both adoptive parents consented to be listed (which would have meant not only finding Jake, but also the unknown adoptive parents). She also suggested CUB and ALMA, where I'd already registered.

ALMA had sent me a welcoming letter, a registration card, and an instruction sheet with "Searching Do's and Don'ts"—mostly for adoptees: "Don't share your search techniques with anyone, including friends, relatives, and especially social workers/county clerks." And "Don't mail personal checks—always use U.S. Postal Money Orders."

When ALMA's newsletter announced a Manhattan meeting to focus on how to use the New York Public Library for the first step in searching, I attended. Later, I received a letter about ALMA's Reunion Registry: "The Registry is of particular importance to natural parents as well as to other natural relatives of adoptees because it represents one of the few opportunities available to find their children. In addition, the chances of an individual natural parent being matched are greater than the chances of an individual adoptee being matched, because there are more adoptees than natural parents searching."

Down at the bottom of the letter, in a different-color ink, someone had written: *There is an Index of Births in the City of New York located in Room 315N, N.Y. Public Library, 5th Ave. & 42nd St., Manhattan, NYC. You can use this index to verify the date of birth.* What was unsaid, but what I learned at the meeting, was that using the index meant finding the original birth certificate.

The Genealogy Room at the New York Public Library is a small room behind the general reading room, a large and splendid space that doesn't even hint at the tiny space behind it. The Genealogy Room is small and silent, with one person at a desk who wasn't terribly encouraging, but was willing to show me where the registries were kept. I was the only other person in the room. The registries are huge books, kept in chronological order in bookcases. The birth certificates within each book are not filed by number, or by date, but rather by last name.

I found the birth certificate fairly quickly. It was incredible to see that official piece of paper—so impersonal and so powerful. It felt as if I were seeing a piece of The Baby. It was proof that she had existed, that she had once been mine.

I still have the sheet of paper on which I wrote down all the information the birth certificate held: her last name, and "female," in the space where her first name should have been. Why didn't it say "Jessica," along with her birth date and place, and most important, the birth certificate's number? With that number, it might be possible to find her new, altered birth certificate, and thus her adopted surname. If she had married, and now used her husband's name, I wouldn't know what to do next.

But along with my ALMA and CUB papers, and newspaper clippings about other agencies and searches, I also had the names of private detectives who specialized in finding people (in those pre-Google days): missing husbands and fathers, lost friends and lovers, birth mothers, adopted children.

I had written the information from the birth certificate on the top sheet of a pad of paper. On the next sheet I listed *Americans for Open Records, People Search News,* and *National Adoption Clearinghouse,* with addresses and phone numbers for each one. At the bottom, I wrote: *Original birth certificate: Court of Jurisdiction.* I thought that meant I had to contact that court in order to see the amended birth certificate, which would give me her adopted name, and the names of her adoptive parents.

On the next page, *The State of New York Department of Health, Birthparent Support Network,* and *The New York State Adoption Information Registry, Vital Records Section.* On the last page was written *Louise Wise Services,* with two addresses, one on East 94th Street, and another—yes!—on West 68th.

Finally, I called Louise Wise again. I remember standing in a phone booth almost trembling as I dialed the number. I told whoever answered that I was a birth parent searching for my child, and that I wanted her file to state that I wanted to be found. Yes, I was told, we'll note that in the file. Thank you for calling.

Why didn't I write down the date of that call? The name of the person I spoke to? For that matter, why didn't I write a letter instead of calling? I have no idea. But I remember that the voice on the phone sounded neither particularly interested nor especially helpful. Or perhaps nothing that could have been said to me would have sufficed, unless it was simply my daughter's name and address— and that was something not likely to have been given.

22. JIL

FINDING FAITH

The day after my meeting with Ruth, we left for a three-week stay on Cape Cod. Our rented house was a ranch, a simple, compact L with a big garden on a cool, sunny hilltop in Truro.

But despite the charm of the house, the garden, and the Cape itself, my head was spinning. Maybe I had never had a really clear picture of myself; maybe I had always been confused about who I was. But now I had *no* sense of myself at all: It was as if I'd just awakened from a coma, with a bad case of amnesia. All this new information! I felt as if I were trying to incorporate actual physical pieces of myself—a new arm or an extra foot—and there wasn't any place to put them.

I was obsessed with every shred of information I had learned from Ruth. Somewhere around the twentieth time I brought it up, Lenny announced that he needed to get off my hamster wheel.

"You're just saying the same things over and over," he told me.

"But it doesn't make any sense! I just can't believe it!" I cried.

"You've said that—a lot."

"But it doesn't!"

I had a shadow life that might have been, that ran alongside my life like an alternate reality, with a different mother, another father. If there were so many possibilities, then which one was real?

I thought about that as I sat on the beach at Head of the Meadow, staring at the cold waves. I thought about it while biking from Wellfleet to Nauset, walking the cranberry bog, eating fried oysters at Clem and Ursie's.

Janey came to visit, and I told her the story, sitting on the curb in front of George's Pizza as the annual Provincetown Gay Carnival parade marched by.

"I wonder if either of them ever had more kids? Maybe I have half-sisters and half-brothers."

"Um, hmm," she said.

"Do you think they could still be in touch with each other? I mean, they were married once—lots of married people stay in contact after they divorce."

"Maybe," she said, distracted by a float of bearded Marilyn Monroes.

"Do you think she would want to hear from me? She didn't register at Soundex, although maybe that's because of him. Maybe he didn't want to register. So she couldn't. Do you think I should register at another place?"

"Maybe," she said again, as ten men in evening gowns drifted by, tossing Mardi Gras beads.

But no matter how much I talked or thought about it, the story of "the baby" refused to become the story of me.

The two famous stone lions in front of the main branch of the New York Public Library on Fifth Avenue and 42nd Street are called Patience and Fortitude, named by Mayor Fiorello LaGuardia in the 1930s for the two qualities he believed New Yorkers would need to survive the Great Depression. I had walked past the lions hundreds of times, but I'd never been inside the majestic building until a warm day in early October, 1996.

In the six weeks since we'd returned from the Cape, I'd found reason after reason not to go. I had kids to get started in a new school year. I had clients to connect with, freelance assignments to write. But most of all, what I had was ambivalence. I had ambivalence the way Midas had gold. I was terrified of finding more pieces of me floating around, pieces I would somehow have to incorporate into myself. These pieces of me felt like thick shards of glass that I would have to swallow.

I found out later, while reading every book I could find about adoption and reunion, that very few adoptees move through the search smoothly. It was usually a matter of fits and starts, an awkward stumbling, picking up a piece of information, trying to incorporate it, slowing down, swallowing it, digesting it, waiting, moving ahead, stopping, going forward again.

I walked to the information desk in the lobby. I was frightened of asking questions. Questions were forbidden. Answers were locked away: They were not mine to access. Trying my best to look like a disinterested journalist, I approached the desk.

Me (nervously): Where are the birth records for the 1950s?

Library Lady (without looking up): Third floor, room 315B.

Saying "Thank you," I beat a hasty retreat, before she could change her mind and call security.

Room 315B was behind the main reading room, the grand space where writers and researchers work. Room 315B was smaller, and mustier, and the librarians behind the desk were busy, and very intimidating.

Me (nervously, again): I'd like the birth records for 1954, please.

Library man (brusquely): You have to fill this out.

Oh no, I thought. This is where I reveal why I'm here and sirens go off and library security escorts me from the building.

I looked down at the many-times-copied form. There were two lines. *Information requested,* it said. Then: *Name.*

"Birth records, New York City, 1954," I wrote, adding my name, and slid the paper back.

His eyebrows rose. "All of them?"

Was that against the rules? "Yes," I answered, my voice going up at the end, like a question.

He shrugged, "Okay," and vanished. A minute later he returned, struggling with two enormous volumes in cracked blue leather. "Here you go," he said.

I staggered to the nearest chair, at a long wooden table with a green-glass shaded lamp, and stared at the two huge books in amazement. *Birth Records, New York City, Department of Health,* the covers said. A thrill ran up my spine. I had gotten away with it!

I opened the top book and almost choked.

The page, about two feet long and so thin it was nearly transparent, was covered, top to bottom, in tiny type. There were seven columns: last name, first name, gender, birth month, birth date, borough of birth, birth certificate number. There were at least a hundred listings per page, hundreds of pages per book. And there were two books: A–K and L–Z.

The tiny type spun in front of my eyes. The listings were alphabetical by last name. I had assumed they would be organized by either date of birth or birth certificate number, both of which I knew. But I was looking at thousands, tens of thousands, maybe hundreds of thousands of babies born in New York City in 1954, all of them listed by last name.

And I didn't know my last name.

I was going to have to look through the birth certificate numbers on every single listing until I found the one that matched my own. I put my head in my hands and stared at the books. Then I took a deep breath and thought about it. Looking at the numbers would be dizzying and far too slow, and it would be very easy to miss the right one. Looking at only the borough of Manhattan births would not narrow it down enough, since it seemed logical that a very large chunk of the births would have been in Manhattan. Looking for November births seemed like the smartest way to approach it: It would eliminate eleven-twelfths of the births, assuming they were distributed evenly throughout the year.

Since I'd spent my life in the back of the alphabet—my maiden name began with *S*, my married name with *P*—I decided to start with *Z* and work my way forward. I put my amended birth certificate next to me, so I could refer to the number, opened the back cover of book two, and began.

First I ran my finger down the column labeled "Month." If I hit a November birth, which was often, I slid my finger over to the "Day" column, which eliminated roughly twenty-nine out of thirty entries. But if it read "15," I moved on to the "Borough" column—that weeded out about 80 percent more. If that read "Manhattan," I inched over to "Gender," which eliminated about half of those. If that said "female," then, holding my breath, I looked at the birth certificate number.

The first ten or twenty times I hit a November birth I got excited. Then I began to realize just how many babies had been born in New York in November 1954. By the hundredth time I found a baby girl born in Manhattan on November 15, I stopped feeling anything but the pain in my eyes from squinting at the tiny type for so long.

Four hours later, my eyes were blurry and sore. I had a headache and backache from leaning over the musty book. All the excitement I'd started with had drained away, and I was hungry and tired.

I called Lenny before I left the building. "I'm starving and I have a headache. And that's all I have."

"You should have started at the beginning of the alphabet," he said confidently.

"Why?"

"I think it's an *A* or a *B. C* at the latest," he said. "I have a feeling."

My husband was famous for his "feelings." He had a "feeling" about the right road to take in a place he'd never been before. He had a "feeling" about how good a restaurant would be, or what stock to invest in, or whether or not a book would be worth reading. The fact that he was as often wrong as right never shook his certainty. And his lack of self-doubt was tremendously convincing to me.

"Okay," I said, and a week later I said good morning to Patience and Fortitude and headed for the windowless cave of room 315B. This time I came prepared with an energy bar, a pack of gum, a bottle of water, and three chocolate kisses. I laid out my supplies, unfolded my birth certificate, and opened the book labeled A–K.

It took ten minutes.

On page 27, my scanning finger stopped at Month: November. Then Day: The 15th. I slid to the next column. Borough: Manhattan. Then Gender: Female. Finally, I checked the Birth Certificate Number: 1007643. I checked again. 1007643. I looked at my amended birth certificate, sitting on the table next to me. 1007643.

It was me.

My heart started pounding and all the air whooshed out of my lungs. I could hear my heartbeat throbbing in my ears, as if I'd just climbed a steep hill, fast.

Slowly, I moved my shaking finger to the next column: Surname: Aylford. *Aylford!*

I said it silently, and then whispered it in amazement: *Aylford!* It had a nice sound, breathy and strong. It made me think of a Jane Austen character, the vicar who comes to tea, or the squire who strolls through the park on Sunday. So elegant! So British! I was born an *Aylford*?? I could no more see myself as an Aylford than as a moon maiden or a circus clown. I could have been born an Aylstein or an Aylberg or even an Aylwitz—but an Aylford?

I looked down. There was a name in the very last column, the name I never knew existed, the name I had been given at birth, the name that was mine, and mine alone.

I slid my finger over to the last column, which read, "Female."

I was confused. Ruth said I had a name. She heard me guess the possibilities. Why would she do that if there was no name? What did the nice foster mother call me all those months?

My disappointment turning to anger, I pushed back my chair and stood up. What was wrong with these birth parents who couldn't even be bothered to give a baby a name? Maybe they chose the name when she was pregnant and told Ruth, then something happened at the hospital that stopped them from using it? Maybe there were complications after the delivery, and my birth mother went into a coma? Or maybe they couldn't agree on a name: They were already divorcing, right?

I had a lot of theories, but I still had that awful, ungenerous "Female" in the big blue book. It stung—hard, concrete evidence of being unwanted.

I closed the book and stared at the chocolates, the gum, the bar, and the water. I hadn't touched any of them. I'd expected to be in the library a long time.

Enormous revelations had occurred, my ground had shifted once again, and only about fifteen minutes had passed. Despite feeling angry and let down, I was energized and very curious.

In the small notebook I'd brought, I wrote *Aylford* at the top of a blank page, then handed the birth record book back to the man at the information desk.

"Do you have old phone directories for Manhattan?" I asked him.

"Next room," he said, without looking up.

The woman in the next room pointed me toward several shelves of ancient, crumbling books. I found 1954 and flipped the book open to the As. *Aylan... Aylcromb... Aylford.* There were two entries: Sara Jane Aylford at 13 East 71st Street, and Edward Aylford at 1 East 57th Street—my birth parents? But weren't they still living together when I was born?

Phone books in the 1950s, I discovered, listed professions along with names. Next to Edward Aylford's number was the tiny abbreviation, "advtg." Ruth had told me my paternal grandfather was an advertising executive. Edward Aylford had to be my grandfather.

I had to force myself to breathe slowly. This was all happening so fast!

Edward Aylford—such a patrician name! I pictured a tall, elegant man with a cane, who looked like Fred Astaire.

Was Sara Jane my birth mother? It was possible. She couldn't be Edward's daughter, because Ruth had told me my birth father's sister had died. But Ruth also said that my birth father's father had been married "several" more times after he and my paternal grandmother divorced. Maybe Sara Jane was one of the other Mrs. Aylfords? I wrote "Edward—paternal grandfather" and "Sara Jane—birth mother?" and their 1954 addresses in my notebook, then checked the current Manhattan directory. There were no Aylfords.

I returned to the woman at the information desk.

"How can I get information on someone if all I have is a name?" I asked.

"Are they alive?" she asked.

"I don't know."

"Famous?"

"I don't think so."

"American?"

"Yes," I said, although I wasn't totally sure.

"Try the Master Biography Index and the Genealogy Index, in case they've done anything noteworthy. They're in the back room on the left. Also look in the

New York Times Personal Name Index, in the back room on the right. If they've ever been in the press or won an award of any kind, they'll be in there."

The Master Biography Index included three Aylfords.

The first, Henry VanderWater Aylford, was a banker, born 1869, died 1931.

Joan Aylford, a poet, was still alive, and roughly the right age to be my birth mother. The nonidentifying information sheet had said that my birth mother enjoyed writing. But would a published poet keep using the name of a man she was married to so briefly and so long ago? It seemed unlikely.

The third was a scientist, Marion K. Aylford, born in 1933. My birth father, Ruth said, was a photographer. Could he somehow have ended up as a scientist?

In the *New York Times* Personal Name Index, I found Donald Aylford, a police officer in New Jersey who was killed in 1975 by a sniper named James Carhart. Though I couldn't figure out where Donald might fit into the puzzle, I read the articles about his killing anyway.

Then, paydirt! A 1975 obituary of Edward Aylford, advertising executive, prominent enough to merit a chunky obit in the *Times*. Born in 1908, graduated from the University of Chicago in 1927, had a bunch of jobs in advertising (starting as a copywriter—my job!), then at the ABC radio network. Went back to advertising in Chicago and New York. A lieutenant commander in the Navy in World War II, he died January 28, 1975 of a heart ailment at New York Hospital (where I was born!).

The last sentence set me trembling: "Mr. Aylford is survived by his wife Rebecca Barnes Aylford and his two sons, Steven Barnes Aylford and John Aylford."

I thought it through. Rebecca Barnes Aylford was the last wife of the "several" that Ruth had mentioned. And if Steven's middle name was Barnes, then he must be Edward's son with Rebecca, this last wife. But my birth father was the child of his father's first marriage. John Aylford was my father.

I sat back, breathless. I had the name of my birth father. Without even realizing it, I'd gotten caught up in the hunt. And I wasn't ready to stop. I felt titillated, and I wanted more. I had my birth grandfather's name, his address when I was born, and even his phone number. I might have my birth mother's name, Sara Jane, as well as that of my birth father. *John Aylford*—I said it once, and then again: What a handsome, forthright name. Just the kind of a name a father should have.

Before I left the library, I headed back to the telephone book collection. The current books for Westchester, Nassau, Suffolk, Syracuse, northern New Jersey, and western Connecticut yielded not a single Aylford. Wherever they are, I thought, they're not here anymore. I wonder where they are… and if I can find them.

John Aylford, John Aylford, John Aylford. For days I walked around repeating the name like an incantation, like Barbra Streisand in *Funny Girl:* "Nicky Arnstein, Nicky Arnstein, Nicky Arnstein." I kept imagining faces and forms to match this beautiful name. They always ended up looking like Fred Astaire: long and lean, graceful, but with thick, dark hair and green eyes. Was this because my father—the only father I knew—was long and lean, dark-haired and graceful? When I was a little girl, we entered father-daughter dance contests at Catskills' hotels. My tiny feet on top of his shiny black dress shoes, we swanned our way through "Begin the Beguine" together. It felt like flying, scary and thrilling. But as I wandered through the days humming *John Aylford, John Aylford, John Aylford,* it never occurred to me that perhaps the father I imagined was invented to match the father I already had.

It wasn't until early January, 1997 that I took the next step. Although I wanted more information, I already felt flooded by what I had. Just knowing the names of my birth father and grandfather, their eye color, their hobbies, was overwhelming. I had started out thinking I wanted a little taste—just a name. Now I felt compelled to move forward.

But I couldn't have taken the next step without making use of an amazing invention that changed the way everyone did just about everything—the Internet.

At the time, I was working two days a week at a teen magazine, writing presentations, brochures, and ads. In the last few months, a new function had been installed on my computer at work, called the World Wide Web. I'd used it a couple of times to look up lip gloss on AltaVista, and the names of the singers in 'N Sync. I had seen an article about how to use the Internet to locate someone living in another state. It recommended using a site called Database America, which could search phone directories from all over the country.

The next day at work I closed the door to my office and opened the Web site. I felt like I was viewing pornography, irrationally afraid that if someone came in and found me, I would be fired. With shaking hands I typed in J O H N A Y L F O R D. I waited a few long seconds and a list of names came up. There were seven John Aylfords, in Louisiana and Maine, Vermont and Virginia. I printed out the list and stared at it: One of these men was my birth father. It seemed so certain, and so completely impossible.

I put the list in my purse, where it gathered dust for several days while I tried to figure out what to do. I knew I couldn't bring myself to call them, even though I had their phone numbers. I couldn't imagine saying to a total stranger: *Hello, my name is Jil and I might be the daughter you gave away forty-two years ago.*

Finally I decided to send them all the same letter. I fiddled with the wording for a few more days, then sat down and wrote what I hoped was a simple, clear letter.

> Dear Mr. Aylford,
>
> This is a very difficult letter to write. You see, I am an adult adoptee currently searching for my birth parents. I believe my birth father's name was John Aylford.
>
> I was born on November 15, 1954 at New York Hospital. I have been told my parents were a young couple who married in the early 1950s after a very brief courtship and then were separated by my father's time in the service. After his return, they realized that their marriage was not going to work. Finding that they were going to have a baby, they made the decision to put that child up for adoption.
>
> I am that child, now forty-two years old. I began searching for my birth parents about a year ago. I believe my birth mother's name was Sara. I know little about her except that her father, a pharmacist, had died several years before I was born of a brain tumor, and she had one sister.
>
> My birth father was trying to make a living as a photographer when I was born. His father was an advertising executive who died, I believe, in the 1970s. His parents had divorced when he was younger, and he had one sister who died in an accident.
>
> Mr. Aylford, I don't know anything about you except that you have the same name as the man I seek. If you are my birth father, please understand that I don't want to cause problems for anyone, or intrude on a life that may not welcome me. I am just trying to put the missing pieces of my life together—to find out who I am and who I come from.
>
> Although I found your telephone number, I hesitate to use it—I don't have the nerve, I guess. As I said earlier, this is a difficult letter to write. I hope that you will write back to me, or call me if you would rather (maybe you have more nerve than I). I would love any information you can offer about my birth family, especially my birth mother. If you are my birth father, I promise I will follow your lead. If you don't want a surprise forty-two-year-old baby in your life, I understand and I won't bother you. I would just like to *know.*
>
> Thank you.

I stared at the computer screen on the desk in my bedroom. I changed the last word "know" to "*know*" then changed it again, then went back to italics. I wanted to be clear: I wasn't going to bust into his life if he didn't want me there. But then maybe italicizing it made me sound too intense? He wouldn't want to hear from some wacko long-lost daughter looking for love, or a daddy, or a new family. I wasn't looking for any of those things—although I had no idea what I *was* looking for.

I stared out my bedroom window. I knew myself well enough to know (*know?*) that once I let too much analysis creep into a decision, I would see not one side, not even two, but ten or twenty or a hundred different possibilities, and reaching a decision would become impossible. I looked back at the screen. *Know:* I left the italics and printed out seven copies, signed them, addressed seven envelopes, folded and stamped and sealed them, and slid them into my purse.

Where they remained for two weeks.

Once mailed, my world might change, forever. But would it change for better or for worse? I tried to imagine all the possibilities. But every time I did, a bunch of alternative possibilities grew, like vines with tendrils and more tendrils, until my brain was strangled by all the possibilities, none of which I felt equipped to handle.

What if the letter found the right John Aylford, and he turned out to be a cold bastard who wanted nothing to do with me? What if he thought I was after his money? What if he didn't know where my birth mother was? What if he *did*? What if she was dead, or sick, or mentally ill? What if he was a white-trash deadbeat and she was a trailer-park whore? Worse: What if they were boring? Did I still want to know?

"I can't decide what to do," I moaned to Janey on the phone.

She had been listening to *what if* for two weeks.

"Listen," she said, in a firm voice. "You had a baby with less thought than this. You got married with a *lot* less thought than this. There's no way you're ever going to know what could happen. You're forty-two years old. They're in their sixties. You're not going to have forever to decide. You just have to do it."

"I do?" I asked plaintively.

"Just mail the letters. You can deal with whatever happens next."

I wasn't sure she was right about that, but the next day I mailed the letters. Then I waited, wondering and worrying.

A few days later, a man with a Southern twang called. "Mah name is John Aylford," he drawled, "I live in Sulphur, Louisiana. But I can't be your daddy 'cause I'm thirty-six years old." He apologized for taking so long to call me, but, he said, "I wanted to ask my daddy if he knew of anyone in the fam'ly having a baby and giving it away, but he didn't know anything about it, so I guess you're not fam'ly to us." He sounded disappointed. I was, too. I thanked him for the call.

"That's quite all right," he said sympathetically. "Ah wish ah could help you. And me and my daddy are prayin' for you."

I hung up the phone, strangely comforted by the sweetness of Louisiana's John Aylford. If this John Aylford was so kind, maybe my John Aylford would be.

Two days later, I got a call from John Aylford in Ohio, who was also very kind. He was also not my father. But Ohio's John Aylford said he would "keep my ears open."

Another John Aylford called with the same news. He sounded disappointed to tell me he wasn't my father, but, he said excitedly, there was going to be a huge Aylford reunion in Seattle that summer, with dozens of Aylfords from all over the country. Since I was born an Aylford, I was more than welcome to come.

I imagined all sorts of Aylfords introducing themselves to each other. "Hello, I'm Donald Aylford." "Nice to meet you, I'm Susan Aylford." "Hi, I'm Bill Aylford."

What would my introduction be? "Hello, I'm Female Aylford. I don't know my first name or how I'm related to you. But I'm an Aylford, too!"

I thanked him, but I didn't think I would go.

I got a letter from John Aylford in Virginia. "I know you have been through a lot," it said. He was also too young to be my father, but, he wrote, "Keep your head held high. God can help you through this." He had gotten a letter from Stephanie Aylford in Washington, who was writing a book on the history of the Aylfords. He passed along her address to me in case I wanted to see if she had any information. "Good luck in finding your father," he said. "And welcome to the family."

After a couple of weeks, I had almost stopped thinking about the letters. Either my John Aylford no longer existed, or he didn't want to be found. The search had reached a dead end. I was disappointed, but also relieved.

At work one afternoon, I was fiddling around with a piece about hot new singers. The Spice Girls were at the top of the charts, with the Backstreet Boys right behind them. I was trying to figure out whether to focus on hot girls or hot boys. I called home to check my messages.

"Jil, this is Jake Aylford calling," a man's voice on the answering machine said. "I just got your wonderful letter and I very much want to speak with you and so does Faith, your mother."

I gasped. Quickly, I hung up the phone, like it was hot. I stood up, and then sat down. I felt my entire body flush. I walked to the door, closed it, then sat down and called the machine again and listened to the rest of the message.

"I got your letter yesterday," it went on, "because I moved to a village nearby from where you sent it so it had to be forwarded. I want to talk to you very badly. Your letter is absolutely splendid. It's about noon. I don't know where you are, maybe you're working. I have to leave in about half an hour. Maybe you could call me tonight after 9:00 p.m."

He told me his phone number and ended with a single word: "Call."

I was shaking so badly I needed two hands to hang up the phone. Even two-handed, I missed the cradle and had to pick it up and put it down again. I stood up and started pacing the small space, trying to take deep breaths.

My letter was splendid, he said. *Splendid!* He wanted to talk to me, and so did my mother. *My mother!* This was too strange, too scary. I grabbed my coat. Running out onto Third Avenue, I started walking uptown, going nowhere. It was a freezing day, but I was sweating, and also shivering—hot and cold, terrified, but thrilled. His voice was deep and masculine, smoky, warm. He sounded smart. He sounded wonderful. He sounded *splendid.* And he wanted to talk to me; he wanted me. I realized how scared I'd been of being rejected, and how much I would have preferred finding nothing at all than finding someone who didn't want me. Fragments of thoughts raced round my brain: *He likes me, I like him, I like his voice, I like his words, he knows her, she wants me, she's my mother. She's my mother!*

I speed-walked back to the office and called Lenny, but he wasn't there. Janey was, and we talked for forty-five minutes, most of which consisted of me repeating the same things over and over, telling her what he said, how he sounded, how crazy it all seemed, how nervous, scared, excited, anxious, terrified, confused, exhilarated I felt. By the time I got off the phone I could at least sit still. I called the machine again to make sure John's, I mean *Jake's* message, was still there. This time there was a second message.

"Jil," the woman's voice said, "This is Bunny. You know me as Faith. I've spoken to Jake. I can't tell you how thrilled I am, how happy I am to hear from you. I've tried to find you or to make myself available so you could find me. Jake is going to call you tonight and I would like very much to speak to you, too, but I'll wait until he has called you. I'm very happy to hear from you and I will talk to you soon. Bye."

I hung up the phone slowly. I had gone from frantic and shaking to a strange state of calm. Why am I so calm? I wondered if it was possible to short-circuit your brain with too much emotion.

Faith, I thought. *Faith*—it was perfect. All my life I've been looking for faith: faith in myself, religious faith, or faith in the people I love. At sixteen, I'd stopped believing in God. The idea seemed as believable as moon men or the Wizard of Oz. I'd been looking for something to have faith in ever since. And now I had found Faith.

I couldn't sit still. I grabbed my coat again and walked blindly west on 42nd Street, past Lexington Avenue and the Chrysler Building, Grand Central Terminal, Madison Avenue, and over to Bryant Park, behind the Public Library where the whole search had started just a few months earlier. I sat down on a bench. The park was nearly empty; it was way too cold for bag-lunchers and newspaper-readers. I could see my breath clouding but I was warm, shivering not from the cold, but from sheer excess of adrenalin.

They had nice voices. They sounded like nice people. They didn't sound like Jerry Springer loonies, but normal and decent, and smart. In my mind, he looked, of course, like Fred Astaire, or maybe Jason Robards, long, lean, beautifully weathered. Her voice was warm and deep, strong, clear. In my mind she looked like Bea Arthur, *Maude* Bea Arthur, not *Golden Girls* Bea Arthur, in a long tunic vest and wide-legged pants, short, shaggy graying hair, tall and straight and clear-eyed.

Beautiful Bryant Park, with its swath of smooth, trimmed grass, green even in winter, was spinning before my eyes. I walked back to my office and called Janey again and told her the latest development. I told her ten times. Then I called the machine and listened to both messages again, and again, and again. Finally I wrote them down, word for word, so I would always remember the first things my birth mother and birth father said to me. By the time I left work I realized I could not possibly charge the company for my hours in the office that day.

It was four long hours until 9 o'clock. Somehow I made it through, ate a few mouthfuls of dinner, spoke when spoken to. At 9 o'clock, I asked Lenny to keep the kids occupied, locked myself in the bedroom, took several deep breaths, and called the number.

He answered on the first ring.

23. BUNNY

FOUND

Nothing is so difficult
But that it may be found out by seeking.

TERENCE

HEAUTONTIMOROUMENOS

The message on my answering machine was brief.

"This is Jake. I've had an interesting letter from someone that I'd like to discuss with you. I'll call back later."

My husband had heard the message already; he'd come home while I was still out, but he listened again, and watched me as I heard it for the first time.

"Oh, my God!" I took a deep breath. "It's The Baby!"

Yes," he said, "I thought so, too."

The Baby had written Jake a letter.

Except that she was no longer The Baby. She had been The Baby in my head for so long that it was hard to think of her in any other way. But the leap to reality wasn't a huge one; it just needed to be taken. After all, babies don't write letters.

Jake called back the next morning—a long wait. As I listened to him talk, I began to recognize his voice—the tone, the shadings, and the enthusiasms—though I hadn't spoken to him in decades. He read me the letter he had received; it was a good letter, clearly, carefully, and thoughtfully written.

Jake and I both wanted to talk to her *immediately*. But somehow—after all those years, we agreed that Jake would call her first. She had written to him, so he would answer: I would talk to her after that. It didn't take me long, after the conversation ended, to realize how foolish I had been—I wanted to talk to her NOW! I didn't want to wait. I didn't care who spoke first or second, as long as I could talk to her.

He had given me her phone number. I called, despite our agreement. She wasn't home. But she was a voice—a real woman. I left a message on her answering machine, telling her who I was, that I wanted so very much to talk to her, and that I hoped she would call me.

But Jake spoke to her before I did. When I called him later to tell him that I had called her, even though we had agreed he would, and his line was busy, I knew he was talking to her.

When I finally got through to him, he said she sounded wonderful. He knew I'd like her. But, he said, she's overwhelmed by everything, and she wants to wait before she talks to you; she'll call you tomorrow morning.

More waiting!

That night Jake and I talked for a long time. He told me The Baby was forty-two years old, lived in New York City, and had two sons of her own.

The Baby was named Jil.

We talked a little about our lives now. He was married to his third wife; he and his second wife had a daughter, and he and his third wife had two children, a boy and a girl. He was working as a photographer; he had worked for a local newspaper for a while, and now did portraits.

Talking to Jake was surprisingly easy. I couldn't still be angry at him for things that had happened over forty years ago. And he was so excited by what was happening. It was not only an adventure: It was also about remembering when he was young and full of hope. He talked a bit about his father, and his death, and wept for a moment. In a way, I wanted to resist—I was no longer enchanted or charmed—and I certainly didn't want to talk long enough that his wife would be jealous of *me*, or of his possible tie to Jil. My focus was Jil. I wanted to learn more about her; I wanted to hear her voice; I wanted to see her. I needed to keep all the threads straight and untangled. Everything was just beginning.

This is what I wrote in my journal that night: "I am so filled with excitement, joy, fear, happiness, desire to love, that I think I will burst. It's like being complete again. Everything is surreal—sur-alive. Sur: beyond, above."

One night, just a day or two later, after all that joy, I had a series of strange dreams. In the first, I was with two men who destroyed everything they saw, while I watched, helpless. In the next, I was trying to save some children in an elementary school while Jake sat nearby, ignoring me and flirting with a woman who had grapes in her hair. In the last dream, I unpacked a large suitcase, and then repacked some of the contents into a smaller bag, deciding to leave as soon as I was finished.

I knew the dreams had to do with being married to Jake. They were about not mattering while he turned in other directions. His charm and seductiveness was like a flashlight or a lighthouse beam, an illuminating glow when aimed at you, dark when it turned away. He didn't turn it on and off deliberately. Watching him from the outside, it seemed as if other people didn't exist any more when he wasn't with them. He wasn't deliberately cruel, but simply unaware. I listened to him remember those times that were so often terrible, remembering them with such pleasure and with a discernible glow. Yes, they were happy times, when we saw parts of Europe for the first time; but there were also times I felt alone, abandoned, unsure, and jealous. If he'd been gone, he'd come back outraged at the suggestion that he'd done anything wrong. And he always came back.

I've heard it said that women have affairs with men with whom they feel the way they did with their fathers, but marry men who remind them of their mothers. As a child, I felt I didn't matter, that I was not heard. I had to shout in my clamor to be heard and seen. The feelings I had with Jake were familiar.

The joy of the phone calls about The Baby was tempered by all this: Was I ready to face it again? Had I truly moved beyond all that? I definitely hoped so. In my dream, I made the right decision; I had used a smaller suitcase, without all the old baggage.

Jake was one thing, from a past long gone, and Jil was something else entirely, apart from everything else in my world: the past, the present, my marriage, my children. Now more than a memory, she was a presence, a new reality waiting to be discovered. She was the living part of my promise: I will always love you.

It was hard to wait for her call. I couldn't imagine what it was like for her, having spoken to Jake, and still waiting to call me. I was on the verge of tears, but I had no need or wish to cry. And I hadn't even spoken to her yet!

Once she called, it was so easy to talk to her; I felt as though I had known her all along and the call went by in a blur. She had two children: Suddenly I'd become a grandmother! She seemed to be so much like me. We laughed at the same moments, and hesitated at the same things.

"It's amazing," I wrote in my journal, "how alike we are. Except I think she's in much better shape than I was at her age—happier and more comfortable. If I'd been able to keep her, she would probably not sound like that. I like her very, very much—her humor, the way she thinks. I suppose there's some recognition of myself in her; but there's more than that. I am so happy that I think I could stand on the roof, lean forward, and fly away. I feel as if I'm held to earth by the lightest of strings. I feel frivolous and joyful. The earth stopped turning, and I am lighter than air!"

Later, I thought about whether she would be tangled up with Jake: Was it to be Jake and me and The Baby, after all these years? I hadn't yet told her about Quint, who, after all, might be her father. For now, I thought that discovering Jake was enough—one step at a time.

We talked about meeting, and I said that however she wanted to do it was all right with me: separately, one of us at a time, or Jake and me together. Though it had to be her choice, I hoped to meet her alone, so we could have a chance to get to know each other. I wanted us to be a presence for each other. I wanted her to be there: friendly, if not a friend; daughterly, even if not exactly a daughter; sisterly, even if not a sister.

Would it be possible? Or was it incredibly presumptuous just to think about it? Was it too late for that kind of closeness? Most of all, I wanted her *there*—a part of my life. I wanted her not to disappear again.

There are no guides to reunions of birth mother and adopted child, no rules, no etiquette books, no hints about good behavior, no lists of what might be forbidden, no way of knowing what would be best. With each step Jil and I took in this uncharted territory, whether we'd thought about it ahead of time or it happened spontaneously, we created our own path and our own map, with its own set of directions. We knew where we had been, and we were learning about where to go: We proceeded carefully, and from the beginning, we did well.

"I'm standing at a point," I wrote in my journal, "where my past and my future cross. I suppose we're always there, at that intersection, the ongoing Now, but this is so precise, so conscious—right in the middle of the spot!"

Amazingly, and suddenly, Jil was no longer my biggest secret, but a presence I wanted to share. Before I even knew her, I wanted to tell everyone: The Baby found me!

Each time we spoke, I wrote the same thing: "She sounds wonderful. Spoke to her Saturday, and today is Tuesday, and it seems so long since we talked! Am I going to go on like this?"

I felt as if I were coming apart—but, even more, that I was coming together. On the phone, even before we met, I recognized her—her humor, the way she laughed. Even our pauses were similar.

This, then, was Jil: a love story. Recognizing that, I warned myself and made three rules:

1. Don't fall in love with her. Love her. But don't *fall* in love. Be steady.

2. Don't expect her presence to fix anything else in my life that needs fixing.

3. Don't abandon the rest of my life, the people I love, in the joy of knowing Jil.

So often it seems easier to write about sorrow than joy; words pour out of my pen as if they were tears.

But when I turn to my journal and read what I wrote in the weeks after Jil found me, I find joy, over and over.

"I feel complete—cured!—restored! and sane. Everything begins anew. This is The Baby! Joy—Jil. I'm filled with mystical joy, and I am very, very happy. I do feel complete—exactly that."

Jil said she has freckles. I couldn't remember whether or not Jake had freckles, but I knew that Quint did. I began to think about picking out photographs to give her when we met. And I wanted to give her something of mine, and something of my mother's. Finally I chose a bracelet my mother had given me for my birthday the summer she died; it seemed to speak of both of us, and it represented a small piece of Jil's heritage. I also decided to give her my old wedding ring, which was part of her story. I'd saved it all these years: the two silver bands, meeting over and over, in a chain, making small connected boxes that to us symbolized our two lives, strong, joined, but still independent. If only I'd been able to live that way!

Actually meeting Jil was the next step. I met her alone, in a restaurant on the Upper West Side where I'd gone many times for tomato soup and bread pudding. It seems an unlikely choice now, but it was the only place I could think of. It was crowded and noisy, but we were engrossed in each other. On the phone, we'd both admitted to often being late for appointments; we were both on time. There should have been background music—a fanfare, several chords. How did we recognize each other? I think we just did. I don't remember the moment of recognition. ("How do you do? I'm your mother. And you are... The Baby?")

My memory plays its customary tricks with an imprecise haziness of things I want never to forget. Snapshots of unimportant moments emerge from my mind, clear and sharp: waiting for the train to Antioch in the old Penn Station; seeing two couples kissing the wrong partners at a party in the Village; carrying a glass of water to my father when I was about two years old, and falling, breaking the glass and cutting my wrist just below the thumb. I still have the scar, a small crescent moon. Then there is a clear memory of my father angry at my mother for giving me a glass to carry.

Though there are dozens of photographs in the uncatalogued, unpaged album in my mind, sometimes the other things, important things, weighty things, life-changing things, are blurs, if they exist at all. I know they happened, but I can't *see* them, no matter how much I want to. I met Jil at a restaurant on the Upper West Side and we talked for hours, but I can't remember the moment we met.

She had my smile, but I didn't recognize the rest of her. Fair-skinned (like my mother), hazel eyes (like me); all of her was lovely. She was a beautiful baby, and she had become a beautiful woman.

We connected on so many levels. There were so many things she said that I simply understood. She said she loves movies, and she uses them as I do, to escape, in moments of unhappiness or crisis. At exactly the same time, we both said: "I *adore* Kevin Kline." From the way we use food to the hand gestures we make, from loving being pregnant to liking the same musicals, we matched: Is everything genetic?

We talked for four hours. It was exhausting, wonderful, amazing, and beyond reality. I thought my eyes couldn't *see* enough of her. I wanted to stare and stare and stare—until I knew who she is, who she was, and could remember all forty-two years of her, could finally know her, see into her. Imagine being on the other end of that! We showed each other our photographs. Her sons are beautiful.

I was left thinking, "Can all of this be true? Is this an elaborate hoax? Am I really awake? Will there be more or is this it?"

At first I thought that even if I never actually met her, I'd be happy just knowing she was well and happy. To some extent, that was still true. But it wasn't enough; now that she was real, I wanted more of her. I didn't want to make up for the lost years, but to explore what remained to us.

That's what we did. We began, and went on from there.

24. JIL

FOUND

He answered on the first ring. Just hearing his voice, I almost fainted from excitement, nerves, and fear. In my bedroom, sitting on the side of the bed, I stood up and sat down, over and over, unable to keep still, unable to figure out what to do with myself, with my tingling nerves, my shaking hands.

"John? John Aylford?"

"Yes." His voice was deep and rich, leathery, a smoker's voice. "Jil?"

"Yes."

Silence: What do you say to a father you have never met?

And then we both started talking, and it was simple, easy, and wonderful.

We talked for an hour and a half. Mostly he talked, and I listened. I wanted to know everything about him: where he grew up, who his parents were, who he loved, what he hated.

Luckily, John ("Jake," he said. "People I like call me Jake") loved to talk. He was a born raconteur. Even the simplest, most off-the-cuff stories had an arc, a shape, funny lines, different voices. He was an actor, a performer, charming and self-possessed.

He was a photographer, he told me, living in Maine. He was on his third wife (who was about my age), and he had two young children with her. He also had a daughter from his second marriage. He spoke movingly of her work with abused children. At one point, it seemed he was near tears.

"I'm impressed," I said. "You sound so… sensitive." I wasn't used to men, especially men of his generation, being so emotional.

"I credit my wife," he said. "Or I blame her, I'm not sure." He laughed. "She's helped me come to terms with a lot of things. She's here right now, in the room with me. She wanted me to call you."

"Wouldn't you have, without her wanting you to?" I asked.

He hesitated. "Sure," he finally said. "When I got your letter, my first thought was to jump in the car and drive to Manhattan and meet you in person. But I held myself back. And then I started to get nervous."

"Why?" I asked, although I was incredibly nervous myself.

"Oh, there are so many reasons," he said and chuckled. "There's so much to tell you. And there are a lot of things I can't tell you yet."

"What do you mean?"

"Not yet. I'm sure we'll have plenty of time now that we've found each other."

I was curious, but I didn't feel the need to push for more. It was already too much to handle.

He told me about how he and Faith met in college, at Antioch, but didn't really get to know each other until they met again at a New Year's Eve party in Manhattan. He was in the Army, stationed in New Jersey, while she was doing some sort of work-study job, also in New Jersey. They married just one month later, February 1, 1953. Soon after, he got shipped overseas to Germany as an Army photographer. Then she followed. I was conceived in Stuttgart (I was made in Europe, a German postwar product!).

"Things weren't right from the start," he said, his voice regretful. "We knew by the time she got pregnant that we were going to split up. It was definitely a mistake." He paused. "I hope this isn't too upsetting for you?" he asked gently.

"No, no," I said quickly. I was *way* past "upset."

"I told her I would stay with her until the baby was born. Until *you* were born," he said. "We came back to New York and she had the baby there. And we made all the arrangements with the agency. I don't really remember much about it. It's a long time ago and it's not one of the happier times in my life. I'm not proud of anything I did."

"What did you do?" I asked.

"So many things, so many wrong things," he said, sadly. "But I want you to like me, so I'm not going to tell you now."

"I already like you," I said. I did; he was funny, smart, and charming. As terrified as I was when the conversation started, I felt wonderful, but completely exhausted, in that crazy depleting way you feel when you've worked yourself into a state of shivering excitement, and then it's done. I was so tired I could barely speak, but I had one more important question.

"Why didn't you and Faith give me a name?" I asked.

"What do you mean?"

"On my birth certificate it just says 'Female Aylford,'" I said.

"That's impossible. Of course we gave you a name." He sounded angry. "We thought long and hard about it, even though we knew whoever adopted you would probably change it. We named you for my grandmother."

"What was my name?" I asked.

"Jessica. Your name was Jessica Anne."

My head spun: Jessica? *Jessica?* Jessica like my baby doll, the one I took to the agency when we adopted my brother? Jessica, like my Barbie; Jessica, the name I picked for a daughter if I had one; Jessica, my favorite name since I could remember?

"What a nice name," I said, nearly breathless. "I've always liked that name."

"Me, too," Jake said. "You see, we have the same taste."

After we hung up I lay down on the bed and watched the ceiling go around. I closed my eyes and almost drifted off to sleep. But my mind wouldn't rest. Jake told me Faith wanted to speak to me (he had gotten her number from a recent Antioch directory and called her as soon as he received my letter). But I told him I couldn't call her then: I was too drained. He said he would let her know I'd call in the morning. We said good-bye, and then I got up and went to help my children with their homework.

The next morning I felt shell-shocked, like someone who's drunk too much and slept too little. I got the kids off to school and retreated again to the bedroom to make another terrifying, strange, surreal phone call. Like Jake, she answered on the first ring.

Her voice was soft and deep, musical, warm. The first thing she said to me, after "Hello," was: "I'm sorry. I hope you can forgive me."

"For what?"

"For giving you away." She sounded as if she might cry.

"I don't feel there's anything to forgive." And I didn't. Being adopted was my life; it was part of me. She might as well apologize for my not being born winged, or French.

"I'm so sorry," she said.

"Don't be," I said. "I'm not unhappy. I don't think about having a different life. It seems inconceivable."

We talked for an hour. She lived in Rockland County, just across the river from where I grew up. I thought of all the times we'd driven across the long, elegant Tappan Zee Bridge when I was a kid, going to visit my aunt and uncle in Rockland County. I could have passed her house, seen her walking on the street—my other mother, my shadow life.

She told me about her husband, a musician and recording industry consultant. She told me about her work: She was a writer and editor, working on her first solo book. A writer! *A writer!!*

She told me about her kids, her daughter (*I have a sister!*), who lived in Manhattan and was a poet, and her son (*I have a brother!*), who was living at home and going to school. She had never told her children about the baby she gave away long ago.

"I couldn't tell them. I was so scared they'd be afraid I would give *them* away—that if I'd done it once, I could do it again." She paused. "And I was so ashamed of what I had done. I didn't want anyone to know about it."

"Do they know now?" I asked.

"Well, a strange thing happened—an incredible coincidence. In her junior year of college, my daughter became friends with a girl in her creative writing class. My daughter knew I'd been married before, and she knew his name. She figured out that this girl's father was my first husband, Jake. Her friend knew her father had been married before, and she also knew the story of the baby that he'd given up. She told my daughter about it. That's how she found out."

"Was she upset?"

"Yes, though she didn't tell me about it right away. I suppose she was angry that I'd kept it secret from her. She didn't understand. So she kept *her* knowledge secret from me. She didn't tell me she knew for two years." Faith sounded sad. "She still doesn't understand why I never told her."

"What about your son?"

"I told him last night," she said, her voice growing lighter. "He was angry at first, and a little suspicious, too. How could I be sure you are who you say you are, that sort of thing. But after we talked, he understood. He's very happy for me."

She told me she'd signed up with several registries, but didn't want to go any further, not really feeling she had a right to intrude on my life. She made herself available in case I was searching.

"When Jake called yesterday," she said, "it felt like a door had opened in my life. I felt like I was at peace for the first time in a really long time."

She told me more about her life, her interests, and her family. But she also asked me lots of questions. She asked me what I was like as a baby, what kind of childhood I had, what my husband was like, and if I was happy. She asked me what I looked like.

I told her my height, coloring, and added, "And I'm overweight."

"Oh, I'm not overweight," she said. "I'm fat." And I loved that, I *loved* that.

Talking to her was just as easy as it had been with Jake, but different. It felt more like a real connection was being made. I wasn't listening and appreciating; I was sharing. She felt like an old friend rediscovered, and when I finally had to get off the phone to go to work, I was almost reluctant, although I needed some peace, and some time to make sense of everything.

She asked when we could meet. "I want to get in the car and drive into the city right now," she said, echoing Jake, but when I hesitated she added, "But I understand if you need to go slower."

"I do," I said. "It's a lot to take in."

I must have sounded nervous, because she quickly added: "You set the pace. I won't even call you. You call me."

"Thank you," I said.

But she called the next day. "I know I said I would wait for you to call, but I just wanted to tell you one thing," she said.

"Okay."

"For the last forty-two years there hasn't been one day that I have not thought of you. Not one."

I didn't know what to say. "Thank you," was all I could think of.

I certainly hadn't thought of her every single day—how could I, when I never believed she existed? But *I* was real to *her*, because she carried me inside her for nine months. She saw me, held me, and fed me. I was real to her in a way she had never been to me. She has other children, which is normal. A mother can have more than one daughter. But a daughter can only have one mother. And I already have mine. Faith said there has always been something missing from her life. Maybe there has always been something missing from mine. But she knew what was missing, because she saw and touched it. I never knew what was missing. I never saw it at all.

Two days later I wrote her a letter and sent her some pictures of myself and my sons. In our third phone call, I explained that I wasn't going to tell Damien and Alex about finding her.

"I can't tell my boys because I'm not going to tell my parents," I said.

"Why not?" she asked.

"I think it would be too upsetting."

In fact, I thought it might be devastating to my mother. It's not like we had a warm, close relationship, the kind of bond that meant I could tell them and they'd be happy for me. Our relationship was strained, and I feared this would only make it worse. And I felt sorry for them: My mother had never recovered from the loss of my brother. After he died, she removed every photo of him from the house, closed the door of his room and never cleaned it out. Even all these years later, she never spoke about him. I worried that this new revelation would make her fear that she was losing another child.

If I wasn't going to tell my parents, I couldn't tell my children. They were very close to their grandparents, and I couldn't ask them to keep a secret from them. So I only talked about it to Lenny, Janey, and a couple of other close friends. I talked about it obsessively, over and over, in long phone calls and letters and e-mails. I was crazy about it, itching and agitated and exhilarated all at once, a lunatic. I hadn't felt like this since I was much younger. It was like the crazed intensity of college, of falling in love, of drunken dancing, full of newness and excitement.

I told Faith I was sorry I was keeping her a secret.

"I understand," she said. "But I was going to be such a wonderful grandmother."

She told me she thought I was being very generous, not hurting my parents. I didn't feel generous; I felt confused and uncomfortable keeping secrets from my children. But I didn't know what else to do.

Though I was trying to take it slow, in the next week Faith and I spoke on the phone nearly every day. She wanted to meet, but I wasn't ready. I was on emotional overdrive, swinging wildly from one mood to another. Slow down, I kept saying to myself, take breaths, and stop spinning.

In between phone calls and e-mails to Faith, I spoke to Jake. He was planning a trip to New York to meet me, sometime in the next few weeks.

One night on the phone, Janey asked me if I could go back to when I mailed those letters (*three weeks ago! impossible to believe!*), would I stop myself from doing it. I almost said yes. It was all so very scary and unknown, so turbulent. But how can you deny yourself knowledge about yourself? How can you not take the risk?

I read an article in *Newsweek* written by an adoptive mother whose grown daughter had found her birth mother after a long search. The author and her husband had supported their daughter in her quest, but when their daughter found the woman she called her "other mother," the adoptive mother was caught off guard by the intensity of her emotions. She was jealous, hostile, and felt terribly threatened. Eventually, they worked it out, although she still had pangs of jealousy. Her point: Think long and hard before you act. Make sure you analyze where this might lead and what you might feel about it, because otherwise your emotions may shock and swamp you.

But I could have thought until my head fell off my shoulders, and I would not have been able to conceive of the feelings I was experiencing: joy, fear, anger, sorrow, excitement, terror, happiness, and confusion, coursing through me, knocking me sideways. I couldn't sleep, couldn't eat, and could barely stand still. I looked in the mirror ten times a day and asked, "Who are you? Who *are* you?"

It was time to meet. We chose Sarabeth's, a restaurant on Amsterdam Avenue near my house. A gemütlich café with yummy pumpkin muffins and a country-cheery charm, it seemed like a safe spot for a very dangerous enterprise. I wasn't ready, but I didn't think I ever would be. I had come this far, almost by accident. I had to see it through.

On a cold January day, only a week or so after that first phone call, I walked down Amsterdam Avenue to meet my mother. I was having some trouble with my legs. On 91st Street and 88th Street and 84th Street I had to stop and lean on a building or a mailbox so I wouldn't fall down. My heart was racing, and I seemed to be having difficulty breathing. A ten-minute walk took me nearly half an hour. I was terrified.

I wanted to get there early, so I could arrange myself and be sitting calmly when she arrived, but all the stopping to catch my breath and recalibrate my legs had eaten up a lot of time. I swung the door open and walked into the restaurant. There were only a few people there, and none of them were women sitting alone, looking expectant.

A waitress approached. "Are you meeting someone—an older woman?"

"Yes," I said hesitantly, wondering if she'd left, almost relieved. Maybe I could just go home and be normal.

"She's in the ladies' room downstairs," the waitress said. "But that's your table." She pointed me toward a little round table against the wall.

I took off my coat and hat and squeezed myself into a corner seat, trying to slow my breathing. I looked around the room nervously. I saw a hand on the banister of the stairs. A hand, then an arm, then a small, round woman who looked nothing like *Maude*. She was wearing a dark skirt and a tan sweater, and her hair was white and soft. No vests or long tunics, no big chunky statement necklace—nothing Bea Arthur about her at all.

Was this her? Could it be? She was walking toward me. I stood up. What do we do now, I thought frantically: Are we supposed to hug? Cry? How could I not have thought about this, made a plan? She looked not one bit like my fantasy image. She was small, soft, and gentle-looking. She walked up to me and put out her hand, a small, plump hand, with short fingers, and dimpled knuckles.

That's my hand, I thought, *my little chunky child's hand; my tiny fingers, my hand.* I took it in my own, our two small round hands together.

"Jil," she said. "I'm Faith."

And she was.

She brought pictures, thank goodness, a whole pile of them, which gave us something to do: her son as a little boy, with curly hair, looking remarkably like my son, Alex; her daughter, dark-haired, against a wall of books. My sister!

There were pictures of her younger self: in a sculptor's studio, looking at the bust of a head—her head, she said; a lovely portrait, taken by Jake, of her leaning on a windowsill, light from outside buttering her face. But the strangest picture was of her pregnant with me. Although it didn't show in the photo, she said that here, curled up in a big chair in her living room, smiling, she was a few months' pregnant. This was inconceivable.

She said, "When I was pregnant with you..." and it was the strangest thing I'd ever heard.

I showed her photos of myself as a child, a teen, in my twenties and thirties, and then photos of my children and my husband. I avoided photos of my parents, it was just too strange.

We talked; it was easy. Although my chest felt tight and my hands shook, I had no trouble speaking. There was so much she wanted to know, and she was a very good listener. She stared at me hard, but it was a tender stare, like she was soaking me up. She held her head to the side slightly, her pointy chin (my pointy chin!) upturned. She listened hard and asked good questions. It felt nice to have someone care so much about what I said—like being stroked.

It made her sad to hear that I didn't have a very happy childhood, and that I didn't get along well with my mother. Back in 1954, the agency said her baby was going to an engineer and his wife, liberal Democrats, educated people. None of this was true.

Our talk bounced along easily, for two hours, then three, from movies to theater, cooking, books, travel, children, and husbands. We liked the same films, and the same Broadway musicals, and could quote the same show-tune lyrics. We both loved to cook (and eat); we both felt lost without a book. We both thought Kevin Kline was the most talented man in America. We talked about the authors we loved: Jane Austen, Edith Wharton, E. M. Forster, the Brontës.

We'd both done a lot of volunteer work in our children's schools, writing and producing newsletters and brochures. We had the same hazel eyes; the same strange, uncontrollable curl at the same widow's peak in the middle of our same broad foreheads; the same small, wide feet; the same way of turning our heads and holding our cups and tapping our fingers when we were annoyed or bored. We even had the same strange habit of stroking the water tumbler sitting on the table; we both liked the feel of the damp, chilled glass. She was more like me than anyone I've ever met, which was the strangest thing I'd ever encountered.

"I have something for you," she said, opening her purse. It looked like a big carpetbag. We don't have the same taste in purses, I thought.

She handed me a box. Inside was a beautiful silver bracelet, delicate and antique-looking. "It was my mother's—your grandmother's."

The bracelet was lovely. I put it on.

"And this was my wedding ring." She handed me a small silver ring, chunky, with little connected boxes all round. "Jake and I had the same one. It was meant to signify the joining of two lives."

The ring had a '70s look, like something I would have chosen if Lenny and I hadn't gotten plain gold bands. I wasn't sure why she was giving it to me—I had no connection to her and Jake as a couple. I barely had a connection to them as individuals. Was the ring supposed to mark the beginning of me? I said, "Thank you," and slid it onto my finger.

She showed me diary pages that she had written almost twenty years earlier, about me: "My first child, my daughter, is twenty-four years old, and I have never seen her. That is not exact. I have not seen her since she was four days old." The papers talked of what she remembered—a tiny birthmark on my nose, feeding me a bottle. She wrote of the pain it had brought her: "Her absence is a part of my life." And the fear it left her with for her own children: "When they leave me, I am always, in some way, terrified," she wrote.

I had often felt that way about my children. Sometimes Alex walked into the school building, or Damien went to visit a friend, and I was convinced I would never see them again. It was as if they were not real to me unless I could touch them. But I had felt that way about my husband, too: At any point he could walk into a store, a gas station restroom, a hotel lobby, and—*poof!*—vanish from my life. Not that he would die, but that it would be as if he had never been, a vanishing so complete that people would not believe he'd ever existed. It was more than a fear of abandonment; it was a fear that the people I love do not really exist at all—like the birth mother I never believed in.

She told me the story again, of how she met Jake, how they married, how it all fell apart. The tale seemed so far away from me, not just in years, but from my life. I had to remind myself that it was *my* story, about how I came to be. I looked at her speaking and thought: *I came from her; she bore me. I grew inside of her!* It was completely impossible to believe. I might as well have come from a bottle, like a genie, or sprung from the cabbage patch.

She said, as Jake had, too, "There are things I can't tell you yet." And for the same reason: "I want so badly for you to like me."

It bothered me that she was withholding information about *me* from *me*.

Four days later she called and said she wanted to tell me the whole story.

"Why did you change your mind so soon?" I asked.

"I'm trying to learn how to be brave."

I suggested that we meet for lunch the next day.

We went to Sarabeth's again. The walk was easier this time, no collapsible knees or heart palpitations. But I was nervous about what she was planning to tell me. I'd tried and tried to imagine what it could be: Was I a twin? I wasn't the only child she and Jake had given up for adoption? She and Jake were cousins?

Like the walk, the lunch was easier, too; this time we actually ate something. She didn't bring up her secret at first, and I didn't want to push. We talked about her family's health history—for the first time in my life I had a medical history!— about motherhood, about our own mothers. But it was clear we were both waiting for something. After she finished her omelet, she said she was going to the bathroom, and then would tell me the story.

It began in Germany, after she had followed Jake to Stuttgart, after she already knew that their marriage was a mistake. There was a lot of ending and starting over, trying to make it work and then separating.

"Jake had a friend, a guy named Quint," she said, the wintry sun outside the window bathing our table in afternoon light. "He was from New York, a terrific fellow, smart, funny, and talented. The three of us were very close."

She told me about how Jake went into the hospital with a strange infection and ended up staying there for a month. She was sure he postponed his discharge from the hospital because he didn't want to return home to her. She felt angry and abandoned. And during the last week Jake was in the hospital, she slept with Quint. Once or twice, she couldn't remember exactly. Somehow Jake knew about her infidelity. By the time she found out she was pregnant, Quint had left Germany. She almost had an abortion before she and Jake decided to try, once again, to make their misbegotten marriage work. But he insisted that she give the baby up for adoption.

"At the time I was sure the baby was Quint's," she said. But that belief had nothing to do with timing, cycles, or sex. It was based on her feeling that Jake could not be the father because he was not emotionally capable of being a father.

Jake never believed he was the father of the baby, either, maybe because he agreed with her assessment of his emotional maturity, or maybe because he was so angry at her for sleeping with his friend. But even though he never believed the baby was his, he stayed with her through the pregnancy, went through the counseling sessions at the adoption agency, was there when she gave birth, and for a few more months after I was born. She was even more certain that the baby was Quint's when I was born with a large freckle on my nose, just like one Quint had—a freckle that has disappeared somewhere over the last forty-two years.

"Why?" I asked her. "Why would Jake stay with you if he knew you cheated on him, and was sure you were having someone else's baby?"

"I don't know," she said. "I think he wanted to be the good guy. He had done some pretty rotten things in the time we were married, and this gave him a chance to redeem himself, I guess, to make himself the hero instead of the heel."

"Did you ever see Quint again?" I asked.

"About a year after you were born, I ran into him at a party. I told him I'd had a baby, and that I thought it was his. He was pretty shocked, understandably."

She glanced at me, her eyes shining. "He was a good friend to me at a difficult time in my life. I never blamed him for anything."

"And you still think he's my father?" I asked. I was trying to take it all in, but I no longer believed we were talking about me. This was someone else's crazy life.

"No," she said. "I don't."

I wasn't surprised. She only slept with Quint once or twice; she lived with Jake. The odds were in his favor. And now that she'd seen me… "You look like Jake's mother," she said. "You have her chin, and smile."

"But why does Jake want to meet me so badly?" I asked. He was already planning to come to New York, and wanted me to clear my schedule so we could spend lots of time together. "Why is he now so convinced that I'm his daughter?"

"I don't know," she said, shaking her head. "I think it might be that he can't bear the idea of being left out of this story. He's a romantic, and this is a very romantic tale. He wants you to be his baby."

We examined the odds. I had Quint's freckle. But the freckle was gone. I had Jake's mother's smile. At least Faith thought I did; I couldn't see it. I started wearing glasses when I was six. Jake and Faith had perfect vision; Quint wore glasses. I had green eyes and blond hair. Jake was dark, Quint was light. But Faith's eyes were light; I had her eyes. Jake was creative, a photographer who had done some writing. I loved photography, and I was a writer.

"What does Quint do for a living?" I asked her. "Do you know?"

She looked carefully at me, and drew a breath. "Yes. He's Quint Phillips."

I was too stunned to speak. Finally, I sputtered: "The writer? Quint is Quint *Phillips*?" I thought about the books and movies he'd written, the television shows he'd appeared on, the *Oscar nomination*.

She was looking at me anxiously, as if waiting for tears.

I burst out laughing. "Quint Phillips? That's ridiculous. I can't believe it."

"It's true," she said, confused at my laughter, which was quickly becoming inappropriate. Two weeks ago I had two parents, the same ones I'd had for forty-two years. Then I had three, then four, now five! They were going to love me at the card shop on Mother's and Father's Day.

"Does he have any children?" I asked, still chuckling.

"I don't think so," she said. "I'm not in touch with him anymore. I haven't seen him since that party forty-one years ago."

The laughter started to die down.

"Are you okay?" she asked.

"I guess so," I said, wiping my eyes. I liked Jake; our talks on the phone had been wonderful, long and emotional and intense, and I was looking forward to meeting him. I wanted him to be my birth father. And now maybe he wasn't. I wasn't angry at her or disappointed in her, but I was disappointed to hear that there was another character in the story—and that maybe Jake wasn't mine at all.

That night, I told Lenny the new piece of the puzzle.

"I'm not sure I want to know the truth," I said. "Jake wants me to be his; he believes I *am* his, so maybe I should just leave it at that."

"Do you really think you'll be able to put that out of your mind?" Lenny asked.

I thought about it. Would I be able to respond to Jake the way I wanted to if that question remained? And what was this whole thing about? My parents were my parents, the people who raised me, for better or worse. Faith and Jake/Quint were something else—I wasn't sure what. The people who made me? If *what* they are to me was important, then I needed to know the truth. If the point was to find my birth parents, then I needed to find my birth parents, not the man who was married to my birth mother when she conceived me.

Faith told me Jake's wife wanted us to have a DNA test immediately, before we got to the point where we might be too disappointed with the results. If his was the sperm, then fine, journey over. But if it wasn't, I had to do this again, with another stranger—and a famous one at that. Would I try to contact a man who once or twice slept with a woman he probably doesn't remember forty-two years ago? There was only so much courage I could summon.

"I can't believe it," I told Maureen the next morning over coffee. I had kept her informed of every step in my search , even though I sensed that she was less and less interested. While she had cheered me on at the beginning ("Your birth mother will welcome you—I know it!"), she seemed uninterested, almost irritated, by what had happened since then. "I can't believe Jake might not be my birth father."

"What did you expect?" she said dismissively.

"What do you mean?" I asked, stung by her tone.

"I never believed that story—a nice married couple, even if they're having problems, don't just *give away* their baby. An educated, middle-class, *married* couple, just handing their baby to a stranger? It doesn't happen. I always knew there had to be something else."

She was right, I suddenly realized. And I thought of a story Faith told me the first or second time we talked, of riding down in the hospital elevator with Jake, holding me in her arms, to go to the agency and give me away. She begged him, pleaded with him to stay with her and keep the baby. He said no. I should have wondered then: Who does that? What man gives away his child, the baby he has made with his *wife*? I should have wondered, but I just accepted the story I was told—then and now—and didn't wonder at all. That, in itself, seems strange. Maureen questioned it; I never did. So what else was there that I hadn't questioned?

That night Jake called and I told him Faith had spilled the Quint Phillips beans. He was angry.

"I didn't want you to know that until I met you," he said. "I wanted to be the one to tell you. I wanted you to know me a little first."

"I do know you," I said. "I don't have to meet you to know you."

"I know, I know… but… I wanted to feel the connection."

"Why?" I asked. "Why is it so important to you?" Was it because, as Faith suspected, he wanted to be part of this drama, this juicy story?

"I've thought a lot about that," he said. "I think it's because I behaved so damn badly back then. I want to take responsibility. I want to be the grown-up I couldn't be then."

It made sense to me, all of it: the drama, the responsibility, the stupidity of these young people who made a baby and messed up their lives and didn't even know who did it. I understood what they did, and even why they did it. In my head it made sense, but in my stomach it was an ache, a pain. They messed up their lives and messed up my life and really, deep down, I didn't understand it at all.

I got off the phone and lay down on the bed. All my life, I'd wondered about my identity, wondered why I had so little sense of self, why I felt so unknown, so invisible, even to myself. But now that it seemed I had answers to some of those questions, I felt like I knew even less.

I started to cry for the first time since the day Jake called after getting my letter. I cried and cried and cried, without thinking at all, flooded with feelings I didn't even have names for, purging the emotion of the last two weeks, the strangest two weeks of my life.

25. BUNNY

GETTING TO KNOW JIL

We know the truth,
not only by the reason, but also by the heart.

BLAISE PASCAL

THOUGHTS

The almost immediate connection between Jil and me seemed like more than two people liking each other: It was quite mystical, like the immediate connection two strangers sometimes feel, as if they recognize each other from a previous life. It was more than seeing a genetic echo of me in Jil, although that was part of it; and it was more than the healing of a wound, though that was important, too. Far beyond those things, there was the sense of recognition of someone I'd always known, but had lost. "I once was lost and now am found," a hymn of grace.

That didn't change as we began to know each other better; what did change was the feeling of unreality. More and more, knowing Jil felt real.

But now I needed to tell Jil about Quint. I was frightened that I'd be judged, which seemed inevitable. I wasn't just a confused young girl whose husband wasn't ready to have a baby. This story was different: I had done something wrong when I slept with Quint, no matter how many reasons I had for doing it. I had cheated on my husband, and gotten pregnant. I could change the setting of my personal kaleidoscope, but the facts remained.

"Oh, please God," I wrote in my journal, "I was a child!

"Is that an excuse? Do I *need* an excuse for then, if I do what's right now? The right thing is to tell her as quickly as possible, and let her search continue a little longer. I know she thinks Jake is wonderful, and he thinks the same about her. They *want* to be related. And she believes they are. This is going to be difficult for her."

And then: "What will she think about me? What do *I* think about me? It was such a long time ago. I barely recognize myself—that thin, dark, lost young woman. Is it really fair to be held accountable for something that happened so long ago? Is it really fair *not* to be held accountable?"

Before we met, Jil told me she had freckles—like Quint, not Jake.

Jil gave me a book someone she knew had written about a birth mother and her lost child. I read it eagerly, and recognized my feelings, told in someone else's voice. The adoption was the loneliest thing I'd ever gone through. Finding out that others had the same feelings of terror and loss was a revelation. Why had it never occurred to me before?

A baby is never quite a reality while you're carrying it, but for this woman—and for me—even the pregnancy was hardly real. We both watched it happen to someone else. The difference between us was that she remembered everything that had happened to her; it was painful, and she wanted to forget. I still hoped to remember.

The imperative now was to tell Jil about Quint, which I knew would be painful for her. She seemed delighted to think Jake was her birth father; now he might not be. In a way, she had only half a story, and half of a complete set of parents. She had to begin all over again, and I hoped the story I told wouldn't be too difficult, too hurtful. And I wondered what she would think of me, knowing the whole story of my marriage and pregnancy. From another point of view, geographically, Jake was relatively far away, while we were here, in the midst of a storm of personal history. He was safe and dry and untouched. She was out in the weather, and, less so, I was, too.

After we left the restaurant where we met, I told Jil that I felt I had an *A* branded on my forehead, for "Adulteress."

"No," Jil said. "*A* is for Adoption."

Though Jil and Jake had spoken on the phone several times, they hadn't met yet. Before they did, Jil asked me to visit her house. No one else was there; I loved the house—lots of bright colors, warmth, a feeling of family and of love. There were drawings and paintings by her children, Alex and Damien, everywhere, big, bold, bright colors, done by happy children.

Afterward, as I drove Jil to Alex's school where she was to meet him, she said, "I'm really sorry I didn't feed you," because we hadn't had lunch. Without thinking, I said, "I'm really sorry I gave you away." It just came out of my mouth, without a moment's thought. I meant it, though I knew she wouldn't be the marvelous person she was if the adoption hadn't happened.

Jake drove down from Maine to spend a weekend in the city. He and Jil liked each other enormously, as they had on the phone. For Jil, Jake was "decent, warm, charming, and romantic." She didn't see the other side; but then, for a long time I hadn't, either.

They talked about the possibility that he was not her father. They decided that the only thing to do was have a DNA test.

The next day, after they'd had the test, but before there were results, the three of us met at a bar near Jil's house. Jake and I got there first so we could talk for a few minutes alone; we hadn't seen each other in decades. "If we were still married," I thought, "we'd be Mr. and Mrs. Jack Spratt—he's so thin! (And I'm so not.)" I teased him about the toothpaste tube—the only thing we'd ever really argued about. He didn't like being teased.

On her way to meet us, Jil stepped on a piece of paper folded in half on the sidewalk. It stuck to her shoe. She unpeeled it, and read in a large headline: "They are your parents." It was a flier advertising a play. She was delighted. The results of the DNA test seemed like destiny.

Jake told a lot of our stories to Jil, who seemed to love hearing them. He remembered different things than I did, which is one of the great things about remembering together; you get to see more pieces of the puzzle. But he also seemed to have forgotten many things that had stayed in my mind: the name of our hotel in Paris, or the name of the street where we changed our money: Rue du Roi de Sicile. He remembered Pierre, though, and that his place was called Pierre's Coca Cola Bar. I wondered how Pierre had ended up. Did he make a fortune? He certainly had been a schemer—a survivor, a charmer. He had probably been arrested for something or other, and had died in jail. No! He escaped! He paid someone, bribed someone, knew someone, and escaped! He had offered to find me an abortionist! What would have happened if I had said yes? No Jil, for sure. And no me, maybe.

About a month after the day Jake had called with the message about a letter from a stranger, my husband and I had dinner with Jil and her husband, Lenny. Though I had a raging cold, and sneezed my way through dinner, I loved being there. I liked Lenny enormously. He has a great face, and beautiful eyes. He seemed kind and smart and sweet. He's also funny—an irresistible combination. They make a good couple: He's thin, wiry, and dark, and Jil is plump—soft and zaftig—and fair. They seem right together.

There we were, the four of us, in the middle of Queens, eating good Greek food in a restaurant with white lace curtains. "Who wrote this script?" I asked in my journal the next morning.

"I still don't want to stop looking at her. I have to pull my eyes away, stop myself from memorizing, implanting every line in the lineaments of this face....

"What richness! I feel so fortunate. She could have been anybody, and instead, she's Jil."

Less than two weeks later, Jil wrote me with the DNA test results: Jake was definitely not her father. She sounded upset and disappointed, but, she said later, not surprised.

I was surprised; in fact, I was shocked. Then I realized I would have been surprised either way. If Jake been her father, I would have been both glad and sorry, and that's how I felt now about Quint, too; I'd rather leave all that behind me. On a very different level, because Jil is so much fonder of her father than her mother, I was afraid Quint might easily eclipse me. He's a well-known writer now, and comes with an aura of glamour and success. I knew not all of this thinking was rational; that it was, at the very least, very self-involved. But there it was.

Jil and I e-mailed each other almost daily. For a long time, I saved our notes. I have them still, a tall pile of paper that was another kind of beginning, through the written word rather than on the phone or in person. At first, the e-mail notes were an exploration, and a reaching out and a revealing of self, part of getting to know each other in ways both trivial and profound, the first cement applied to our growing relationship. Our e-mail conversation continues, and still gives me an enormous amount of pleasure.

Through all of it—the first telephone calls, the meetings, and the e-mail notes—it wasn't terribly long before I realized that it would never be possible near the end of my life to find the daughter I'd lost close to the beginning. The Baby is what I lost, and The Baby could never be given back to me; I could never find her, no matter how long or deeply I searched. But it was thrilling to get to know Jil, even so.

She can never take away all the pain and all the loss that I felt about The Baby. Nor can I take away her sorrow and anger. Those feelings were real; they were there. They're considerably softer for me now because of Jil, but when I look at the photographs she gave me of herself when she was a baby, there is still, and always will be, a profound sense of loss. Though I can be joyful at her presence in my life, nothing can completely erase the memory of what was.

It must have been the same for her. Getting to know her was indeed a healing process, although it didn't always feel that way. Often, it felt more like a gift, an enormous gift, unconnected to all that had gone before—and to the pain that had now become only a memory.

26. JIL

FATHERS

A week later, Jake came to New York. Since he wouldn't arrive until late in the evening, we planned to meet for breakfast the next day; but when he called to say he'd arrived, and to confirm our breakfast plan, neither of us could wait. We decided to meet at the bar of a restaurant on my corner.

I hadn't gone *out* at 10:00 p.m. since college. I was so excited I all but ran down the street. From the phone calls and letters, I felt I knew him already. I'd even seen pictures—*he did look like Jason Robards!* I loved his letters, so dramatic and intense. Even his handwriting was romantic. I'd gotten an envelope filled with photos of him and his family just a day or two earlier.

"I want to say the right thing," he wrote, "but I have so many conversations in my head with you I sometimes get to feeling presumptuous. It is also partly that it has been so easy to talk with you on the phone—astounding, really, when you think about it—that I feel I am writing to someone I *do* know."

Sometimes he sounded like a long-lost love: "What we need badly is to meet—to talk about us, and about a thousand other things." But he also warned me: "Hyperbole is my middle name. I promise to try to curb it, at least until you know me better."

When I walked into the restaurant, there he was: tall, lean, with wire-rimmed glasses and a dark moustache. He looked like Jason Robards crossed with Kurt Vonnegut. He had a great smile, crooked and flirtatious, and a seductive way of leaning in and locking eyes. We hugged madly, like two old, dear friends, then sat and talked and drank and smoked and laughed. It was a continuation of the long, rambling, easy conversations we'd been having on the phone, and the connection was palpable. We loved the way we made each other feel. At 1:00 a.m. they put the chairs up on the tables, and sadly, we said good-night.

He was only in New York for a few days, and I spent nearly every minute with him. After breakfast on the second day, we went for the DNA test, which was a simple swipe of the inside of our cheeks with a swab. We'd have to wait a few weeks for the results. But by lunch on day two, we were convinced we didn't need any test to tell us what we were to each other: This connection had to be based on something: blood, genes. It was fate.

"It has to be, right?" I asked at least ten times a day.

"Of course," he answered every time. "It has to be."

We joked about it: If it turned out he wasn't my birth father (and he would be, of course), he would adopt me. I'd been adopted before, I could be adopted again.

Or I would adopt *him*. We pondered the possibilities.

The next afternoon, he and Faith met at a bar in my neighborhood. I decided to give them some time alone first. Both of them said they wanted me there, to ease the tension, but I insisted on coming a half-hour into their reunion.

Walking there, nervous, feeling as awkward as the first time I met Faith, I stepped on a piece of paper that stuck to my shoe. I pulled it off just outside the entrance to the bar; it was a leaflet advertising a local play. "They're your parents, for heaven's sake," it said. Fate? Clearly.

The meeting felt awkward. What a trio we made: mom and dad and adult daughter—insta-family. I could tell that Jake was nervous; he told long meandering stories that didn't seem to be about much: children on a bus, going to school, their expectant faces like sunflowers; mothers fixing buttons, tying shoes; the loveliness of New York in winter. Faith was quiet. I was uncomfortable. I wanted to have my relationships with them, but I didn't want to be part of their relationship. It seemed like they were disappointed with each other, and their disappointment disappointed me.

The next day at lunch at a little Mexican restaurant, Jake told me the story of his sister's death. It was a tobogganing accident, he said, when she was sixteen and he was nineteen. Though he wasn't there, Jake knew so many details—the moon on the snow, the friends calling to each other, the car that came around a corner too quickly—that I began to wonder how he could know all this, and remember it fifty years later. He began to get choked up, and then to cry. I watched him as he dabbed his eyes, rubbed his jaw, stared mournfully out the window, and then glanced back at me, as if checking the audience's reaction.

This is a set piece, I thought, he's done it before. I was engaged by his performance, but not moved by his story. I could never imagine talking this way of my own sibling's death. I told people about my brother's suicide, but I'd never gotten this emotional in the telling. It felt wrong to me, showy and fake.

Jake had brought some of his work. Later on, in my apartment, he laid out portraits, wedding pictures, and headshots for newspapers. He seemed both proud and hesitant: proud that he'd chosen his best work to display, and hesitant because he wanted me to like it, to approve of him. At one time he'd had big dreams. Though he was doing good work, it wasn't the work he'd planned. Was all this—me, Faith, the history—pulling him back to a time in his life he didn't really want to remember, a hopeful time that made the reality of the present seem disappointing?

He looked around my living room, at the pictures of my kids, our families, places we've traveled.

"You took all these?" he asked.

"Yes," I said, "except for that one," pointing to a smiling shot of Alex on the beach taken by a friend.

"They're very well done," he said appraisingly. "You've got a good eye."

I was inordinately pleased. A pat on the back from my birth dad!

"Must be genetic," he said. I agreed.

When he left for home the next day, I gave him a Valentine's Day present for his wife, and an old book of poetry I'd had since high school.

A few days later I got a letter from him with more photos.

"As I headed north," he wrote, "I had the constant feeling I was making a big mistake, that I was headed in the wrong direction."

We talked on the phone and wrote long letters to each other. He didn't have e-mail yet, and he loved writing letters. He was good at it. He thought I was, too. He wrote, "I feel positively exalted reading your letters," and I nearly swooned. And then, he promised, no matter what the DNA test said, "I'm not going away."

In another letter, he told me of his reaction to the first letter I'd sent him, the letter I sent to all the John Aylfords. He picked it up and looked at the return address: He didn't know anyone named Picariello in New York. Was it from a former student? He opened it and at first he wondered if the letter was a con. Then he got to the next-to-last paragraph and began to pay attention.

"It was truly like waking up from a very complicated and confounding dream, and I said the word 'Jessica' out loud. Then I was instantly out of my chair, bursting with joy and gratitude and curiosity and awe and many unnameable feelings that maybe only you and Bunny could name. The last word, the only word in the whole letter in italics; I stared at it over and over in admiration."

It seemed a million years ago that I'd written that letter. But, in reality, it was only a couple of months earlier that I sat staring at my computer, changing "*know*" to "know" and back again. I was a completely different person then, I thought.

He sent photos of me taken when he visited, and wrote, "These snapshots are not exactly memorable. I had to have something, though, even though it wasn't the time or place. Sometime I hope you'll let me do it right."

And then: "I could make a career of writing to you. Your letters are so astounding, so rich with everything you are. " But it was hard, he wrote, to find the time to write. "Maybe the answer at the moment is to try to write frequent short letters instead of infrequent long ones. Can you please be a little patient with me as I try to work this out?"

Was I already a burden? But how could it be? I was "astounding," he said. "What I would like best of all is to live around the corner from you," he wrote. "Jil, I miss you so."

I wrote back and mentioned walking the dog early one morning and seeing all the buildings along Central Park West gleaming in the sunlight from the east. He sent me a yellowed copy of a local newspaper from 1960 called the *Brooklyn Heights Press*. Above the logo on the front page it said, "A Photographer's Affair with Brooklyn Bridge—Page 9." Inside were four faded photos of the bridge, and a quote from Jake, saying that dawn was when he loved the bridge the most, "when it looks like the city is burning up in the rising sun and the tops of skyscrapers catch the light first like flares on Wall Street."

In the letter he wrote, "I am sending you this because of the thing you saw when you were taking your dog for a walk in the park, the flaming tops of the buildings. Even though it's something that happens all the time, I don't think I ever heard anybody else ever mention it like that. I felt as though I'd written the line…. I told my friend Tim about it, kind of as an example of our instantaneous attraction and ease with one another (you and me, I mean), our being on the same wavelength, our thirst for talk, as if we had known each other all our lives. I claimed you might have heard me talking through the womb, and he agreed…. We had to find each other, and we did."

A few days later, the doctor called with the DNA results: There was no possibility that Jake was my father.

How could it be? How could we feel this way about each other and *not* be connected? I called Jake. He had little to say, just disbelief—but not disappointment. Disappointment would have implied that this made a difference, and we were resolute that it would not.

That night I wrote him: "What it boils down to for me is fear that our feelings will change with this change in 'status'—fear that my feelings for you will change or (the bigger fear) that yours for me will change. This may seem strange to you, but I would like you to promise me that if your feelings do change, you will tell me, to free me from wonder and doubt. Besides whatever you are to me in my heart, you are, officially, my birth stepfather. You cannot imagine how I felt when I saw your name in the 1954 book of records. These moments are like totems, or charms. They have incredible power. I say my birth name to myself over and over. It means a great deal to me."

A few days later, Lenny and I went out to dinner with Faith and her husband, who looked like a '50s movie star, one of those crew-cutted boy-next-door-handsome guys like Glenn Ford or Van Johnson. I was nervous; Faith was more nervous. Thank goodness for Lenny, who could meet the pope and the president (simultaneously) and not blink. Over halloumi cheese and skordalia at a little Greek restaurant in Astoria, Queens, we chatted about food and travel and books and movies. At one point, I asked the men if they saw a resemblance between Faith and me, and they both nodded vigorously.

Lenny noticed Faith staring at me; she grinned. "It gives me so much pleasure just to look at your wife," she said. I felt bathed in warmth.

The thought of meeting Quint Phillips did not bathe me in warmth. But having come this far, I was determined to go all the way. Surprisingly, I found an address for him in the Manhattan phone directory, as well as a telephone number, though I was much too nervous to call. What would I say? *Hi, Quint—er, Mr. Phillips—this is the baby that you may remember being told you might have conceived in Stuttgart in 1954.*

I wrote what I hoped was a gentle letter, explaining who I was, and that thanks to the modern miracle of DNA, I was sure he was my birth father. I asked him to call me. One sunny cold afternoon, I took it to his building on the Upper East Side. It wasn't what I expected: modern, showy, with two doormen and a concierge. It looked like a building for rich transients and wealthy foreigners, not lifelong New Yorkers. The concierge was friendly to me, an obviously nervous woman. Maybe he thought I was a recently released mental patient, or one of the people who stalks famous men, like the woman who kept moving herself into David Letterman's house.

"Does Quint Phillips live here?" I asked. What a stupid question, I thought, there's no way they're allowed to say who lives in a posh building like this.

But he answered immediately. "Yes, he does."

I handed him the letter, and he walked it over to a bank of mailboxes.

I thanked him and left. In the little pocket park next door, I sat for ten minutes, just to get my breath.

I went home and waited for the call. When it hadn't come three days later, Faith decided to call him.

"Maybe he's afraid you're some kind of stalker," she said. "Or that you're after his money."

My motives were so clear to me; it seemed unimaginable that he would think anything different. Faith left a message on his machine: "I know you've received a letter from Jil, and I want to talk to you about her."

He called her back that afternoon. "Who's Jil?" It turned out that he'd been in Los Angeles for the past week and had no idea what she was talking about.

It hadn't occurred to Faith that she would have to tell him the whole story, but she did.

He called me an hour later, "Jil, this is Quint." His voice seemed strangely familiar from hearing it on television. He seemed relaxed, as if we were talking about a job or a play we'd seen.

At one point I said, "You seem so calm," and he answered, "What did you imagine I would do, burst into tears?"

"Aren't you shocked?" I asked. "Surprised?"

"Not really. I've always had it in the back of my mind that something like this might happen."

I found that hard to believe—he seemed so distanced from the whole idea of me. I couldn't imagine that he'd ever thought about it at all.

He asked me a few questions about the search and how I found him, where I lived, where I grew up. I asked him about his parents, his family. His replies were brief: He'd been married twice, no kids, and had lived with the same woman for the last twenty years. He had never told her about me, and said he would wait until he got back to New York to tell her in person.

"How do you think she'll react?" I asked.

He chuckled. "I can't even imagine."

At the end of the short conversation, he said we could get together when he was back in New York and have lunch and "stare at each other." Then he gave me his number in LA and said that I should feel free to call him and "add or subtract anything" if I wanted to.

As I said good-bye and hung up, I realized I'd had more emotional conversations with my dry cleaner.

A week later we met for lunch at the Museum of Modern Art. "So we can smoke," he said, when he called to set it up. "It's one of the few places left."

I was standing outside the museum, nervously waiting, the sidewalk crowded with tourists and office workers on their way out for lunch, when it suddenly occurred to me that I might not recognize him. I should have found a recent photo of him online, I thought: too late. There were dozens of women standing around, waiting for friends, lunch dates. He couldn't recognize me. I was supposed to recognize *him*.

I was nearing a full-fledged panic attack when a small man in a baseball cap walked up. "Jil?" he asked.

We kissed politely and made our way to the museum restaurant. I felt ridiculously awkward. I prayed I wouldn't dribble or drop my fork.

We had both brought some family photos—good props. He spread his out on the table. There was his father, dark and masculine, sitting with little Quint on the lawn of a grand home, while his mother, a beauty, stood next to a car. There was an adorable little Quint in boarding school uniform, the freckle on his nose clearly visible. I showed him pictures of myself as a child, a teen, my husband and children.

He told me he had no siblings, no cousins. "In fact, you're my only blood relative," he said.

"Not exactly," I said, pointing to a photo of my sons. "You have two grandsons."

"I guess I do," he said indifferently.

He was more surprised by my interests, which were the same as his. I told him that from earliest childhood I wanted to be a writer. I told him about going to film school, writing poems and short stories, acting in high school and college. He shook his head in amazement.

He told me about his childhood, which sounded lonely, growing up in New York City, with well-off parents who ran with a heady crowd and didn't seem all that interested in their only child. He talked about finding out in college that his father was Jewish, which was a shock, and about getting started in show business. When I asked him about meeting Jake and Faith, he didn't seem to remember much. It was a long time ago, he said, and over so quickly.

After lunch, I thought I'd walk home through the park to calm down. I entered at Seventh Avenue and 59th Street, so wired and tense I almost missed a beautiful white bird, sitting in the middle of a swath of lawn—an egret in Central Park? It opened enormous wings and glided smoothly away over the baseball fields.

I exited the park at 91st Street and Central Park West and suddenly had all the wind blown out of me. I stumbled to a bench and fell onto it. Staring across at the elegant twin towers of the El Dorado, I started to cry. All the pent-up energy of meeting Quint had escaped like air from a broken balloon, flown off like the egret into the sky, and I crashed. I felt weathered, depleted. I sat there sniffling and moaning softly for ten minutes, then picked myself up and shuffled slowly home.

I wasn't working full time, and both my kids were in school, so Faith and I saw each other frequently, nearly every week, sometimes twice a week, writing endless e-mails in between. We were enthralled with each other. "You are wonderful, wonderful," she wrote to me in her almost daily e-mails. "You are wonderful, too," I wrote back. We said it to each other so often, we finally acronymed it: YAW and YAW2. I knew someday reality would hit; I would figure out that she was just a person, flaws and foibles along with all the wonder. But at the beginning it was like falling in love, and falling in self-love, too. This is who made me! This is what I am made of! And it is remarkable and delightful.

We marveled continually at how alike we were. After a few weeks, we started keeping "The List of Similars." We both...

Hated heights, especially small ones—couldn't go higher than two steps on a ladder.

Never vomited.

Had the same smile, chin, larger lower lip, triangular smile.

Revered *Seinfeld*.

Loved food, joyously, passionately, exuberantly, excessively.

Loved to cook.

Had difficult mother relationships (like 99 percent of the women in the world).

Loved movies, theater, books, travel.

Loved show tunes.

Laughed at the same things.

Used (overused) the words *wonderful, amazing,* and *weird*.

Were compelled by the freakish and freaks, not personally, but voyeuristically.

Wrote words in the air or under the table when annoyed.

Adored small, cheap, totally unpretentious restaurants.

Liked to go to the movies alone.

Belonged to women's groups of various kinds (writing, reading, creative, consciousness-raising).

Were education activists, deeply involved in our children's schools.

Liked strong/spicy foods: garlic and onions, mustards and chutneys, Indian food and spicy Thai or Vietnamese.

Liked to stroke, pet, and otherwise fondle appealing surfaces, like a cool water glass or a velvet scarf.

Loved Kevin Kline, John Cleese, and homemade baked beans—not necessarily all together.

Disliked cloves, because they reminded us of the dentist's office.

Made the same hand gestures with the same small, plump hands.

Hated to go to sleep at night for the same reason: the fear of loss of consciousness that is like death.

Had absent, much-loved fathers and domineering mothers.

Loved being awake alone at night and feeling the sleeping, breathing, warm, safe quiet house.

Were overweight, and hated it.

Were gold-medal pouters as children.

Rereading the e-mails years later, our voices are so similar I have to look at the e-mail address on the top of the page to tell which of us has written. Sometimes I think we are like a science experiment: Nature versus Nurture. How much like a mother will a child be, if raised by a completely different person? Was I romanticizing this? Was I deluded? I look at the List of Similars and think about it all—the music, the books, the strange habits… *Kevin Kline*! Even as a disciple of the "Everything-is-socialization" school of life, I know nature has won this contest, plump little hands down.

For several weeks, I didn't hear from Quint. I wanted to talk to him, but wanted *him* to call *me*. I was like a teenage girl waiting for a call from the captain of the football team. My anxiety was aggravated by his celebrity. He had way groovier people than me to hang out with, I figured. He could go out to lunch with Warren Beatty or Bruce Willis. Why in heaven's name would he want to go to lunch with me?

I knew he was leaving for Los Angeles in a few days so I finally picked up the phone. We made a plan to meet the next day at a bookstore on Madison Avenue, and then have coffee. I arrived early, and perused book jackets while I waited for him to show up. "Reading for free?" he asked, sneaking up on me from behind.

He bought a book, asked me if I wanted anything. (So much, so much, I said silently.) Walking to the café, we talked about our mutual foot problems (he had just come from the podiatrist). Over cappuccino, we discussed movies. Other than *The Third Man*, which we both loved, our opinions were nearly always opposite: The ones he loved, I could barely stand; the ones he despised, I adored. What would we put on our List of Similars: bad feet and cigarettes?

Our taste in books was entirely different as well. I asked him what book he would take if he were to be stranded on a desert island and he chose Proust's *Remembrance of Things Past*, because he wanted to reread it, and because it's long—a very practical choice. We talked about the books we loved as children. The first books he could remember liking were the Oz books, especially *The Marvelous Land of Oz*, and the character of Tip, who changes magically from a young boy to a grown woman. I loved the Oz books, but always found that change, and *The Marvelous Land of Oz*, deeply disturbing.

I asked him what he was like as a child.

"Secretive," he said quickly.

"Solitary?" I asked.

"Yes, although I had friends. But definitely secretive."

He did not invite personal questions, nor did he ask them of me. Instead, he told me the story of his career, from the Army to a flat in Greenwich Village to his early struggling years, to work in television, then movies. He was a good storyteller. We left the café around 5:00 p.m. and walked down Madison Avenue toward his apartment.

At the corner, I gathered my courage to ask something more personal.

"How do you feel about…" I couldn't think of a word.

"Our situation?" he said. I nodded. "I don't know."

"It's so hard to look at you and Faith and truly realize who you are to me," I said.

"I'm sure it's hard for you. You're putting together the pieces of who you are."

He was right. "But," I said. "Faith is really the only one of us who's lived with the reality of this. You and I are new to it. So why does it seem harder for me?"

"There's no downside for me," he said, which wasn't really what I had asked. "It doesn't matter to me if people know or not."

Was that the most important element to him?

He'd told his girlfriend and his closest friend, an actor I had a huge crush on when I was in college, and a couple of other good friends in LA. "And, of course, the whole world will know after I take out that ad," he said, smiling.

"A full page in the *Times* would be nice."

He laughed. "Kind of costly, don't you think?"

"Hey," I teased. "You didn't pay for college, and you didn't pay for my wedding. I don't think a full page in the *Times* is too much to ask."

He seemed tickled.

"So where do we go from here?" I asked.

"I didn't know I had any options."

"There are always options."

"Like what?"

I enumerated: "We shake hands, thank each other for a lovely time, and never see each other again."

He shook his head. "Ridiculous."

I breathed a sigh of relief. "Option two: We move in together and try to relive the last forty-two years."

He laughed. "That might be problematic. How about option three: We just keep going?"

As we strolled the last block down Madison Avenue, I took his arm, which felt like an enormous act of bravery. We kissed at the corner and he told me he would call from LA. I took hold of his collar and said, "I like you."

"You're genetically predisposed to like me," he said.

"No," I said. "I'm genetically predisposed to *want* to like you. The fact that I do is a bonus."

As I walked away I realized that the only right answer to "I like you" is "I like you, too." That wasn't the answer I got.

Every meeting with Quint exhausted me. He made me nervous, insecure, itchy for something I never got. It was as if I were constantly reaching out and grabbing smoke. Although our lunches—always lunch or coffee, never dinner, never even a suggestion of a movie, a show, meeting my husband, my meeting his girlfriend— were friendly and pleasant, there was little warmth. He told wonderful tales, stories of celebrities and movie sets, but seemed uninterested in my life, my family. He was friendly, but distant.

With Faith and Jake, I'd realized immediately I could ask them anything. Quint felt far away. All I wanted was for him to like me. Why was I so needy, and so damn insecure?

Every time we met, I had to stop somewhere on the way home and compose myself. Depleted, my throat sore from too many cigarettes, ashamed of myself for feeling like a lovesick teenager, I would wonder whose life I had stepped into. I was living in a bad miniseries, I decided. Life doesn't imitate art; it imitates soap operas.

Jake had stopped writing and calling. I wasn't comfortable calling him because he was nervous about his children answering the phone and asking who I was. I got frustrated and angry when he didn't respond to my letters. I was surrounded by disappointing father figures.

But Faith was there, solid and loving and responsive. Everything we learned about each other just spun the connection between us tighter and tighter. I wrote her: "As much as I look forward to a time when things between us are natural, I do enjoy the thrill of now when it is new. The rush of emotion—it's like having a baby or falling in love or that rare meeting of friends that doesn't happen often in adulthood. If I didn't have children and a husband, I probably would have moved in with you by now."

There seemed to be nothing we couldn't say to each other. She wrote: "I can't stand the idea of having lost you, of not having seen you when you were a baby and a child and a girl and a young woman—and of not having been there when you were unhappy and alone. It is very difficult to ask you to forgive me. Having been found is redeeming, but it doesn't take the pain away. Yet it's absolutely wonderful. When you ask me to make three guesses about my birthday gift, I want to say: You, You, and You."

Her e-mails were long and juicy, filled with stories and details. I wrote her: "Do you know what I do first when I get an e-mail from you? I scroll down without reading a word just to see how long it is—like counting all the chocolates in the box before you eat a single one, getting ready for something delicious. Then I read it. Then I read it again. Then I open a reply and keep yours open next to it so I can make sure to respond to everything in the right order, and fully."

In the fall of that year, Alex started second grade and Damien started high school. I met Quint for lunch in September. He had been to China and brought back two presents for me. I was very pleased that he brought me gifts, but the gifts themselves disturbed me: a set of plastic place mats with Chinese art reproduced on them, and a blindingly bright purple sweatshirt with a yellow satin flag appliqué, neither of which I would ever wear or use. They seemed like gifts for a completely different person.

I tried hard to be happy that he thought to bring me a gift at all, and thanked him. But the gifts depressed me. They seemed to be emblematic of the fact that we had not connected at all. He thought I was someone else, someone who ate off ugly plastic place mats and wore garish sweatshirts. It made me wonder why I was there, having lunch with this strange, chilly man. What was the connection between us? Were we trying to make something out of nothing? Was he really anything more than a sperm donor?

Faith told me that Jake was coming to New York for a memorial service, and had called to set up a visit with her while he was here. I didn't hear from him. What had happened here? Where had he gone? Had I done something? No, I concluded, his feelings had changed after the DNA results. And all that blather about our powerful connection—what was that? Charm and sparkle and bull? I was angry, so angry that when Jake finally sent an e-mail, two days before arriving, my first reaction was to tell him I was busy. But after thinking about it, I decided I did want to see him, and e-mailed back to set a time.

It was a strange meeting. He brought me more photos, but this time they were of Quint from when they were in Germany, sitting at a typewriter, in uniform, at a table in a restaurant. It was like he was trying to step out of the picture by introducing me to the new star of the show. He told stories from their time in the Army, his marriage to Faith, what went wrong. It made me unhappy and confused. Was he giving me up? Walking away? Did I care?

He seemed sad to me now, all the charm worn away, like gold plate rubbed off dull lead. He started to tell me the story of his wedding night, something clearly sexual, and I stopped him. "I don't want to know about that," I said. "Of course, of course," he muttered, shaking his head. It felt like he didn't know who I was, or why he was with me.

Later, Faith told me that Jake said little about our meeting, except this: "Jil is the best thing that happened to me this year."

Then why did it feel like he was walking away from me?

By October, my relationships with my birth fathers had disintegrated to cards: postcards from Quint, and a note from Jake, who apologized for not keeping in touch. I met Quint for another lunch. He told me for the third or fourth time that I was his only blood relative. I reminded him again that he had two grandsons.

"Oh, right," he said, as if this were irrelevant information. "What are their names again?"

The last time I heard from Quint was a postcard from Cuba. "Lunch when I get back," it said behind a colorful picture of Havana. I never heard from him again. From time to time I see him on television. Once I went to the movies without knowing he had written the film, and when his name appeared on the huge screen, I gasped so loudly that a woman two rows down shushed me. It was like something secret and shameful had suddenly burst out into the open. Sometimes when I come upon him on television, I change the channel quickly. Sometimes I stare hard, trying to see a resemblance. I never do.

But over the months and years, I felt more and more connected to Faith. The first year, for our birthdays, we took each other to the theater. It occurred to me sadly that I would never think of taking my mother to a show. We had never discussed a book we'd both read. In fact, we rarely discussed anything, because most discussions ended with me feeling criticized and angry.

One weekend around Thanksgiving, my kids slept at my parents' house for a night. My mother and father brought them home on Sunday and stayed for dinner. Walking down the hall toward the kitchen, I heard my mother whispering to Lenny, the whisper I'd heard my whole life from around a corner, up the stairs, down the hall.

"He's just like *she* was at that age," I heard her say, and I knew she was talking about Damien, now a teenager, and me. "I really pity you."

I didn't even hear Lenny's answer. I turned on my heel and went upstairs. *I am wonderful, wonderful,* I said to myself. *Wonderful*—and strangely, I thought of the story of the ugly duckling.

I went into Alex's room and took the book of Hans Christian Andersen stories down from the shelf. From the beginning, the story says, the poor little bird was doomed—his egg was bigger than the others in Mother Duck's nest and took longer to hatch. Mother Duck was advised to abandon the egg, but she waited patiently. At last he emerged, but she knew something was wrong with her baby. "How big and ugly he is," she said.

Though Mother Duck hesitantly accepted her ugly offspring, the rest of the duck community was less tolerant. They pushed him and bit him, chased and harassed him, called him a "hideous creature." His siblings wished the cat would get hold of him; the girl who fed the ducks kicked him aside. Eventually, even his mother gave up on him. "I wish to goodness you were miles away," she said. The poor little ugly duckling felt shame, he felt different… he felt *defective.*

He left home and tried to live with the wild ducks, who thought he was "frightfully ugly," but grudgingly accepted him as long as, they warned him, "You do not marry into our family." He fled and hid, cold and alone, searching for a place to belong.

In the spring he flew into a garden where he saw three swans drifting in the water. Overcome with a strange melancholy, he swam fearfully up to them. "Kill me!" he begged, and bowed his head. But when he bent his head to the water to die, he saw, for the first time, his reflection, and recognized the truth. He was really a beautiful swan. He was accepted by the swans. Children fed him, and people called him handsome. "I never dreamed of so much happiness when I was the ugly duckling," he said.

I stared at the watercolor image of the beautiful swan. It was the adoptee fantasy, come true: I have found my family and they are better, more powerful, more beautiful than those with whom I was once forced to live. My mother didn't understand me, but it wasn't because she didn't want to. And it wasn't because there was something wrong with me; it was because she couldn't. She wasn't supposed to; I am not hers. I am not defective, I am not flawed, I am not wrong. I am a *swan*.

27. BUNNY

EVERY WOMAN IS A DAUGHTER

Children begin by loving their parents;

as they grow older, they judge them;

sometimes they forgive them.

OSCAR WILDE

THE PICTURE OF DORIAN GRAY

There was a little girl

And she had a little curl

Right in the middle of her forehead.

And when she was good,

She was very, very good;

And when she was bad,

She was horrid.

Those are the lines that both Jil's mother and mine felt perfectly described each of us. I actually *had* a clump of hair that curled onto the middle of my forehead.

What the rhyme meant in earlier years was approval. When I was good (when I did what my mother wanted me to do), I was very, very good. The rest of the time I was horrid. On my own side of the forehead, I wanted to do what I wanted, no matter how far from my mother's wishes that might be; but—and this is a huge BUT—I still wanted to be approved of. I wanted to be considered "very, very good" simply because I was me.

I never doubted that my mother loved me. She just found me different—and difficult. She felt it was her responsibility to mold me—to fix me—and to equip me for all of life's difficulties yet to come. A refrain I heard many times: "I'm your mother. I love you. But no one else ever will if you behave that way."

The struggle between us was simple: She wanted me to match her expectations, and I wanted to be me. Neither of us was quite fair, and between us, we made an unhappy circle—my mother would have approved of me if I had been different, and if I really wanted to be approved of, I knew I had to be.

I knew my mother found me to be a difficult child; and somewhere, somehow, I thought she must have good reason. The seesaw was always between good and horrid; I never stayed in the middle for very long.

My mother gave me many good things: Her love, even without her approval, was first. Second was the intensity she provided that helped me make my own mold—sometimes, yes, in opposition to her, but no less valuable for all of that.

My father was different. I'm not sure that I would describe him as "approving," but he was definitely accepting, and that mattered a lot. He worked very long hours—like Jil's father—and wasn't home at reasonable (for a child) hours. Partly because of that, he was like an adoring uncle, a personal Santa Claus, rather than a disciplining father. I don't remember him ever telling me not to do something, except once: At the height (or depth) of adolescence, he asked me to try not to upset my mother so much.

I think there are many daughters who, like me, adored their fathers and struggled with their mothers. Daughters are so often angry at their mothers, and forgiving of their fathers. Fairy tales tell the same story: It's the wicked stepmother who won't let Cinderella go to the ball; it's the jealous queen who tries to murder Snow White in the forest. Hansel and Gretel are sent away by their stepmother, but clever Gretel saves them by pushing the witch into her own oven (oh! the symbols!). In "Beauty and the Beast," as in so many tales, the father is loving but weak.

The story line of *The Prince of Tides* is a striking example. The father was a bastard—violent, angry, and not quite sane; the mother protected her children as best she could. The cure for the grown child comes when he is able to tell his father than he loves him, and to tell his mother that he's angry at her. Yes, it's more complicated than that, but this is what it boils down to. The grown child needs to break through father-anger to love, and mother-love to anger. The triumph is love for the father and, at best, forgiveness for the mother.

For small children, mothers have an enormous amount of power. It isn't difficult to understand a child's anger: She sent me to my room, she won't let me stay up late, she makes me eat food I don't like, she's always telling me what to do. The relationship is harder for daughters and mothers; from a Freudian point of view, after all, they love the same man; but that's only a small part of the story. Aside from sheer chemistry, sons are part of "the other" for their mothers, and many boys are much more openly loving than are their sisters, who save their adoration for daddy.

The long and short of it is that mothers can be dumped on. Even in cases of childhood abuse, the mother is often blamed for not keeping the child safe; and she's as much resented for that as the perpetrator is for whatever he may have done. The exercise of power has to do with control and guilt; safety has to do with love.

As parents, most of us start out wanting to do well. We each want to be the best mother of all, the most loving, the most approving, supportive, understanding. No one wakes up in the morning and thinks, "Today I'm going to mess up my children." But it happens anyway, and mess up we do.

When my children were small, I thought I was a perfect parent. Now I know I wasn't. Further, and not just to excuse myself, I believe there really isn't any such thing as a perfect parent, not even a *nearly* perfect parent. There isn't any way a child's needs can be perfectly met: No one has enough love (or time) to fill every moment of childish desire, demand, and want, and children, on the other hand, live in a world of perception and emotion that is by definition childlike, and to an adult, too often irrational and inexplicable. For parents, the scales of love—the balance—is elusive. Too much love is smothering; too little can be fatal.

It cannot have been easy to have been my child. But I think one of the best and hardest things about being a mother is that, as you go along, doing what you think is best, you are full of earnest conviction, eagerness, and—yes—love; meanwhile, your children's currents are often running in another direction. That's just the way it is. That's why if you think about what you've done wrong as a mother, you'll have one list, and if you ask your children, and they're willing to tell you, they will have a completely different one.

I wish I could do motherhood over again. I'm an adult now: I wasn't always then. Growing up turned out to take much longer that I thought it would; I think, somehow, one expects it to happen by a certain date: maybe with your first vote, or after graduation from college, or maybe to come along with your first full-time paycheck. Certainly it's not a wedding present. Nor is it in a box wrapped in pink and blue paper to be opened at the baby shower.

Growing up, it turns out, requires work, as well as determination, persistence, dignity, courage, and humor—and just plain time. It would have been much better if I had finished the process before I had children, but I didn't. Yes, I wish I could do motherhood over. I definitely have a list of things I regret, moments that will make me cringe forever, much that I wish I could undo or redo. But we're stuck with who we were, and what we did or left undone.

Losing Jil was the first thing I did wrong for my children. Her loss reverberated through everything else, sometimes consciously, most often below the surface of awareness. I was still a child when that happened, but I'm responsible for it even so; and I hope I've been forgiven.

I can imagine—though I'd much rather not—not knowing Jil. After all, there were a great many years, more than four decades, when I *didn't* know her. But I cannot imagine that she doesn't exist.

I would not want anyone to read what I've written here and think I believe that for a woman who is pregnant with a child she can't keep, adoption is a better option than abortion. No matter what your belief about the moment of conception, there is always a choice to make. No one makes it easily; no one chooses abortion with any pleasure. But for most of those who do, the pain does not linger throughout their lives: They aren't haunted by memories or birthdays. Yes, that bit of life, smaller than a walnut, might have been a child: but there's a vast difference between "might have been" and the reality of a baby. The loss of a healthy newborn is a hurt that never leaves. I'm not saying that either option is correct; but I do believe that adoption is, finally, more difficult, more painful, than abortion—which is not a reason not to choose it. The choice I made was a relatively passive one, and left a residue of many years of sorrow and pain; but it is a choice I am so incredibly glad I made.

In her memoir *Borrowed Finery*, Paula Fox writes about her childhood and the ways in which her parents literally abandoned her. She grew up to have a child she was unable to keep, a daughter who was adopted as an infant. When they met as adults, they recognized each other immediately, as Jil and I had in that crowded restaurant on the Upper West Side. "I walked off the plane," Fox writes on the next-to-last page of her book, and describes meeting her daughter in the airport waiting room. "I found her beautiful. She was the first woman related to me I could speak to freely."

On the last page, Fox continues, "I have had splendid close friendships with women. What I had missed all the years of my life, up to the time when [we] met, was freedom of a certain kind: to speak without fear to a woman in my family."

Jil's existence, The Baby separate and real, was as urgent in its effect on me as her demands to be born, and the sharp spasms of my own womb had been twenty-four hours earlier. Her leave-taking, as her birth, was slow and painful, and her absence inevitably became a part of my life. But what Jil and I have now is so rare and so special, so full of closeness and joy, that in some ways, it's hard to remember the missing decades. How incredibly lucky I am now to have Jil as part of my life. I am filled with gratitude for all that we have and have always had—and our amazing good fortune in searching and in being found. I am grateful for Jil, both The Baby who was, and the woman who is.

28. JIL

MYSELF

The phone rang at 5:00 a.m., waking me.

"Your mother's breathing became very labored during the night," the resident on duty at Mount Sinai Hospital said. "We told her we thought she needed to be ventilated. She asked if we would sedate her to do that, and we said yes. She agreed, and we did the procedure. But we need to do some further tests, and we need your permission as her health care proxy."

"I don't understand," I said, sitting up, struggling to be calm. "I just saw her last night, and her breathing seemed okay."

"Yes, this began around midnight," he informed me.

The doctors had told her that they thought she might have clots in her lungs, but my mother had refused to do a CAT scan, as she had refused almost all treatment except painkillers; but after the doctors and I argued with her, she'd agreed to it. "But the CAT scan results showed that her lungs were clear," I said.

There was a pause. "What CAT scan?" he asked.

"The pulmonary doctor thought she had blood clots in her lungs so they did a CAT scan, and my mother told me it was clear."

"Your mother never gave permission for a CAT scan," he said. "We wanted to put her on blood thinners, just to be safe, but she wouldn't take them. We'd like to do the scan now—we need your permission for that, too."

I was stunned, but realized that this made perfect sense. My mother didn't capitulate. She just wanted to make me stop nagging her.

I didn't know what to say. It was perfectly obvious that my mother didn't want any treatment; but how could I say no to the CAT scan I'd been begging her to have for days? Especially since this wasn't even what was wrong with her. She was in the hospital for treatment of her *cancer*.

The doctor could hear my confusion.

"Look," he finally said. "I understand your mother can be…" He paused to search for the word: "challenging. We can deal with the immediate problem and help her breathe. Then we can talk about where to go from there."

"Okay," I said. "Do the CAT scan. I'll be there in about half an hour."

"Thanks."

"One more thing," I said. "Have the test results from the surgery come in yet?"

We'd been waiting for more than a week. The immediate results, taken in the OR, were fairly positive. The section tested showed that the tumor was a slow-growing type that would respond well to treatment. But, as the surgeon told me three times, we had to wait for the full test results to know what we were dealing with, especially with a tumor of this size. Despite his warning, I was trying very hard to be positive, if only to stem the tide of my mother's negativity. It was hard to be hopeful when my mother lay behind a frozen wall of silence, waiting to die.

My stomach was in a knot that had become permanent these last few weeks, ever since my mother called and said to come see her; she wasn't feeling well.

Her voice on the phone frightened me; the sight of her frightened me more. Sitting in the white leather bucket chair in the living room, she looked shrunken and stiff. She'd aged ten years since the last time I'd seen her, only two weeks before. She'd lost weight and her hair, always an immaculate blond helmet, was disheveled, one side flat against her head, the other puffed out, as if she had been napping. My mother does not nap. Her hands quivered in her lap like moths, and when she stood up she was bent over, hunched. Her skin even looked different, puckered, dry, and parched. How could someone change so much so quickly?

She had been to the doctor, she told me. I was hushed, shocked, by this announcement. My mother had never had a physical, a Pap smear, a mammogram, a check of her cholesterol, or a bone density test. Once, when I asked her if she was going to have a colonoscopy, she looked at me, lowered her eyebrows, and said, "What are you, nuts?" That was the end of that discussion.

She only *had* a doctor because years ago, her insurance company required a primary care physician's name on a form. Someone said they had a doctor who was "nice," so my mother put his name down. Surprisingly, he *was* nice, nice enough to keep my mother as a patient, even though she never allowed him to do more than take her blood pressure.

Now she had terrible pain in her abdomen, low down, below her stomach. When I asked her how long she'd had this pain, she swatted the air at me. "A while," she said. I pressed her.

"Days? Weeks?" I asked, incredulous. "Months?"

"Yes," she whispered, "a long time."

A CAT scan revealed that there was a "mass" that the radiologist said looked like an enlarged uterus.

"I haven't had a uterus since 1946," my mother said.

The nice doctor gave her the name of another doctor he wanted her to see. A gynecologic oncologist, she said once, and then we dropped the second half of his title. A gynecologist was as scary to my mother as an oncologist was to most people. The two words together were too much to bear.

"My doctor is going away," she told me for the fourth time. She was worried that the nice doctor wouldn't be around to care for her.

She had an appointment with the unnamed-type-of-gynecologist on Wednesday.

I told her I would go with her. "No," she said. "You don't have to do that."

"I *want* to do that."

"I need to save you," she said. Save me from the bad stuff, I wondered? No, save me *for* the bad stuff. "I'll need you later on." She had this all planned out. There wasn't even a diagnosis yet, but she had envisioned the tragedy that would follow, and my character wasn't onstage yet. I was being saved for the big scene in the last act, a small role, but key.

I made a pathetic attempt at optimism.

"Mom, why don't you try *not* to assume this is something horrible? It could end up being not such a big deal."

She didn't even hesitate. "I know what this is—I just *know*." My mother has always "just known" about everything: what boys really wanted, why drugs and liquor were bad, why *goyim* don't make good husbands, why Jews are smarter, why Israel is good and Arabs are bad, why her family is superior to other families, why margarine is better than butter, and why so many college graduates are "educated idiots."

She stared out the window as the afternoon grew darker. "I told the doctor I won't do chemo. Surgery, maybe; I might do radiation." She said this calmly, as if she were picking from a list of possible spa treatments. Though there hadn't even been a diagnosis yet, she already knew what she had, and how she would treat it.

As my husband and I got up to leave, my father watched from the top of the stairs, waving a big hand gently. He had taken to saying "I love you" a lot, which made me feel like a little girl. My mother waved from the dark room behind her. All I could see was a small silhouette against the big picture window.

In the last two days before her appointment, my mother did not get out of bed. A week earlier, she took Aleve for the pain. Now she was taking codeine, and it did nothing to alleviate her pain. It seemed incredible that something could progress from manageable with over-the-counter medication to invulnerable to prescription codeine in a mere two weeks.

The doctor's office was on Fifth Avenue, a very posh address. My mother had to lean against the wall to walk, slowly, with my father on the other side holding her up. She was pale, and her eyes were flat and dull.

In the small examining room I helped her to undress. I had never seen my mother naked. Folding her white panties, hanging up her pants, easing off her shoes, I was nauseated by the intimacy of this act.

I helped her into the thin cotton gown and onto the table. Her skin was icy and she was shaking. I was shaking, too. When the nurse came in to take her blood pressure and ask a few questions, we were both relieved to have another person in the room. I turned away to move to the far end of the little room, out of their way.

"No," she said. "Stay here by me."

I moved up near her head as the doctor entered, brisk but warm, introducing himself and making friendly chitchat before moving on to the serious business.

The standard questions elicited less-than-standard responses.

"When was your last Pap smear?" he asked.

"I've never had one," my mother said.

"When was your last mammogram?"

"I've never had that, either."

"Your last pelvic exam?"

"1950," my mother replied.

He looked up from his clipboard. "1950?"

"Yes," my mother said. "I had to get a physical when we went to the adoption agency to adopt my daughter." She looked at me. "They made me." Her voice was flat. "They have to make sure you're telling the truth about why you can't get pregnant."

"And you were telling the truth," he said, to confirm.

"I wasn't telling anything. I didn't know why I couldn't get pregnant."

He was confused.

"I had surgery when I was seventeen," she explained, "because I had very heavy periods, very painful. When the doctor from the adoption agency examined me, he told me I didn't have a uterus or a left ovary."

The doctor didn't react. "And how is your health generally?" he asked.

My mother said, "Ha," and rolled her eyes, as if this were one of the dumber questions she'd heard lately. "I'm in a lot of pain," she said.

He looked at the CAT scan. "Yes, I'm sure," he said. "But before this all started?"

"Okay, I guess," my mother replied. "I don't go to the doctor, so I don't know. But fine."

After I helped my mother put her naked feet into the stirrups, he said, as every gynecologist on earth says, "Okay, let's have a look."

My mother reached for my hand and I took her icy fingers in mine. It was the shortest pelvic exam I'd ever witnessed. The doctor briefly ran his hand across her abdomen, shrouded by the paper blanket, and said, "You can sit up," and to me, "Why don't you help your mom get dressed, and we'll talk in my office."

Silently she dressed and silently we sat and waited for him at the small round table in his cluttered office. There was a huge framed photo of the doctor crossing the finish line at the New York City Marathon. His hair was dark and he looked younger.

The doctor came in and pulled a chair up next to us.

"You have a very large abdominal mass," he said, and my mother nodded slightly. "I'm fairly sure it's malignant." Her expression did not change. "It's pressing on several organs and that's causing the pain. I can't tell where it started, but it needs to be removed."

He paused. "It needs to be removed right away. I can call the hospital and get you a room for tonight and I can do the surgery tomorrow morning."

I was stunned. My mother was staring at him, her eyes wide. She didn't look frightened, just frozen, pulled tightly into herself. Her hands were pressed into her lap, her arms tight against her side. It looked like she was afraid she might spring apart into a thousand pieces if she relaxed at all.

"Can we wait?" I asked. "Does it have to be tomorrow?" I hadn't even formulated questions to ask.

He looked from her to me. "It has to come out, or it's just going to get more painful."

"How big an operation is it, and how long is the recovery?" I asked.

"Until we're in surgery, I won't know exactly how many organs are affected. But maybe none are; it may be contained." He looked at my mother. "Once you've healed from the surgery, we'll talk about further treatment."

My mother finally spoke. "I won't do chemo," she said.

"We can talk about that later," he said. "Obviously, you don't have to do anything you don't want to. In the meantime, I need to make the arrangements with the hospital. It'll take some doing to get you a room today."

He looked at her, then at me. "Shall I have the staff call the hospital?" he asked.

We both looked at my mother. "I don't know," she said.

"Is there something you don't understand?" he asked patiently.

She shook her head.

"Mom," I said. "You're in terrible pain."

"That's why we need to do this right away," the doctor said.

She stared back at us, unspeaking.

The doctor stood up. "I'm going to leave you alone to talk about this. Take your time. If you have any questions, come find me."

I saw no path other than the surgery: My mother couldn't go home and lie in bed, starving and barely breathing. I wanted my mother to be in the hospital where other people—expert, responsible people, *people other than me*—would help.

"I'm getting Dad," I said.

My father was so scared he could barely walk from the waiting room into the office. After he sat down next to her, and I explained what the doctor had said, he took my mother's hand. Somehow, despite her unshaken belief that this was the end, he was still hopeful. He begged her to go to the hospital, and then started to cry.

She looked at him, and then turned to me. "All right," she said. "Tell them I'll go." It sounded like she was talking about prison, or the guillotine.

If life came with a pause button, this is where I'd hit it. But that's not how life works: You don't know you're at the top of the ride until you're racing downward, and you can look back and say, "Why didn't we stop right there?"

First, of course, there was the question of money: My parents had no credit cards, so I put the entire doctor's fee, thousands of dollars, onto my American Express card. It was the largest item I'd ever purchased.

Then we went to the hospital—my mother and me. My father was dismissed. "You go to work." He was happy to do so. "We'll call you later," my mother said to him as I helped her out of the car at the Madison Avenue entrance to Mount Sinai. This set the tone for what was to follow: My father went to work, and I entered the darkness with my mother.

It took hours and hours, and by the time I left the hospital, it was dark outside. I had to remind myself that the doctor's appointment, which already felt like weeks ago, had only been early that morning.

In the vast waiting area the next day, the oncologist found me. The surgery took longer than expected because the tumor, which was huge, was pressing on every major abdominal organ.

"This has been growing for a long time—years, probably."

"So if she had gone to the gynecologist this would have been discovered?"

He lifted his palms to the air. "If she had gone for any kind of checkup, this would have been discovered by any doctor, just by palpating her abdomen." He sounded frustrated.

"Can you tell what kind of cancer it is?" I asked hesitantly.

"Ovarian."

"Ovarian? She only had one ovary left." It seemed like some sort of cosmic joke: After tearing everything out of her and leaving her barren, the one thing she had left caused this?

"Yes," he said. "I'm not even sure why they left it behind. Nowadays they might do that to keep some hormonal supply. But back then a hysterectomy was almost always total. But I don't understand why she had that surgery in the first place."

"No one does," I muttered. "So what happens next?"

He explained that the preliminary tests done in the operating room were good: The portion of the tumor that had been examined looked to be a slow-growing type, and her cancer might respond well to treatment. "If she agrees to treatment," he added. I was impressed—he listened and remembered her statements.

But, he added, "Of course, those results are only preliminary. We need to do a lot more tests, and that takes a few days."

I heard his warning, but I tried to focus on the fact that preliminary tests were positive. Maybe there was some light at the end of this darkness.

The next few days went well. My mother woke up, then sat up and began to eat. She was in a small room for two patients, but had no roommate, so there was plenty of space when we visited: my husband and son, even my father. I went to the hospital every day after work, and sometimes in the morning as well. I told her over and over again that the preliminary tests were positive. Her only answer was, "Wait till we get the rest of the tests."

Other than that, she was fairly quiet. She made unpleasant remarks about the nurses, and complained about the poor care. She expected me to make things happen, to yell at nurses, to make demands, to do for her what she had done for me. But I was not her. When she snapped her fingers, people jumped; when I snapped my fingers, people chuckled. Her attitude toward hospitals, toward life, was hyperaware and confrontational. *Don't be a schmuck!* was her mantra. It was a profoundly negative and primed-to-fight-stance. Things will always go wrong, she thought, people will screw up, the system will fail. You damn well better be constantly on guard, ready to fight, always maneuvering, commanding, and demanding. Now I was supposed to fill this role. But I'd never had the stomach for it; it was just another way I couldn't be the daughter she wanted.

She asked hourly for painkillers. She'd rarely ever taken an aspirin, and now she wanted morphine. "It doesn't matter now," she said about reversing a lifelong stance. I didn't ask her what she meant.

On the fourth day after surgery, Lenny and Damien left town for a long-planned trip to eastern Europe and Alex went to visit a friend in New Jersey. It was Easter week, the city was quiet. Damien and Lenny came to visit her in the hospital the morning before they left and she told them to be careful, to be safe. It's the same thing she'd said before every trip, anywhere, even around the corner to buy a carton of milk. But her energy wasn't in it. Her own danger had distracted her.

The day after they left, things started to go wrong. There was an infection in her system that couldn't be identified. She refused to take antibiotics. Her lung function was poor. Her legs were swelling too much. There was a steady flow of doctors in and out of her room: A pulmonary specialist was brought in, two different oncologists, an infectious-disease specialist, another gynecologist, an endocrinologist. My father visited for a few minutes, all that he could stand of the hospital. As he was leaving, he leaned over to kiss her. She patted his hand. "You've been a good husband," she said. It sounded like good-bye.

The next day she was moved to what they called a "step-down room," a unit with four patients and its own full-time nurse. "This gives her a little more attention until we can get everything straightened out," a doctor explained.

There were so many doctors now that I wasn't sure which one to talk to. I came every day; she wouldn't allow anyone else to visit. My father was excused. My husband and sons were away. The one aunt and uncle she still spoke to were in Florida, and couldn't travel. She had no friends left, having pushed them all out of her life after my brother died. I tried to get to the hospital by 7:00 a.m., to catch the doctors as they did rounds. But it seemed as if every time I managed to find one of them, and get him to hold still for a question, more often than not I was told that it was not his area; it was someone else's department. Or he would give me a quick rundown and then launch into the list of things he wanted me to persuade my mother to do: a CAT scan of her lungs, an IV of antibiotics, blood thinners. I almost laughed at them.

I was there every day, but it wasn't enough. I didn't yell at the staff to clean the floor or get her more blankets. I didn't make the painkillers arrive on time. I couldn't get them to heat up her tea. She didn't want to eat; but even so, why couldn't I make sure there was only white meat turkey? I couldn't scream at people, or throw fits and make demands. I was a failure at the most important test of my life.

I hired attendants to stay with her, so she would have someone there to look out for her, to badger the nurse or demand painkillers—to fight the fight she couldn't fight for herself, and I couldn't fight for her. She complained about how stupid they were, how incompetent.

The hours in the step-down unit passed slowly. I brought my knitting with me; and in just a few days I started and finished an entire baby sweater for a pregnant friend. One of the doctors, an internist, was also a knitter. We compared projects.

"Must be a *fayegleh*," my mother said when he left the room.

"But Mom, he's married."

She gave me a withering look.

My mother answered the doctors' questions in monosyllables, but she managed a sentence here and there for the nurses. A new one came on duty one evening and introduced herself: "Hello, I'm Shonda."

"That's a lovely name," my mother said.

The nurse smiled and thanked her. When she left the room, my mother said, "You should always pay them a compliment, butter them up a little, you get better treatment." Then she added, "What a stupid name."

Each day she looked worse: paler, thinner, in more pain. She'd stopped eating, and refused an IV line. She asked me for lemon ices; I brought her two each time I came. She would take a few spoonfuls before pushing them aside. One night, she told me to give her a sponge bath. She didn't ask; maybe she was afraid I would say no. She ordered. "Don't the nurses do that?" I asked, horrified.

"I don't trust them," she said. "You do it."

I got a bowl and a sponge from the nurse and washed my mother's pale, splotchy, scarred body. I tried to be gentle, but my hands were shaking. "Get it down there," she said and struggled to pull her legs a few inches apart. I couldn't look at what I was doing; it was the closest I've ever come to leaving my body.

When I left that night, it was after 10:00 p.m., and the city was dark. "Take a cab," my mother said. "You shouldn't have stayed so late."

"I'm okay," I said. "It's just across the park."

"Be safe," she said. It was the last thing she ever said to me.

"Did the test results come in yet?"

On the phone in the dim morning light, I could hear the doctor rummaging through papers, looking for those long-awaited test results.

"They're here, and they're not good," he said.

"But the preliminary test…"

"That was just one test. These are different. I'm sorry. Why don't we talk about it when you get here?"

As the taxi spun through the dawn darkness of Central Park, I thought about how I'd crossed this park every day for almost two weeks, which felt like two months, or two years. Though the park was beautiful, my stomach tensed as we got closer to the black stone monolith of Mount Sinai. I dreaded every second of every minute in the hospital with my mother. I was there to fill the role of loving daughter; but I was not that person. I felt incredibly alone. It was Easter, and with so many friends and family out of town, I'd barely had time to tell anyone about my mother's situation.

One person I did tell was Faith. She had never tried to be a mother to me; but in many ways, she was something better. When people asked me if I felt as if she were my mother, I always said no; she was more like an aunt, but an aunt you're friends with, too. She was the best of friend and family, and in some ways, the best of mothering. She thought I was perfect or at least she made me feel that way. I tried not to contrast it with how my mother made me feel.

At this point, my parents knew about Faith, Jake, and Quint. I had told them several years ago, when I couldn't stand keeping the secrets any longer. My mother actually opened the door to my confession, by offering to give me my adoption papers and original birth certificate, papers I never knew she had. The word *adoption* had not been spoken between us for decades.

I sat in the living room and told them that I'd found my birth parents, keeping the story straight and simple, being careful to start by telling them that they were my parents, my only parents. My mother sat up very straight, saying nothing, her arms at her sides, her hands clenched. My father said only one word: "*Korvah*," the Jewish word for "whore," when I told them about Faith sleeping with Quint when she was married to Jake. My mother shushed him.

When I finished, my mother said, speaking for both of them, "We understand. It's only natural that you should be curious about this." It sounded like something she read in a pamphlet: "How to Talk to Your Adopted Child about Her Search for Birth Parents."

She told me, for the first time, that she remembered visiting me when I was in foster care those first months. The foster care mother seemed very nice, she said. She lived in Queens and had a house full of beautiful plants.

And they asked you to keep my first initial, I reminded her. That's why you named me Jil. No, my mother said, absolutely not. I had that name picked out years before you were born. I just liked it. They never asked us anything.

The next day I told my kids. Alex had met Faith a few times, as a friend of mine. He thought she was a nice lady, but couldn't figure out what connection she had to him. "Is she going to be my grandma instead of Nana?" he asked. No, I told him, Nana is your grandma.

"So is she Nana's mommy?" I explained it again, and he got it, sort of.

My parents never mentioned my birth parents, or adoption, again. But a year later, we were having dinner when my mother said suddenly, "How is Faith?"

I was confused: At first, I heard "faith" with a small *F*. "Fine," I said. That was all. The papers they gave me were a fascinating piece of my puzzle—legal papers of abandonment.

"I didn't abandon you," Faith said when I showed them to her. The word upset her. In her story she did what was best for me. But I didn't mind the word. It was plain and honest. In order to be chosen, you first have to be abandoned—like Moses, like Superman. In order to be found, you must first be lost.

At the hospital, I found my mother in the intensive care unit. I'd prepared myself for the sight of her, plugged with tubes and wires, deathlike. But she looked surprisingly calm and peaceful, calmer than she'd looked since before all this started.

"Your mother isn't in any pain," one of the nurses told me; I was grateful. I hadn't even thought to ask.

"Will she wake up?" I asked.

When she said, "No, we're keeping her completely sedated," I was even more grateful, and then ashamed of being so glad my mother was unconscious.

In the tiny unit, with its half-closed curtain, I sat down and checked out the machines, beeping comfortingly, monitoring oxygen, blood pressure, and breathing. The whoosh-shoosh of the ventilator was soothing. Morning sun shone through the window.

When the doctor arrived, he closed the curtain, pulled up a chair, and leaned forward to explain the situation. The CAT scan they did before I arrived showed that there were pulmonary embolisms, which explained the breathing problems. In addition, there was a serious infection in her abdomen, which wasn't uncommon after such an extensive operation. Now that they had full test results, they knew we were dealing with the worst possible form of ovarian cancer.

"So what do we do?" I asked.

"Well, we could put her on blood thinners to deal with the clots. But we also have to try to clean out the infection with another operation. In her weakened condition, it would be very precarious. Plus we'd have to take her off the thinners for the surgery."

If the surgery dealt successfully with the infection, and if she survived the surgery, there'd be a long and very difficult recovery. Once she recovered, she would face very aggressive chemotherapy, for a cancer that had been allowed much more time to spread while she waited to recover from two surgeries—if she agreed to any chemo at all. And even the most aggressive chemo would maybe buy her a year of life, most of it spent in the hospital or in some sort of recuperative facility.

I tried to make sense of all this. But too much had changed too quickly, and there were way too many *ifs*.

The doctor went over it again. It sounded even more awful the second time.

"Do you want to talk it over with your father?" he asked.

That hadn't even occurred to me. My father had never had a vote on a decision in his life; my mother was always the general, always in command. In her absence, I was in charge, though I didn't want to be.

"Does your mother have a living will?" he asked.

"Yes." My mother had made and signed one just a few weeks earlier. It was exceptionally direct: no life support, no extraordinary measures, no prolonging the process of dying in case of an incurable physical condition. I'd been carrying it, along with the health care proxy, in my purse for the last two weeks. I showed it to him.

"Well, her wishes seem pretty clear."

"What happens if we do nothing?" I asked.

"It's hard to say. She may live another few hours, or days, maybe even a week. If we take her off the ventilator, it would most likely be only a few hours, a day at most."

"Will she be in pain?"

"No, we'd keep her sedated."

My mother's opinion on the subject of prolonging life had always been a thousand percent clear: no way, no how—no machines, no surgeries, no treatments. But that was all theoretical; how could I know what she would want when it was a harsh reality? How could I make this decision for her, and for my father?

I asked the doctor, "What would you do?"

I expect him to say something like, "I can't answer that." Instead, he paused, and then said: "Your mother didn't want anything like this to happen to her," as he nodded at all the beeping, buzzing machinery. "Her prognosis is bad—just about as bad as it could be." He looked at me—really *looked* at me. "I would let her go."

I was stunned and grateful, so grateful, for his honesty and candor, and for giving me permission to do what I believed my mother would want.

"Okay," I said.

He nodded, and got up. "The palliative care team will step in now," he explained. "But I'll be around if you need me, or you can call." As he slid open the curtain and stepped out of our little enclosure, he told me, "I think you're doing the right thing."

I was more grateful for those words than I could say.

That afternoon I met with the palliative care team in a small room off the ICU. Every member of the team—a doctor, a social worker, nurses—was warm, supportive, and understanding, there to make a dreadful experience as bearable as it could be. They'd been briefed by the other medical personnel, and seen my mother's files and living will. We're in it together, they seemed to say.

The doctor who headed the team explained that everything possible would be done to keep my mother sedated and free of pain. An intense, slender woman, warm and gentle, she had steel in her, I could see.

"Will your father be here?" she asked.

My father. Oh my God, my father. How was I going to tell him? The last time he saw my mother, a few days ago, she was sitting up in bed, talking, complaining. Now she was unconscious, with a breathing tube down her throat, and a death sentence on her head.

"He's away right now," I said. He had gone upstate to spend Easter Sunday with his business partner's family. "He'll be here in the morning."

"Does he know what's been decided?"

"No. I'll have to tell him."

The next morning my father and his partner came to the hospital. Jimmy had worked with my father for more than forty years, since he was a seventeen-year-old boy. He called my father "Pop," and my father loved him like a son, almost better than a son, because there had never been conflict between them, just a sharing of the most important thing in my father's life—his work. When I thought of him, I imagined him as the son of my father's first marriage—to his contracting business.

The three of us sat down at a long picnic-style table in the hospital cafeteria. At age eighty-five, my father was skinnier than ever, but still in good shape. I leaned forward and took his hands in mine.

"Dad, I have some really bad news."

My father flinched, as if he'd been slapped. "Is she gone?" he asked, his voice cracking.

"No," I said. "But it's not good."

Before I could say another word, he began to cry, covering his face with his big hands. "Oh my god, oh my god," he said. "No, no, no."

I'd steeled myself to stay calm, but I couldn't. I started to cry, too.

"It's not good, Dad. The cancer is very bad," I said, struggling to get the words out, to keep from becoming hysterical. Jimmy moved closer and put his arm around him. I reached across the table for one of my father's hands. "It's much worse than they thought at the beginning." He moaned.

"Dad, she's unconscious now. She's on machines, and you know she wouldn't want that," I said.

He was bent over, his face nearly touching the table. His shoulders shook. It was the saddest sight I'd ever seen: my big strong father, bent over, weeping like a child onto a hospital cafeteria table, because his daughter was telling him that his wife of nearly fifty years would soon be gone.

I wanted him to tell me I'd made the right choice; but I realized he couldn't even hear what I was saying, much less absolve me of responsibility. I was in this alone.

"I've got to go," he said, struggling to his feet. "Take me out of here," he cried to Jimmy, as they stumbled toward the exit, my father leaning heavily on his oldest, closest friend, the man who is more of a son to him than I have ever been a daughter.

That afternoon, I met again with the palliative care team, who'd been in and out of the intensive care unit where I sat vigil, talking to my mother. "We don't know what she can hear," the doctor had told me. "We do know that there is some consciousness, some recognition. The sound of your voice may be comforting."

The sound of my voice has never been comforting when she's conscious, I almost told her. But who knew? If it was possible, I'd try. At first it was very strange, talking to my pale, still, unconscious mother while the machines beeped and whirred; but it quickly became quite comfortable. I told her how sorry I was that this was happening. I promised to take care of my father when she was gone. I told her how much her grandsons would miss her. It was the best conversation I'd ever had with my mother.

In the meeting, the doctor asked how my father was. I didn't even know how to answer that, and I was too exhausted to try. Terrible, horrible, heartbroken.

"Is he going to come and say good-bye?" the doctor asked.

"I don't think so," I said, explaining that my father "isn't strong enough" for hospitals.

She thought for a long minute. "I don't want to tell you, or your father, what to do. But there are other things you should think about. Later on, he may regret not coming to say good-bye."

"I don't think so," I said.

"He may not," she replied. "But someone may ask him if he got the chance to say good-bye. Or he might see it in a movie or a TV show, and feel really bad that he didn't do that."

I thought about it and decided she was right. Chances were good that someone would ask that.

She leaned across the table. "If it would make it easier for you or for your father, I could help. I could explain to him beforehand what he would see, and answer his questions, and go with him if he wanted me to."

It would never have occurred to me to ask her to do these things. "Yes, thank you," I said. "Thank you."

I asked my father to come to the hospital in the morning, in case he wanted to say good-bye to her.

"I don't know," he said. Then, to my surprise, he added, "Maybe."

The next morning, in a small private waiting room, the doctor pulled up a chair and told my father very simply and directly what he would see. Jimmy sat on one side of him, and I sat on the other.

"You can talk to her," the doctor told him softly and slowly. "I believe she will hear you. You can kiss her good-bye if you want. It won't hurt; she isn't in any pain. But I think she'll know you're there."

"Can she smell this?" my father asked as he pulled out a bottle of Opium perfume, which he'd wrapped in a paper towel. Opium had been my mother's scent for three decades. "It's her favorite. I thought it might make her feel good to smell it."

The doctor didn't blink. "I think she can."

I started to cry: This was the sweetest, saddest thing I'd ever heard.

We stood up and walked into the intensive care unit, down the row of curtained partitions. "You come with me," my father said. I thought he meant me, but realized he was talking to Jimmy. The two of them went behind the curtain and pulled it closed. The doctor and I looked at each other, and then moved away so we couldn't hear what my father was saying. I was a little embarrassed that I was on the side of the curtain with the doctor, and not the other side, with my parents.

In a minute, they pushed the curtain aside and came out. "I'm done," my father said, his face ashen. They walked down the hall and out of the hospital.

That afternoon, Faith asked me what Lenny, Damien, and Alex were planning to do.

"I don't know," I said. "I haven't told them."

"You haven't?"

"I didn't know if I should interrupt their trip. There's nothing they can do, anyway." I thought I was being kind, a loving wife and mother, saving them from all this pain.

"I'm not sure you're right about that," Faith said. "Think about how you would feel if you were away and something like this was happening. Wouldn't you want to be given the choice about what to do? Wouldn't you be angry if the choice were made for you?"

I realized that she was right. I would be furious if I were kept in the dark; I wasn't thinking clearly.

"I don't even know if I can reach them. I'm not sure their cell phones work over there. And my cell doesn't work in the ICU. Even if they get my message, they can't reach me."

"I think you should try," she said.

They were in Sarajevo, leaving for Zagreb that night. I called the hotel and got no answer. When I called again, someone answered who didn't seem to speak English very well. I left a simple message: Check e-mail. I knew there was occasional e-mail access in the hotel because Damien had sent me a message a few days earlier. I sent them an e-mail explaining what had happened, giving them the choice of whether to come home or stay, and asking them to call me at a specific time later in the afternoon.

Remarkably, they got the message a few minutes later and were able to check e-mail right away.

Later Lenny told me their discussion of what to do was very brief.

"I want to say good-bye to Nana," my son said, which made me so proud of him. They called as planned a few hours later to tell me they were going to try to get home as quickly as possible. There were more flights leaving Zagreb than Sarajevo, so they were going to take their scheduled flight to Zagreb that evening and try to continue on from there.

Then I called Alex. At fifteen, I was afraid he would find it too upsetting to see his grandmother like this. But I felt the decision should be his.

"I'm coming home," he said. "I'll be at the hospital in the morning."

That evening, I met again with the palliative care team, and told them my younger son would be at the hospital in the morning, but that it might take my older son and husband longer to get home.

"I feel really uncomfortable asking this, but I would like my mother to be…" I didn't even know how to ask. I didn't want Lenny and Damien to fly around the world and not find my mother alive when they got here.

"I understand," the doctor said. "You want to give your family the chance to say good-bye."

"Yes," I said gratefully.

"Of course. We'll keep the breathing tube in until they arrive, and we'll talk to the doctors about providing some nourishment in her IV." Then she leaned across the table. "I'm wondering if *you've* had the chance to say good-bye."

"I've been talking to her," I said. "It's… nice."

"Good. Given all the emotion, sometimes people forget to say the things they really want to say. And they regret it later." She pulled a piece of paper toward her. "I've found there are five things that really mean something to people, that they don't want to forget to say." She took out a pencil. "You don't have to say them all, of course—or any of them. But I'll give them to you, just in case."

The words looked like a poem:

Thank you.

I forgive you.

Please forgive me.

I love you.

Good-bye.

In the ICU cubbyhole next to my mother, I looked at the tubes coming into and out of her. I was used to them, even the one that went into her nose and was dark with backed-up blackish-green bile. I stroked her hair, stiff and coarse, and held her hand, strangely warmer than usual.

Saying good-bye to my mother meant saying good-bye to the dream I've always had that, at some moment, probably near the end, we would somehow manage to get past our anger and disappointment, and really talk, in a way that would not make me tense, waiting for her criticism, her dismissal. She would say I love you, and I would say it, too. Most important, she would say, "It's not your fault." I always knew this was complete fantasy. Yet I still imagined it would happen.

Now she was saying nothing at all.

"Mom, I hope you can hear me," I told her. "I really, really hope I'm doing the right thing. I want to say thank you; I know you did your best. It didn't always work out so well, but your intentions were always good. I'm sorry we were never… I'm sorry I wasn't the daughter you wanted. I'm so sorry." I started to cry. "For all the stuff that didn't work between us. I forgive you. I hope you forgive me. I'm trying to do what you would want me to do. I'll take care of Dad. I'll take care of your grandsons." I put my hand to her pale cheek. "I hope you get to see Mema and Poppy, and Uncle Bernie, and Kenny. I hope they're there, somewhere, waiting for you."

The next morning Alex came to the hospital and sat in the ICU with me. I don't think I could have done that at his age—spend an entire day watching my grandmother die. But he did, and I am forever grateful.

After flying twenty hours, from Sarajevo to Zagreb, from Zagreb to Frankfurt, from Frankfurt to New York, Lenny and Damien arrived at the hospital with their luggage that afternoon. We talked for a while; then Damien was alone with his Nana for a few minutes to say his good-byes—then Alex. After both boys went home, Lenny said his good-byes, and we watched as the nurses took all the tubes out of my mother and turned off the ventilator. After all the hours and days of listening to its calming whoosh, the ICU cubicle was strangely quiet. We pulled in another chair and Lenny and I waited. Exhausted from his twenty-hour round-the-world journey, he soon fell asleep.

I watched the monitors and my mother. Her blood pressure slowly dropped. The numbers went lower and lower. Her breathing slowed, then sometimes stopped, then started again. I stood next to her, unafraid of my mother for the first time in my life. For once, I felt I'd done right by her. I'd given her husband, who loved her so dearly, a chance to kiss her good-bye. I'd given her grandsons, who also loved her, their chance to say good-bye. I was standing by her, doing what I believed she wanted me to do.

It was the best I could manage. She would always be a mother duck, and I would always be a swan. But I would be the best swan I could.

Her breath got softer and softer as the numbers dropped lower and lower. It was as if she were waiting, too—waiting for this to be finished. Lenny stirred in his chair; seeing me standing, he came to my side. We watched, together, holding hands, as my mother drew another breath, and another; and then stopped.

Two years later: The pain started over a weekend, a sharp, piercing pain in my stomach that was worse every time I bent or stretched. I waited a week for it to go away. When it didn't, I went to the emergency room, thinking I might have appendicitis. I spent nearly eight hours in the ER, flipping back and forth between scared witless (it's cancer, I'm dying) and surprisingly calm (it's nothing, just indigestion), until finally a doctor took a look at my cold naked tummy and said, "You've got an incision rupture."

"What do you mean?"

"The surgical incision you had has ruptured," he said, pressing gently on my navel. "Your hernia surgery…"

"I've never had a hernia," I said.

"Well, it sure looks like it. I can see the scar, very faintly. And you can feel the rupture." He put my hand on the middle of my stomach and pressed gently. Sure enough, there was a knot, like a peeled grape, just under the skin.

I thought he was crazy. But a few days later, the doctor I went to for a second opinion said, "It's an incision rupture." Peering closely at my navel, he went on: "You can see the scar."

I asked my father if I'd ever had surgery as a baby or small child. "No, of course not," he said. When I pressed him: "You were never even in the hospital. You were always perfectly healthy." Did the adoption agency mention anything about surgery? What about my foster mother, the lady with the beautiful plants in Queens?

"No, nothing."

I asked Faith as well.

"Do you remember the doctors in the hospital saying anything about a hernia when I was born?"

"No, definitely not; you were perfect."

But the third doctor confirmed it. "Definitely a surgical rupture," he said. "Right here."

A few weeks later I had a small piece of mesh sewn into my abdomen to hold the rupture together. I left the hospital after only a few hours with a bandage patched onto my stomach and an excuse to stay home from work for a few days.

Faith called daily to make sure I was okay. Friends called; my dad checked in. My kids took good care of me, as did my husband. I felt cared for, and loved.

When I went back for my one-week checkup, I asked again what it was. Surely once he opened things up, the surgeon would find that he and the other doctors had made a mistake.

But they hadn't. His theory: I had most likely been born with a hernia and had it repaired before I was adopted at five months old. Perhaps that was why I stayed in foster care so long—to make sure the surgery was a success.

I felt like I'd been abducted by aliens. I had surgery I never knew I had. It was from another life, when I was Jessica. There was no one to ask: *What is that red line across my stomach?* No one to tell me what happened.

There may always be pieces of the puzzle that fit or don't, that make sense or don't. I may know where they fit, but I may not. And just when I think I have all the pieces, something new will come along and scramble it all over again.

How do you become who you are? How much is in your blood and how much do you pick up along the way? What is inside you, unalterable and fixed? How much do you know about who you are, about how you came to be? What does it mean to be a daughter, a mother, a family? What is learned, and what can never be taught?

Some pieces of my life have never lost their sharp edges. I don't believe in the things that often provide answers: destiny, fate, predetermination… God. Was I born a blank slate, to be written on at will? Did I put myself together from bubble gum and glue? I now know who I came from, but I still don't know how I came to be.

Our lives—Faith's and mine—were marked by adoption. She lived with the shame of what she had done, as I lived with the wound of what had been done to me. Faith says she would not want anyone reading this to think she believes adoption is a better option than abortion.

I would not want anyone reading this to think I don't believe in adoption, despite how it affected my life. What I do not believe in, however, is pretending that adoption and biological birth are exactly the same thing—that adoption is the magic wand that books like *The Chosen Baby* would have us believe, that makes a child you adopt identical, somehow, to the child of your womb. It is not the same thing. That does not mean, however, that adoption isn't beautiful, or wonderful.

In order to be found, you must first be lost. But when it comes to adoption, we focus on the finding, and pretend the loss does not exist. And there is so much loss—loss that deserves attention, respect, and recognition. The loss of the birth mother, of her child. The loss of the adopted child, of her biological family. The loss of the adoptive mother, of her fertility. For adoption to work—to really work, not just be a bandage over a wound—we must acknowledge the wounds, mourn the losses, open them to the light, and accept the scars.

In the 1950s, adoption was marvelously simple. Today the world of creating families is becoming more and more complex, with foreign adoptions, private adoptions, mixed-race adoptions, special-needs adoptions, not to mention all the interventions of infertility treatments and surrogacy. People can now adopt frozen embryos—the sperm from one man combined with the egg of one woman—implant them into the womb of another woman, and raise them as part of yet another family. We have moved so far from what once was a simple process that defining motherhood itself may soon be impossible. Is it the woman who created the egg? Carried the fetus? Raised the baby?

I would never deny any woman the breathtaking joys of motherhood. But we can't ignore, and shouldn't pretend, that all these things are purely positive, with no scars, no problems to overcome, no primal wounds, or no reasons to mourn.

Giving birth is a simple process, but in the end there's nothing simple about it. Biology may not be destiny, but it's a hell of a lot more powerful than any of us give it credit for.

I am so grateful for having found Faith, for being able to try to put together the pieces of who I am. But in the end, despite all the pieces and the discoveries, I'm still not sure what I was born, and what I was made, how much was a product of genetics and how much was the result of my upbringing. The big things in life, I've come to realize, don't have easy answers. And sometimes they don't have answers at all. What is nature and what is nurture? Why am I who I am? I don't think I'll ever know.

I've been very lucky to have so many wonderful pieces to put together. If there are still a few rough edges, a few pieces out of place, that's okay. I don't regret having been adopted, because I'm pretty happy with who I am, and the way my life has taken shape. I can't really imagine myself any other way. I accept that sometimes life is simply random, and that sometimes there are no answers.

In the end, we are who we are. And that's not a bad thing.

TOP LEFT: Bunny and her mother—about 1971.
TOP RIGHT: Bunny at about ten years old: "There was a little girl and she had a little curl . . ."
BOTTOM: Bunny in her twenties.

Epilogue

"I'm so sorry."

That was just about the first thing Faith said to me when I found her thirteen years ago.

"For what?" I asked.

"For giving you away," she said.

To me it never felt that there was anything to forgive. For one thing, I'd been told my whole life, since before I can remember, that adoption was "for the baby's own good." I believed that, and once I knew Faith's story, I agreed: I don't think she had a better choice. But also, it's impossible for me to imagine being anything else. I am adopted, I have green eyes, I am female—these are the incontrovertible facts of who I am. I could move to Rome, I could convert to Bahai'sm, I could even have gender reassignment surgery. It doesn't matter: I'd still be an adoptee.

While we were completing the editing of this book, Faith was diagnosed with what turned out to be terminal cancer.

"I'm so sorry," she said to me, again, one morning on the phone.

"For what?" I asked, again.

"I'm sorry we didn't have more time together," she answered.

This time I agreed.

Thirteen years sounds like a lot, but it wasn't enough. Thirteen years wasn't enough, thirty years would not have been enough, a hundred years would not. No amount of time is enough to say, "Now I am done with this person I love. Now I can manage to live happily without her."

When Faith was first diagnosed, it seemed like an unpleasant bump in the road. She told me about it on the phone, making light of it.

"When this is over," she said, "we'll have lunch. We'll go to a show. When this is over, I'll have you and Lenny here for dinner."

"When this is over" lasted through vicious chemo that landed her in the hospital for two weeks, weakness that put her in a wheelchair, pain that wracked her body, a second opinion that hurt worse than the cancer, more treatments that didn't seem to be working, a second hospital stay. Despite the amazing list of similarities between us—passion for Kevin Kline! tiny hands! love of show tunes!—we did not share the quality of optimism. I was terrified. Faith was calm, upbeat, uncomplaining. When I asked, on the phone, how she was feeling, her answers were either "Fair" or "So-so" or, on really bad days, "Not so great." And they were always immediately followed by, "But how are *you*?" When I asked what I could do—make soup or bring books or get DVDs—her unvarying response was, "Just call me." I called almost every day.

After the third, and worst, opinion, hospice care was called in, first at home, then at a facility in the Bronx. I went to visit. The receptionist gave me the room number, but when I walked into the room and saw a stranger in the bed, I walked right out. I double-checked the room number, then the chart hanging on the wall. I seemed to be in the right place, but it wasn't until I saw a small photo of Faith and her husband on the nightstand that I accepted that this was indeed my birth mother. Her head was nearly bald, her skin pale and tight over the bones of her face, her mouth a gaping darkness. There was so much less of her—less hair, less weight, less being.

I knew she wouldn't be awake; her son, my half-brother, had told me she hadn't awakened in several days. Her breathing was deep and sluggish and reminded me of my mother's profoundly slow breathing as she lay dying in the ICU four years earlier.

I spent an hour sitting by her side. Twice she opened her eyes and stared, her eyes blurred as if clouded by cataracts. Her mouth moved, and gargled noises emerged. It seemed as if she were trapped underwater, lost in a dense blanket of fog that she couldn't break through. I wanted to reach out and grab her, pull her up through the water, back into the world.

She died just a few days later.

I conjugate my loss: I have lost Faith, I have lost, I am lost. This feeling is strange, confusing, and all I can think to do with it is call Faith and talk about it, or send her an e-mail. I cannot quite conceive that there will be no response. I feel as if I am at sea, alone, adrift with my loss. I was not part of her family, she was not part of mine. Over the years, I met her husband and son only a handful of times. Her daughter, my half-sister, refused to meet me, for reasons I have never understood. Faith met my husband and children several times, and a few close friends, but she lived her life with her family and I have lived my life with mine.

We saw each other more often than I saw any of my friends, and most of my family, and we talked or e-mailed at least three or four times a week. We were our own private island, each other's therapist, pen pal, safe house, and long-distance lover—the person who knows no one else in your life, so you can therefore tell her everything. But she was more than just the recipient of every confession. Maybe because we never had to go through all the mother-daughter drama, we were able to connect as friends, and as something more, something I've never been able to define, but it was extraordinary and unique and wonderful. I will miss talking to her, and I will miss hearing her deep, musical voice. I will miss her wisdom, her warmth, her enthusiasm. We were enormously similar, but I always thought of her as a better version of me: kinder, smarter, more compassionate.

I know how fortunate I am to have found Faith—not just to have found this missing piece of my life, but to have found this particular person, this remarkable connection, this warm and enriching relationship. It is one thing to love someone you are related to; it is something else entirely to genuinely like and appreciate her.

Losing Faith leaves my world a little grayer, and a lot emptier. I have lost a friend I could always turn to, always count on. I have lost someone who made me feel loved, and safe, and welcome. Faith thought I was perfectly wonderful, wonderfully perfect. I thought she was, too. I feel an enormous loss for what she was, and for what she was to me. I will miss her greatly.

J.S. Picariello
September 2010

TOP LEFT: Jil with her mother.
TOP RIGHT: Lenny, Jil, and Damien at 14 months.
BOTTOM: Jil and Kenny.
OPPOSITE: Bunny examining a bust of her head. The photo was taken by Jake.

ACKNOWLEDGMENTS

Heartfelt thanks to a crucial few: To Faith, for wisdom, love, and understanding. To the dearest of old friends, Joanne Rubin and Jeri Darling, who listened and listened and together became Janey. To Neva Sharon, for keeping the letters and a long and valued friendship. To Dr. Diane Meier, a remarkable woman and caregiver. To Helen Morris, who always gets it. To my sons, Damien and Alex, who make me laugh and make me proud. And to Lenny, who always believes in a better me than I ever believe in myself. *Alla famiglia!*

—JS

About the Authors

After graduating from NYU film school, **Jil Picariello** became an advertising and marketing copywriter, working for several ad agencies and a long list of major magazines, including *New York, People, Parenting,* and *Reader's Digest*. A New York native, Picariello holds an MFA in creative writing from The New School. She lives in Manhattan with her husband and two sons.

Bunny Crumpacker was the author of seven books, including *The Sex Life of Food* and *Perfect Figures*. She also wrote a children's book, two books based on food pamphlets published from 1875 to 1950 (a chronicle of American cooking in those years), and was the coauthor, with her husband Chick Crumpacker, of a book about jazz. A New York native, Crumpacker worked as a caterer, editor, newspaper columnist, and school community relations officer. She and her husband, a record producer, lived in the Hudson Valley, just north of New York City.